Welcome to the *EVERYTHING*® series!

These handy, accessible books give you all you need to tackle a difficult project, gain a new hobby, comprehend a fascinating topic, prepare for an exam, or even brush up on something you learned back in school but have since forgotten.

You can read an *EVERYTHING*® book from cover-to-cover or just pick out the information you want from our four useful boxes: e-facts, e-ssentials, e-alerts, and e-questions. We literally give you everything you need to know on the subject, but throw in a lot of fun stuff along the way, too.

We now have well over 100 *EVERYTHING*® books in print, spanning such wide-ranging topics as weddings, pregnancy, wine, learning guitar, one-pot cooking, managing people, and so much more. When you're done reading them all, you can finally say you know *EVERYTHING*®!

FACTS
Important sound bytes of information

ESSENTIALS
Quick handy tips

ALERT
Urgent warnings

QUESTIONS?
Solutions to common problems

THE
EVERYTHING®
Series

Dear future biker:

Motorcycles and the people who ride them have come a very long way since their simple beginnings. Along the way, they have experienced a great deal of negative publicity and Hollywood hype. In response, fine organizations like the American Motorcyclist Association have presented motorcycles and the folk who ride them as safe, sane, and squeaky-clean.

I have never thought of myself as either a glamorous Hollywood type or as squeaky-clean. Come to think of it, I can't say that I have ever met anybody that would fit either of these stereotypes. I am a full-time motorcycle enthusiast, and part-time author, and writing this book turned out to be a challenging and fun experience.

Looking back on what I wrote, I believe I accomplished what I intended. *The Everything® Motorcycle Book* is the whole story, with both the ups and downs of motorcycling—the hobby, sport, and, most of all, lifestyle. I hope you will enjoy reading it as much as I have enjoyed writing it.

Ride and live free,

THE
EVERYTHING®
MOTORCYCLE BOOK

The one book you must have to buy,
ride, and maintain your motorcycle

A. J. Drew

Adams Media Corporation
Avon, Massachusetts

Dedication

For Dozer and the owner of that breakfast buffet.

Acknowledgments

Thanks to my mother, Ann, and my brother Steve for giving me the time to finish this project.
Thanks to Dozer, Trouble, and Animal for insights shared along the way.

EDITORIAL
Publishing Director: Gary M. Krebs
Managing Editor: Kate McBride
Copy Chief: Laura MacLaughlin
Acquisitions Editor: Bethany Brown
Development Editor: Julie Gutin

PRODUCTION
Production Director: Susan Beale
Production Manager: Michelle Roy Kelly
Series Designer: Daria Perreault
Layout and Graphics: Brooke Camfield,
Colleen Cunningham, Michelle Roy Kelly, Daria Perreault

An Everything® Series Book.
Everything® is a registered trademark of Adams Media Corporation.

Published by Adams Media Corporation
57 Littlefield Street, Avon, MA 02322 U.S.A.
www.adamsmedia.com

ISBN: 1-58062-554-1
Printed in the United States of America.

J I H G F E D C B A

Library of Congress Cataloging-in-Publication Data
Drew, A. J.
The everything motorcycle book : the one book you must have to buy,
ride, and maintain your motorcycle / by A.J. Drew.
p.   cm. — (The everything series)
Includes index.
ISBN 1-58062-554-1
1. Motorcycles. 2. Motorcycling. I. Title. II. Series.
TL440 .D67   2002
629.227'5—dc21   2002003932

Illustrations by Barry Littmann.
Photo research and acquisition courtesy of Irene Durham.
Photographs in interior and insert reprinted with permission and courtesy
of the Seattle Support Group © unless otherwise noted.

This book is available at quantity discounts for bulk purchases.
For information, call 1-800-872-5627.

Visit the entire Everything® series at everything.com

Contents

Introduction

There are plenty of external, superficial reasons for owning a motorcycle. Sport, recreation, and transportation top the list. But if you go just a few layers deeper, closer to the heart of the matter, you will see that these reasons are more like excuses. You can easily find other sports and safer modes of recreation—and when it comes to transportation, a good economy car beats the motorcycle hands down. So why buy a motorcycle?

Have you ever read *Jonathan Livingston Seagull* by Richard Bach? If you haven't, then you might not understand what riding a motorcycle is all about. Even if you rode a motorcycle to the bookstore in search of this title, you should still read about Jonathan's life. The one word that sums up what Jonathan was looking for, and the one word that sums up what you express when you choose to ride a motorcycle, are the same word—freedom.

In a society intent on tightening its grip of conventionality, you have often felt the need to run hard and fast to avoid the trappings of conformity. You have fought long and hard to retain individuality. That is really why you want to ride a motorcycle. Not because it will fulfill your desire for freedom and individualism, but because it will give you a way to express this desire in a way that nothing else can.

Motorcycles express this freedom in many ways. In a world where everyone is in a hurry, motorcycle touring can turn a vacation into an experience that will provide memories and stories for a lifetime. In a culture where every house looks the same, motorcycle customizing offers a chance to demonstrate your unique style. In a workplace where the ups and downs aren't all that fun, off-road motorcycling can provide a fast-paced release of pent-up tension. The pure enjoyment of riding motorcycles can be all that, and more.

You are not alone. Within the motorcycle community you will find many of similar mindset, decent people who share your thirst for freedom, and you will be able to find them easily because they are all there, atop motorcycles. Contrary to the Hollywood depiction of the

Lone-Wolf biker, the community that shares your interests is genuinely social and highly accessible.

There are literally hundreds of motorcycle organizations with a diverse focus of interests. No matter what your particular two-wheel love is, you will easily find others who share that interest and who can give you a head start on your new interest. There are organizations that concentrate on touring, customizing, off-road riding, and even racing. Fantastic resources for motorcycle enthusiasts are available at many levels: very affordable and widely accredited rider safety courses for the beginner, advanced studies for the experienced, even racing schools which will improve upon your road skills and get you ready to be a road racer.

The Everything® Motorcycle Book is a self-explanatory guide to the machines and the people that make motorcycling great. It will help you get the most out of your relationship with two-wheelers and the folk who love them. It will point out the pitfalls experienced by those who have traveled this path before you, and guide you through one of the best decisions you could make—to join the ever-growing number of people who proudly call themselves bikers.

CHAPTER 1

Motorcycling History: From Motorized Bicycles Onward

It is important to know the history and even prehistory of motorcycles to understand how they are built and how they function, as well as the role they have played and will continue to play in our society. How did motorcycles evolve into the machines they are today?

Before Motorcycles Roamed the Earth

A motorcycle is generally defined as a machine resembling a heavy bicycle with two wheels and a motor, and might also include a sidecar with a third wheel. The invention of this machine dates back to 1868, when Sylvester H. Roper built a contraption that now resides in the Smithsonian Institute's National Museum of American History.

Still, calling Roper's contrivance the first motorcycle might be going a bit too far. Unlike today's motorcycles, this machine was powered by a small vertical steam boiler that was mounted under the seat. The boiler forced steam into two small pistons, which in turn powered a crank drive on the back wheel. Compared to some of the contraptions that would follow, it was very well designed and compact. Roper's machine had an interesting feature that had not been seen before. Twisting the straight handlebar controlled his vehicle's throttle. This concept would later become the twist grip throttle that virtually every motorcycle uses today.

QUESTIONS?

So, what ever happened to Mr. Roper?
He went on to build more steam-powered motorcycles and automobiles. In June of 1896, he was clocked riding a motorcycle at forty miles per hour. Riding at the speed that could only be called amazing for his time, Mr. Roper fell from his motorcycle, and died of a heart attack.

In 1884, John Kemp Starley invented the first modern bicycle when he devised the chain-driven rear wheel that propels bicycles. The chain-driven system made it much easier to mount an internal-combustion engine. Instead of designing an entire power train around an engine, you could just replace the pedal drive system with the engine. It wasn't long before some gearhead decided to introduce the chain-driven bicycle to the internal-combustion engine.

Many people credit Gottlieb Daimler as being that first gearhead. In a way, this seems fair, as he was also the inventor of the first successful four-stroke engine. His vehicle was built in 1885. But Mr. Daimler's vehicle was a bit more than a motorized bicycle—about two wheels more. Based around a bicycle frame, the engine and its mounting were so clumsy that Daimler added a stabilizing wheel to either side. His vehicle may be better described as a proto-automobile.

Who Was the Real Inventor of the Modern Motorcycle?

Well, no one can really say. Certainly Sylvester H. Roper, John Kemp Starley, and Gottlieb Daimler played significant roles in the invention process, but the real story took place in the backyards, basements, and garages of the world. The final invention of the motorcycle cannot be credited to any one person because its birth took place almost simultaneously.

1906
Neckarsulm

Photo courtesy of Seattle Support Group.

Who hasn't heard of the Harley-Davidson Motor Company? Formed by William S. Harley and Arthur Davidson in 1903, this company remains the longest continuously operating motorcycle producer in the world. Another popular American-made motorcycle was the Indian, which began rolling off the assembly line in 1902. In England, the Triumph Cycle Company would later produce a motorcycle based on the 1902 plans of Maurice Johann Schulte. These three companies really stand out as having survived the tests of both time and changing economic conditions, but there were actually hundreds upon hundreds of motorcycle manufacturers that seemed to pop up overnight, much like the dot.com boom of the 1990s.

That's how the decade of the motorcycle (1900s) had started. It was a time when motorcycles greatly outnumbered automobiles—it wasn't until 1913 that Henry Ford's Model T made its first appearance. Prior to that, the automobile was prohibitively costly. And when you add high cost to the relatively low power provided by the automobile engines of the time, you begin to see why the motorcycle was the preferred mode of personal motorized transportation. Yes, automobiles existed prior to the Model T, but only members of the top economic levels of our society could afford to drive them.

FACTS

The motorcycle would not continue its domination over the automobile for very long. The popularity of the automobile went up as the cost went down. Before long, the motorcycle industry that had sprouted up just over a decade earlier came crumbling down again, just like the dot.com companies a century later.

The Decline in Popularity: 1914–1941

By the time World War I began in 1914, about half of the motorcycle manufacturers had gone out of business. Industry leaders faced the fact that something had to change, or else the motorcycle would go the way of any product that had outlived its usefulness. If the motorcycle could no longer compete as a utility and transportation vehicle, it would have to be marketed for entirely different purposes. To survive, manufacturers began promoting motorcycles for recreation and sport. Shortly after World War I ended in 1918, the motorcycle had established itself as a recreation vehicle. Fueled by a postwar economy, the promotions had worked.

In 1930, the Great Depression presented the next great setback for the motorcycle industry. Stock prices fell over 40 percent. Nine thousand banks went out of business. The savings of more than 9 million people simply vanished. More than 85,000 businesses went under, and the average wage fell by about 60 percent while unemployment rose to about 25 percent. In the worst years of the depression, more than 15 million people were out of work.

The portions of the motorcycle industry that managed to survive the introduction of the Model T faced a great challenge. How do you sell a sport and recreational vehicle to people who can afford neither sport nor recreation? This time, the challenge could not be met. The vast majority of motorcycle manufacturers became the very first economic causalities. In the United States, the only two motorcycle manufacturers to survive were Harley-Davidson and Indian.

Rebirth of the Machine

Both World Wars prompted rapid technological developments, but it wasn't until the end of World War II that the economic benefits of these technologies would be realized. The postwar economy was brisk. People could now afford to spend on transportation, recreation, and sport once again. Also, wartime innovations were being combined with inventions that had been achieved earlier. Do you remember that steam-powered contraption from 1868? Well, Mr. Roper's twist throttle was reinvented by Glen Curtiss in 1904. It was later reinvented again by the Indian Motorcycle Company and is now the standard throttle on virtually all motorcycles.

Unfortunately, Indian would not survive much longer. Both Harley-Davidson and Indian had negotiated huge contracts during the war, but Harley-Davidson turned out to be a much better contender at the bargaining table. By the end of the war, Indian was cash-poor. In an effort to save the company, Indian's decision-makers did exactly what Harley-Davidson had deliberately avoided. Instead of going to production on the shaft-driven v-twin that they had developed during the war, they tried to produce a motorcycle that was streamlined in cost, in imitation of the British motorcycles that were being brought back to the United States by war veterans. The decision cost them their company. In 1950, Indian was so deep in debts to Brockhouse of England that Brockhouse called the debt, cut the company into pieces, and then sold the lot to Associated Motorcycles (AMC). In the hands of AMC (who also owned Norton, Royal

Enfield, AJS, Matchless, and Velocette), the Indian would last only a few more years. By 1954, the v-twin engine that was the hallmark of American-made motorcycles was replaced by a 700cc Royal Enfield. A few years later, AMC removed the name Indian from their product lines.

QUESTIONS?

Just when did Indian motorcycles go out of production?
The last year that Indian motorcycles were produced is still subject to debate, because a production run was made after their plant was closed, especially for the New York Police Department. It seems that only Indian motorcycles were able to meet their demands.

Even with the postwar economy booming and the innovations in motorcycle mechanics, in terms of technology the motorcycle industry still lagged well behind the automobile industry. Part of the problem was lack of competition. Harley-Davidson was the only manufacturer in the United States. AMC closed its doors by 1960, leaving only the Norton to carry on its legacy.

International Competition

In England, the manufacturers that survived concerned themselves more with keeping up with each other, and did not expend much effort on serious innovation. Meanwhile, the Japanese faced an entirely different set of circumstances. Because the Japanese infrastructure was so damaged by the war, they found themselves right back where the American Motorcycle Company had been around the turn of the century. Japan needed affordable transportation and the motorcycle was vastly superior to the automobile in that respect. At first the Japanese companies were content to produce what the Japanese economy demanded. European manufacturers mostly ignored them because their product amounted to nothing more than motorized bicycles.

The European manufacturers did not recognize that the Japanese mopeds were a great deal more than the motorized bicycles of the 1900s. They were technologically superior to European manufactured motorcycles in just about every way except engine displacement. When Honda introduced its CB450 to the world market in 1965, Harley-Davidson and other non-Japanese manufacturers realized the undeniable truth—the Japanese presented very serious competition. With their state-of-the-art design and reasonable engine size, the Japanese motorcycles quickly rose to the top of a market previously dominated by the technology of the 1920s and 1930s. The CB450 handled like the best of the European designs and could outrun a standard production Harley-Davidson with twice the engine size.

ESSENTIALS

Instead of priming a carburetor, retarding the timing, and jumping up and down on a kick starter while praying that a backfire didn't break your ankle, the owner of a Japanese motorcycle needed to do little more than turn the key and press a button.

The non-Japanese companies tried to compete by offering larger and larger engines with modern conveniences like an electric starter, but the Japanese advancements were too fast. By 1969, Honda introduced the CB750. It was faster and cheaper than any motorcycle that other manufacturers could offer. To make matters worse, the technological advances in the Japanese motorcycles created bikes that almost anyone could master.

How Harley-Davidson Survived

Even when it looked like the Japanese would be the only manufacturers to produce motorcycles beyond the 1970s, Harley-Davidson puttered along, supported primarily by their diehard fans. In 1981, the business-as-usual mentality would change dramatically. That was the year Harley-Davidson executives purchased the company from its parent company, AMF. The new owners set a task for themselves—to improve the reliability of the Harley-Davidson engine and the "rideability" of the frame and suspension.

FACTS

The 1983 introduction of tariffs on foreign imports was championed by President Ronald Reagan. Consequently, many people recognize Reagan's administration for saving the Harley-Davidson Motor Company from bankruptcy.

In 1983, the U.S. government imposed tariffs on foreign manufacturers. With the higher tariffs and the introduction of the newly designed Evolution engine and Softail chassis, Harley-Davidson could once again compete with the Japanese imports while retaining their style and sound.

Harley-Davidson continued to improve the quality of its products. By 1991, all new Harleys featured five-speed transmissions. In 1992, belt drives became universal, and in 1995, Harley finally introduced fuel injection. And despite all these improvements, the company never sacrificed its style, which is uniquely Harley-Davidson. Although Harley-Davidson now offers a competitive product, it does not generally offer the cutting-edge technology found on Japanese motorcycles, and European motorcycles find themselves somewhere between the two.

Hell's Angels and Biker Stereotypes

Consider the average view of the Hell's Angels Motorcycle Club (MC). Not a pretty picture, right? But how many people know that Hell's Angels didn't start out as a motorcycle club? Its history goes back to 1941, with the creation of a squadron within the air combat group called the Flying Tigers, commanded by Arvid Olsen.

From Flying Tigers to Hell's Angels

The Flying Tigers were anything but a regular military unit, so it took something other than regular men to make it work. Officially, the operation belonged to the Chinese government, but the planes were purchased with loans from the United States and virtually every pilot was recruited by the Central Aircraft and Manufacturing Corporation. This was little more than a front corporation set up to recruit volunteers from all branches of the U.S. military. An executive order was signed that allowed Americans to fight on behalf of other countries and the Flying Tigers were born.

"Since the Flying Tigers first spread their wings in the skies above China, the enemy has learned to the fear the intrepid spirit they have displayed in the face of his superior numbers. They have become the symbol of the invincible strength of the forces now upholding the cause of justice and humanity. The Chinese people will preserve forever the memory of their glorious achievement."

—Chiang Kai-shek, Chinese nationalist leader

1915
Harley-
Davidson

Photo courtesy of Seattle Support Group.

Claire Lee Chennault, a colonel in the Chinese air force, was in charge of training the men. Chennault was an American who had been forced out of the Army Air Corps, partly for his unorthodox ideas on the use of airpower. To put it simply, he was a maverick and the men that he trained would become mavericks as well. They had to be. In the days when serving in the U.S. military was considered safe, these men resigned their cushy jobs to fight against a country that was not officially an enemy of the United States. They felt that politicians were too slow in making decisions, and they were willing to kill or be killed for what they believed in. By the time the United States officially entered the war, Chennault had only ninety-nine outdated planes and a handful of American pilots that had never been in combat. But with their free spirits and the sense of independence, the Flying Tigers were on their way to becoming legendary.

So what happens to a bunch of rebel wartime pilots when they run out of war? They buy motorcycles. After the war, Olsen returned to his home in California and traded two wings for two wheels. He had called his fighter squadron Hell's Angels, and he now used the same name to describe other veterans who had switched from planes to motorcycles.

FACTS

The first vehicle to ever have the words "Hell's Angels" painted on its side was the P-40b fighter plane manufactured by the Curtiss Wright Corporation. Arvid Olsen ordered that the words "Hell's Angels" be painted on the side of each plane in his command. Due to the tremendous respect for the accomplishments of the Flying Tigers, all P-40 class airplanes would eventually receive the nickname Flying Tiger.

Although it was a general expression, rather than a reference to a specific group, the motorcycle club that formed shortly after took on the name of Hell's Angels Motorcycle Club. Olsen rode with the club on many occasions, but, in true maverick style, never officially joined.

Like the combat veterans of every war, those returning from World War II were disillusioned by what they found. The soldiers on the battlefield had learned to trust each other with their lives, and members of a unit became closer than any friend could. Returning veterans sought to re-establish such ties with other men. Motorcycle clubs were formed to fill that void.

The Riot in Hollister, California

On July 4, 1947, the Hell's Angels and other motorcycle clubs, which consisted of a huge number of World War II veterans, attended a rally sponsored by the American Motorcyclist Association (AMA), in Hollister, California. Imagine about 4,000 motorcycles rolling into a town whose population was about 4,500 people. The news coverage of the time reported that a full-scale riot erupted in Hollister, that the Hell's Angels absolutely destroyed the town, and that the police had to use paramilitary tactics to restore the peace.

Yet, if you look at the facts, the story doesn't hold. Many of the bikers were combat veterans and far outnumbered the police. If any of the motorcycle clubs had attempted to wage war against Hollister, the town and the police that were called in would not have been left standing when everything was said and done. In reality, however, twenty-nine bikers had been cited for traffic offenses as well as drunkenness and indecent exposure, and that was that.

Although the police reports made it absolutely clear that the event was not the riot that the press sensationalized it to be, Hollywood had other ideas. In 1954, a movie called *The Wild One* would forever change the way people think about bikers and the way bikers think about themselves. The film by Stanley Kramer starred Marlon Brando as a motorcycle misfit and Lee Marvin as nothing less than a full-blown psychopath. If the movie had presented the event at Hollister as it really happened, chances are bikers wouldn't have the reputation they do today. But truth doesn't necessarily sell tickets at the box office. Instead, the movie turned the rabble-rousing of a few bikers at Hollister—no more threatening than what can be seen on today's college campuses after a football game—into devilry, and the motorcycle into a tool of the devil. Like all successful movies, *The Wild One* was followed by a series of movie knockoffs, each trying to outdo each other. The trend of bad-biker movies would continue into the next decade.

The term "outlaw" originally referred to a person who was outside of the protection of law. The term "outlaw motorcycle club" typically refers to clubs that are not affiliated with the AMA. The same is true of the term "outlaw biker."

The Birth of a Tradition

The sixties changed how people think about a great deal of issues, including the popular opinion about motorcycles and their riders. In 1962, Honda declared an all-out war on *The Wild One*'s stereotype of bikers. Their motto was: "You meet the nicest people on a Honda." In addition to the reassuring words, pictures showed normal law-abiding citizens riding Honda motorcycles. The advertising campaign paid off in a very big way, which added to the Japanese domination of the sport and recreation motorcycle market. Honda had almost singlehandedly stirred the sport motorcycle market back to life.

During the time of that advertising campaign, in the early 1960s, Honda motorcycles were little more than a collection of dirt bikes and very small street bikes. Consequently, the face-lift that Honda gave to the motorcycle industry did not extend to the larger street motorcycles, which boosted Honda's sales while keeping in place the stereotypes associated with the Harley-Davidsons. It wouldn't be until the end of the decade that a positive influence could be seen in the field of touring motorcycles.

Easy Rider

In 1969, a movie called *Easy Rider* finally challenged the stereotypes promoted by the 1954 flick *The Wild One*. By today's standards, the movie is rather dull—no kung fu–style fighting and only one gunshot during the entire film. The movie presents the odyssey of Captain America (Peter Fonda) and Billy the Kid (Dennis Hopper), who decide that the status quo of the nine-to-five world is not their idea of freedom. After raising capital via methods which were probably a bit more socially acceptable prior to the war on drugs, they travel across America looking for the promised land of New Orleans and the mecca of Mardi Gras to the tune of the Steppenwolf classic "Born to be Wild." Instead, what they find is that the status quo just won't let them live outside of the system.

FACTS

Jack Nicholson's first major role was in *Easy Rider*, in which he played a lawyer who was fed up with practicing law. Captain America and Billy gave him a ride to New Orleans and he gave them the underlying message of the movie. People hated them because they represented the freedom that the rest of the country craved.

With the release of this milestone film, the public received a different image of road bikers. The characters may have broken a law or two, but they weren't dangerous criminals. They just wanted to find the freedom that the constitution of their country had promised. The feeling struck a chord in the counterculture that had built up around the movement protesting the Vietnam War. It was roughly at the same time that Honda released its major competitor to the large engine market, the CB750.

The timing was perfect for what would forever change motorcycle history. Honda's huge advertising budget shifted to support its new larger motorcycles. Gearheads continued to insist on buying Harley-Davidsons. The interstate highway system that was started shortly after World War II had made great progress. Hollywood shifted its presentation of the biker from misfit criminal to freedom seeker. Returning veterans of the war in Vietnam fueled motorcycle sales and touring became a tradition.

Bikers Today

The image of the young leather-clad hooligan has been fading from most people's minds, yet who could have foreseen that great advertising campaign that featured Malcolm Forbes posing atop his Harley-Davidson? Our two-wheeled friend had begun as an affordable and utilitarian mode of transportation, transformed into a recreation vehicle, and finally found a place as a symbol of high fashion. That's right, the very thing that once marked you as a social deviant now screams social status. Today, motorcycles have invaded Hollywood; celebrity bikers now include Arnold Schwarzenegger, Sylvester Stallone, Bruce Willis, and the current host of the *Tonight Show*, Jay Leno.

Motorcycles have crossed social, as well as gender, barriers. Celebrity bikers include Courteney Cox Arquette (who crossed that line on a Kawasaki Ninja), Rosie O'Donnell (with her Suzuki Intruder), and even Mary Hart, who admits that she is a biker.

Some argue that this social trend drives up motorcycle prices, but the truth is, although the price of owning a new motorcycle has risen, so has the price of just about any consumer product. The real difference between what has happened to the motorcycle and what has happened to many other products can be found in what you get for your money. Virtually every new motorcycle sold today is as easy to operate and maintain as an automobile with a manual transmission. When you consider reliability and the cost of maintenance, it is easy to see that just about everyone benefits from the recent popularity of the motorcycle. Everyone, that is, except the folk who only loved the machine because it made them look like a social misfit.

ESSENTIALS

Today, Hondas are made in the United States by American workers, and a handful of other companies have entered the competition with the two companies that once dominated the market. Today's consumer has a world of choices and is no longer forced to make his or her decision based on stereotypes, mechanical limitations, or the sense of national loyalty.

Computer-controlled fuel injection has made fouled spark plugs almost a thing of the past (they may still occasionally foul in cold weather). Drive shafts and belts have replaced the chain that once required almost constant attention. Electric starts, air suspension, intercoms, radios, passenger armrests, hard saddlebags, turn signals, and other accessories have made the motorcycle more convenient than ever. Although nothing is completely safe, improvements in general design, headlights, brakes, and tires have made them safer than ever. Even the largest Harleys are now equipped with fuel injection and electric starts.

CHAPTER 2

What's Under the Tank

Engine, carburetor, starter, transmission, the clutch. If you don't know one motorcycle part from the next, you've come to the right chapter. Here you will learn about the main parts of the motorcycle, and how they vary among different models. This information will help you make the right purchasing decision and is essential for knowing how to take care of your bike.

Engine Configurations

Motorcycle engine configurations include the single cylinder, the v-twin, the l-twin, the opposed twin, the parallel twin, the inline triple, and even the flat four and flat six, which are unique to the Honda Gold Wing. For a while there was even an inline six, but they proved to be more trouble than their bulky size was worth.

But with all these engine configurations (and there are many other less-prevalent ones not listed here), every conventional motorcycle engine can be placed into one of two categories based on how it works: two-stroke engines and four-stroke engines. No matter how the pistons are arranged, they pretty much do the same thing—they move up and down. The difference is in how many times a piston moves up and down to complete one power cycle.

The Four-Stroke Engine Category

The four-stroke engine is the easiest to explain. On the first stroke the piston is moved downward. The intake valve opens and the fuel/air mixture is drawn into the cylinder in the same way a hypodermic needle draws medicine from a bottle. On the second stroke, the piston moves up to compress the fuel/air mixture. If the timing is right, the spark plug ignites this mixture when it reaches the optimum compression ratio.

The third stroke is the power stroke. After being ignited by the spark plug, the air/fuel mixture expands rapidly in what can best be described as a planned and controlled explosion. Those expanding gases drive the piston down the cylinder much the way a bullet is driven from the barrel of a gun. When it reaches the bottom, the exhaust valve opens to relieve the pressure and the crankshaft swings around for an upstroke. That upstroke drives the piston back to the top of the cylinder and helps force out any remaining fuel/air mixture through the exhaust valve.

The Two-Stroke Engine Category

Although two-stroke engines are functionally much simpler than four-stroke engines, their design is harder to understand. Each downstroke in the two-stroke engine is both a power stroke and a drawing-in of the air/fuel mixture. Each upstroke is both an exhaust and a compression stroke. The two-stroke engine does not place the valves on top as a four-stroke engine does. Actually, the two-stroke engine does not usually have valves in the way a four-stroke engine does. Instead, it has ports in the cylinder wall for both intake and exhaust.

1915 Harley-Davidson

Photo courtesy of Seattle Support Group.

In a typical two-stroke engine, a mixture of air, fuel, and lubricant enters the crankcase through a reed valve, which actually has nothing to do with the function of the piston moving within the cylinder except in that the reed valve responds to the vacuum created by the piston's movement. The mixture is then compressed in the crankcase by the reciprocation of a piston. When one of the pistons reaches the bottom portion of its stroke, it uncovers a port in the cylinder wall and the pressurized mixture floods the cylinder. The piston then compresses this mixture as it moves upward in preparation of ignition. Towards the top of its stroke, the mixture is ignited by a spark plug, which drives the piston down into the cylinder.

ESSENTIALS Two-stroke engines create much more pollution, so they are generally not used on public roads. As you can imagine, there is absolutely no way to ensure that all of the burned fuel is forced out without also leaking some of the unburned mixture into the exhaust.

Here is where it gets a bit tricky, because the end stroke becomes the beginning stroke. As the piston is driven down inside the cylinder, it compresses the mixture of fuel, air, and lubricant in the crankcase, so that when it reaches the bottom, the compressed mixture floods the cylinder and assists in evacuating the remnants of the previous power stroke's burn through an exhaust port.

Two-Stroke Versus Four-Stroke Engines

Both two-stroke and four-stroke engines need a form of lubrication for the moving parts. Four-stroke engines typically have an oil reserve. Oil is pressurized and then sent through small ports to each of the moving parts. Two-stroke engines use fuel that has been treated with a lubricant. The fuel/air mixture carries this lubrication through the crankcase and into the cylinders. Because it lacks an overhead valve system that requires constant lubrication, the two-stroke engine is ideal for harsh conditions—it has no oil reserve to spill and no tiny oil passageways to clog. The two-stroke is zippier because every downstroke is also a power stroke, is more durable in harsh conditions, and requires less maintenance than a four-stroke.

Most modern two-stroke engines do not require the operator to mix the oil and fuel. Instead, they have a separate oil tank. Two-stroke engines do not recycle their oil the way four-stroke engines do, and it is constantly being burned away during the combustion process—so you must check the oil reserve regularly.

On the other hand, a two-stroke engine makes a lot more noise, because the exhaust gases are driven out of the cylinder by the rushing in of the air/fuel mixture and only a partial stroke of the piston. In a four-stroke engine, there is a distinct exhaust stroke that drives exhaust gases out of the cylinder. The exhaust system on a two-stroke engine is far less restrictive than that which the four-stroke engine is able to accommodate. In general, a restrictive exhaust is a much less noisy exhaust.

In sum, each type of engine has specific uses. Two-stroke engines are the choice for off-road vehicles because they are much better suited for harsh conditions, because off-roading is usually conducted where noise is not a factor, because the type of people who engage in that activity know how to take care of this type of engine, and because they are used far less frequently and for shorter periods of time than street bikes. For the same reasons, four-stroke engines are far better suited to the less-harsh conditions of streets and highways.

Good Vibrations: More on Engine Types

When you ride a motorcycle, you feel every single shake, rattle, and roll of the engine. If you have never ridden a two-stroke bike, imagine straddling a giant electric razor. Four-stroke engines are an entirely different story. Unlike the two-stroke engines found on practically every dirt bike, the four-stroke engines come in various configurations. Generally speaking, the more cylinders there are, the smoother the ride.

Single-Cylinder Engine

If you start with the lowest number of cylinders, you first encounter the single-cylinder engine, which has been called the "thumper." Avoid them entirely. In the early days when motorcycles were anything but low-maintenance, the thumper dominated the market because people thought that fewer cylinders meant that fewer things could go wrong. This idea backfired. You just can't balance the force of a one-piston engine—it either has to be extremely light or extremely small. This would be a great design for a two-stroke lawnmower motor, but not for a street bike.

Two-Cylinder Engines

Then there is the v-twin, which is the hallmark of Harley-Davidson. The v-twin was right there at the very beginning of motorcycle production. It is much smoother and generally produces more torque (power at the wheel) than the thumper, but it reached widespread use for a much more practical reason. The v-twin fits the bicycle frames that motorcycles were built on "back in the day."

Two is greater than one—but less than three. The v-twin can be one hell of a kidney exerciser. Harley's 45-degree angle doesn't do much to help this situation. Some models try to give your organs a break with rubber engine mounts, but most of them just let the rider enjoy the vibrations. The main problem with the v-twin is that the closer the pistons are to each other, the more they shake, because the power stroke is always in the same direction and little can be done to compensate for it. Honda was partly successful with a staggered crankshaft, which simulated an l-twin engine, Kawasaki had some luck with using counterbalances, but when you get right down to it, the v-twin is a beast that you will either love or hate, depending on your own personal preferences and tolerances.

FACTS

Today, the v-twin is a classic engine. It became synonymous with "street bike" when the Japanese companies decided to try to dominate the U.S. road market. American bikers coined the phrase "Harley clones" to describe this rush of imports.

Next up is the l-twin, which is basically a v-twin engine with a 90-degree angle. The increased angle helps to direct the power stroke in more than one direction, but the effort never went much further than Honda's crankshaft idea, and as a result these engines are only found on a handful of motorcycles, including the Moto Guzzi.

The opposed twin, a.k.a. the Boxer, offered a solution to the vibrations normally associated with two-cylinder engines. Originally developed by BMW for the German army, this engine design was also used briefly by Harley-Davidson during World War II and eventually cloned by Russian engineers for the same purpose. Today, you can still purchase a Russian-made Ural motorcycle featuring the opposed-twin engine.

The last of the twin-cylinder designs, the parallel-twin engine, vibrates more than the v-twin. Some might even say that it shakes like a thumper, only faster. The parallel twin pretty much functions like a thumper, except that it has two cylinders (rather than one) hammering away in the same direction. Basically, this type of engine is a v-twin with a 0-degree separation between cylinder angles, which increases vibration rather than decreasing it.

Still, the engine was popular for some time. It was originally developed by Triumph motorcycles but would later be copied by BSA, Norton, and others.

The Inline Triple

British companies added a cylinder to the twin in their effort to compete with the Japanese, who in turn were competing with Harley-Davidson. Unfortunately for the British, by the time they worked around the problems inherent to an inline motorcycle engine, Honda had already introduced the flat four. The British motorcycle industry was doomed. Not only did Honda's four-cylinder motorcycle have the advertising edge of sounding bigger, the use of four cylinders smoothed the ride tremendously.

Four- and Six-Cylinder Engines

The inline-four and the inline-six engines that were toyed with in the mid-1970s and early 1980s had a major drawback. They were much larger than a motorcycle could comfortably accommodate. Efforts to rearrange key engine components to provide more room for the rider's legs proved useless—nothing could really be done to comfortably squeeze engines better suited for automobiles inside a motorcycle.

To shorten their engine, Honda introduced a v4, which did offer just as many cylinders as their inline four, but in a smaller package. Still, it wasn't until they introduced the flat fours and flat sixes that the world really stood up and took notice.

ESSENTIALS Instead of having pistons that move up and down as do each of the configurations previously mentioned, Honda's four-cylinder and six-cylinder designs move side to side. Each piston is arranged horizontally and in opposition to the others.

These new engines are very similar to the Boxers that were used during World War II, except that they are liquid-cooled and have four or six cylinders, depending on the particular model. When it comes to low vibrations, these engines are the absolute finest as they decrease vibrations by using both an opposed-engine design and a larger number of cylinders than their bouncy counterparts.

These engines offer one more advantage over others: In addition to being heavier (because they are liquid-cooled), they make the motorcycle easier to handle around turns—thanks to their flat design, the engine's weight is very low to the ground. So what's the catch? Well, if you like the engine you are going to have to like the motorcycle, because these engines are only available on Honda Gold Wings.

Keeping It Cool Means Keeping It Balanced

No matter what type of motorcycle you ride, unless it's a rocket bike, you have an internal-combustion engine between those wheels. What is an internal-combustion engine? Well, *internal* means "inside," and *combustion* means "fire." As you know, fire means heat. So how do you get rid of all that heat inside the engine?

Air-cooling is the oldest and easiest way to get the heat out of the engine. Heat generated as a result of both combustion and friction travels from the inside of the engine to the engine's outer surface without any assistance. There, it dissipates into the air. The faster the air travels across the surface of the engine, the more air comes in contact with the engine's surface, so the faster the heat is dissipated. This might be a wonderful system if you could ride very, very fast and never stop for streetlights. The problem is, the faster the engine works, the more heat is generated.

The solution is to increase the engine surface. This is where cooling fins on classic motorcycles come into play. Sure, they are tough to clean, but they are for a great deal more than just good looks. Adding cooling fins to exterior cylinder walls dramatically increases the engine's surface area. More surface area means more air contact with the surface area. More air contact with the surface area means more heat dispersed.

But even with cooling fins, this passive cooling system simply does not work well enough when the engine is sitting still. So while many off-road bikes continue to rely on little more than passing air to cool their small engines, street motorcycle designers looked for further ways to take advantage of the laws of nature.

Cooling Systems

The oil-assisted cooling system was introduced to address this issue. ("Oil-assisted" because, when you get right down to it, all cooling systems are primarily air-cooled.) The oil-assisted cooling system is a simple concept—engine oil is splashed over internal parts to lubricate and cool down the engine. Oil accumulates the engine's heat and then travels under pressure to an oil cooler in the front of the motorcycle. The oil cooler itself is little more than a radiator for oil. After giving its heat to the surrounding air, the oil returns to begin the cycle again.

Motorcycles equipped with oil-cooled engines require special attention. The operator must ensure that the oil cooler is free of debris that might prevent airflow from doing its job, causing your motorcycle to overheat.

ALERT

Never use automotive coolants (antifreeze) in a motorcycle—it contains material designed to keep the inside of the cooling system clean. Because motorcycle engineering requires different materials, many of these substances are not compatible with the internal workings of a motorcycle cooling system.

Liquid-assisted cooling systems take the oil-assisted cooling system one step further. Instead of using the engine's own oil as a coolant, the cylinder walls are surrounded by a specially formulated liquid that absorbs the engine's heat and then travels to a radiator in the front of the motorcycle. The liquid-assisted cooling system is so effective that it is now used on the great majority of street motorcycles currently in production. In an automobile, this type of liquid is called antifreeze.

It All Boils Down to Balance

On one side of the fulcrum, you have cooling fins, oil, and coolant, which disperse heat. On the other side, you have friction and combustion, which generate heat. If you dissipate heat too quickly, your engine will not run at proper operating temperatures. If you dissipate heat too slowly, your engine will overheat, and stop working permanently. For the most part, only motorcycle engineers need to worry about the thermal balance. What you need to know is that engines and their respective cooling systems were designed to work with each other under certain conditions and with certain regular maintenance. You should not expect a motorcycle designed to maintain optimum engine temperatures via a radiator or oil cooler to function properly when its cooling device(s) are covered in mud, grass, and leaves. If you want to hop hills and throw mud in the air, you should consider a motorcycle whose designers did not feel it necessary to include a radiator or oil cooler.

ESSENTIALS
> Liquid-assisted cooling is a more efficient way of maintaining proper engine temperature, but you will never see an oil-assisted cooling system fail because the owner filled the radiator with the wrong coolant. Liquid-assisted cooling systems mean a more efficient way of maintaining optimum engine temperature, but they also require more maintenance.

Fuel Injectors Versus Carburetors

Carburetors and fuel injectors have the same purpose: producing the fuel/air mixture necessary to make an engine run. They both create a situation where fuel is pushed into the air/fuel mixture. Fuel injectors accomplish this by pressurizing the fuel and then squirting it into the mixture. Carburetors achieve similar ends by creating an area of lower-than-atmospheric pressure (vacuum) and then allowing normal atmospheric pressure to push/pull the fuel. For the most part, fuel-injector intake systems outperform carburetors by a very wide margin.

Carburetor

Carburetors—"carbs" in gearhead lingo—function by introducing fuel into the passing air. Except when the operator increases throttle, the carburetor relies on the vacuum effect. With each intake downstroke of the piston, air is drawn through the carburetor, past the intake manifold (which connects the carburetor to the cylinder head), and, ultimately, into the cylinder inside the engine. The shape, size, and throttle position of the carburetor controls the volume of air that is permitted into the engine.

ALERT

The trick to really understanding how the carburetor works is to forget everything you have ever heard about vacuums because it is probably wrong. You see, there is really no vacuum—the term here is simply a way of describing the difference between two pressures.

When the carburetor is wide open, air is allowed to flow in at its fastest and the difference between external and internal pressure (vacuum) is at its least. When the carburetor is shut, only a tiny amount of air is allowed to pass by the carburetor and the pressure difference (vacuum) is at its greatest. Because zero vacuum would mean zero fuel delivery, the orifice or "throat" of the carburetor is designed to be a specific shape and size to ensure vacuum.

This design is flawed. Because the carburetor relies on the difference between internal and external pressures to deliver fuel, anything that affects that difference will affect the ideal size of the carburetor's throat. When the engine is cold, the restriction needs to be greater because the internal air pressure is greater. So a choke has been added to the carburetor so that during engine warmup and cold riding conditions the operator can temporarily increase the restriction between internal and external pressures.

ESSENTIALS

If a motorcycle starts and idles fine but almost dies on rapid acceleration or when you rev the engine, it's likely that the accelerator pump in the carburetor has failed. Fortunately, the average carburetor can be removed and rebuilt in your garage; rebuilding kits are available for a reasonable price at most motorcycle-parts stores.

Acceleration is another obstacle. When the throttle opens, air rushes in and the vacuum decreases. As the vacuum decreases, so does fuel delivery—and you can't accelerate without additional fuel. To overcome this problem, a device called an accelerator pump is built into the carburetor. Basically, the accelerator pump squirts extra fuel into the throat of the carburetor. Twisting the throttle is like pushing down on the top of the squirt bottle.

ALERT

If your carburetor leaks gasoline from the vent hole toward the top of its float bowl, you should not try to plug that hole. Doing so will prevent external pressure from entering the hole and the carburetor will not work properly. If you choose to rebuild the carburetor yourself, chances are you will find the real problem is grit in the valve that is connected to the float. A poorly adjusted float can cause this to happen as well, but float adjustment does not generally change unless someone changes it.

On a carburetor-equipped motorcycle, gravity is enough to deliver the fuel to the carburetor. From there, vacuum takes over. There is a hole in the top of the carburetor's float bowl, which allows external pressure in. At the bottom of the float bowl is a passage that allows the fuel to escape into the throat of the carburetor. When the pressure is greater in the float bowl (external pressure) than inside the carburetor's throat, the fuel is forced by the greater pressure toward the lesser pressure.

Fuel Injection

Fuel injection is a whole different story. Instead of depending on a difference in pressure to deliver the fuel to the fuel/air mixture, a fuel-injected engine depends on a mechanical or an electric pump, with much higher fuel pressures. Because fuel delivery is much less dependent on the pressure difference (vacuum), there is much less need to control that difference. Chokes don't stick closed and spark plugs are much less likely to foul. Yes, air pressure still comes into play, as the volume of fuel must be matched to the volume of air in specific ratios. But fuel injection does not rely on those pressure differences to deliver the proper amount of fuel to the intake charge.

The first truly workable fuel-injection system for motorcycles was available on the 1984 BMW K1000 four cylinder. Ducati followed in 1988, then Suzuki, Honda, and even Harley-Davidson. But fuel injection still has a very long way to go before it is considered biker standard. If you already own a fuel-injected motorcycle, congratulations! You probably have a very well thought-out piece of engineering that will give you years of transportation and enjoyment. But if you haven't yet made a motorcycle purchase, please read refer to Chapter 5 before you make up your mind.

Electric Starters Versus Kick Starters

With either starter method, the goal is to move the pistons up and down in the cylinders at speeds sufficient to achieve the proper compression ratio for ensuring combustion. Cylinders are never perfectly sealed. On every compression stroke, an amount of air/fuel mixture is lost into the crankcase. When the piston moves slowly, there is more time for this loss to occur. When the piston moves faster, there is less time for the mixture to escape.

Kick Starters

Generally speaking, the kick-start procedure for modern motorcycles is much easier than it was for their predecessors:

1. Unfold the kick lever.
2. Kick the lever downward.
3. Repeat if necessary.

But kick-starting a motorcycle isn't always easy—motorcycles are less likely to start on the first try than a cheap-imitation Zippo lighter. Generally, the older the motorcycle, the worse your chances are. It's not so much the age as the engineering. Trial and error has simply made much better motorcycles all around and the starting procedure is no exception to this rule.

Back in the day, the kick starter was downright dangerous. At a very minimum, you could always expect the lever to slam back into your foot. Actually, the lever could strike you with enough force to break your foot, leg, or maybe even your nose—if you fly over the handlebars. To gauge the danger element for yourself, feel free to find a Harley XLCH Sportster and give it a try, but if you weigh less than 150 pounds, you might want to bring a parachute.

1924
Sunbeam

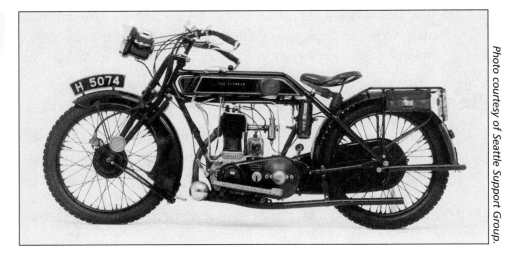

Photo courtesy of Seattle Support Group.

Electric Starters

Electric starters are little more than a less annoying and less dangerous way of doing exactly what the kick starters do, but they do have one major disadvantage over kick starters. The kick starter will continue to work when your battery is dead. While this might not seem like a fantastic advantage, it certainly feels like it at three in the morning after you have killed your battery trying to start a motorcycle with wet spark plugs. If you have a kick starter, you can just swap out your plugs and it will probably fire up like normal. If you have an electric starter, after swapping out your plugs you will find yourself walking your motorcycle to the closest hill and trying to bump-start it by riding down the hill and popping your clutch. And, of course, that hill always manages to be miles away.

ESSENTIALS Almost all modern motorcycles come equipped with electric starts. The only kick starters you are likely to encounter are old motorcycles and a few new off-road models.

Manual Transmission

Manual transmission works by changing the ratio in which the power from the engine is distributed to the rear wheel. In the beginning, this was accomplished without a transmission at all. In the earliest motorcycles, the ratio was absolutely fixed. The engine and the rear wheel each had a pulley that was one set size, and the two were attached by a leather belt.

FACTS

Most motorcycle mechanics consider the oddball automatic transmission/clutch as black magic. Chances are you will never see one of these things, as they were only made as an experiment, for a very short time. They failed miserably, so avoid them.

If the engine's pulley measured two inches in circumference, and the wheel pulley measured one inch, the ratio was 1:2 (one revolution turned into two revolutions). No, I didn't get that backwards. Every time the larger pulley (in this case the engine) turned around once, the belt was pulled two inches forward. Because the belt was also wrapped around the pulley on the wheel, that pulley had to turn the equivalent of how far the belt moved. Being only one inch in circumference, the pulley had to turn around twice each time the belt moved two inches forward.

The Original Clutch

While moving in a range of speeds that the engine could reach, that system was fine. Even with very underpowered engines, a real-world ratio between the front and rear pulleys could be used that would allow the motorcycle to function. The real problem was coming to a stop. After all, if the rear wheel is physically attached to the engine, the wheel stops each time the engine has to stop. To overcome that problem, the first crude clutch was invented. It consisted of nothing more than a third pulley that could be moved to add or release belt tension. To stop the motorcycle, the operator would simply move a lever, which released the movable pulley from the position where it held the belt tight. While at a standstill with the engine running, the belt would simply slip until the moveable pulley was brought back into play. This way the engine was disengaged from the wheel and could continue to run while the rear wheel stood still.

The Evolution of Transmission

Few people realize that this device was also the first motorcycle transmission. Although crude, high-maintenance, and certainly foul-smelling (due to burning leather), the device was able to control the ratio between the turning engine and the turning rear wheel. Depending on how tight a pulley kept the belt, the ratio between engine revolutions to rear wheel revolutions would change between a dead stop (X:0) and the full capacity, which is the raw expression of the difference between engine pulley and wheel pulley (1:2 in this basic explanation).

ESSENTIALS

The modern transmission, however, has come a long way from this early design. The original belt and pulley design lost torque when the belt slipped. In the modern transmission, a properly working clutch ensures a solid connection between the engine and the rear wheel. The single-ration design proved to be far too limiting.

Any given running engine will provide a certain range of revolutions and a certain range of torque. The problem is that without a transmission, those two ranges are never large enough to provide what we need to operate a motorcycle effectively. From a standstill, the part of the motorcycle that comes in contact with the ground (the wheel) needs to receive a large amount of torque to overcome inertia (and get the bike moving), but a low number of revolutions because the bike should not be going very fast.

Simple Newtonian Physics

The first half of Newton's first law states that objects at rest tend to stay at rest. Remember the last time your car ran out of gas and you had to push it to the gas station? When you first started moving, your feet didn't have to move very fast, but it was hard to get the car going. Once it started rolling, however, the pushing part became easy but your feet had to move a great deal faster. Think of pushing the car as torque, and moving your feet as the "RPM" (revolutions per minute).

The modern transmission is a collection of different sized gears that are employed to convert the engine's ability to provide revolutions and torque into a wider and more practical range without wasting as much engine power as the old system of leather belt and pulley. In the smallest (first) gear, the gear ratio in the transmission that is being used is smaller than when in top gear. This causes the engine power that comes out of the transmission to have a higher torque but lower RPM than when it is in top gear. This is where torque comes in—to force the motorcycle to overcome its tendency "to stay at rest." As you use higher gears, the available torque decreases but the available RPMs increase. By the time you hit top gear, there is very little torque needed to maintain speed because of the second half of Newton's law—which is that objects in motion tend to stay in motion.

FACTS

An infamous exception to the standard foot shifter is the "suicide shift." This device is a hand-operated lever that requires the rider to let go of the handlebar to shift gears.

Between 1950 and 1970, virtually all motorcycle manufacturers had taken the manual transmission one step further. Instead of making a transmission separate from the engine, everyone except Harley-Davidson incorporated the transmission into the lower end of the engine housing. This is commonly called a "unitized transmission." Harley-Davidson, on the other hand, still uses a transmission that is entirely separate from the engine. Connecting the Harley-Davidson's engine and transmission is a sprocket on the engine's crankshaft, a sprocket on the transmission, and a chain in between. That chain is called the "primary" and the case in which it rides is called the "primary case." This additional part means one more potential part to break, additional regular maintenance issues, and additional costs.

Beyond the differences between the unitized transmission and the primary-chain way of connecting to the engine, motorcycle transmissions are similar in most ways. A set of gears with different ratios control the amount of available torque and RPMs for differing riding conditions. There is a set of forks, which move those gears, and a peg by your left foot that controls the forks. Most exceptions to this type of construction have been proven entirely too unsafe for continued production.

The Clutch

The clutch has two essential purposes. It allows the motorcycle to stop by disengaging the engine from the transmission and allowing you to stop the motorcycle without shutting down the engine. Secondly, the clutch helps protect the workings of the transmission against damage.

In many motorcycles, there is a very narrow moment when the speed of the turning gears is just right that you can shift without using a clutch. This is called "speed shifting." Although it might sound like a good idea, it is not. You are more likely to do damage to the gear teeth and might even manage to lock the transmission, which could result in personal injury.

ESSENTIALS

If you miss the moment when the engine is not driving the rear wheel and the rear wheel is not driving the engine in your speed shift attempt, the teeth of one gear will slam into the teeth of another gear in one direction or the other. You could easily snap teeth off gears and run the chance of locking up the transmission at speed.

Speed shifting is so dangerous and damaging because when an engine is either accelerating or decelerating, there is a tremendous amount of force being exerted on one side of the gear teeth. This is called being "under load," as opposed to being idle. When a motorcycle accelerates, one side of the gear teeth in the transmission is in contact and under pressure. When you decelerate without using the clutch, the other side of the gear teeth is under pressure. Remember, a manual transmission means there is a physical connection between the engine and the rear wheel. So if not for neutral or a clutch, the engine transmission gears would always be under load when the motorcycle is moving. If the engine is not driving the gears, chances are the rear wheel is driving the engine.

To understand how this works, put a motorcycle in neutral and throttle up to about 3,000 RPMs. When you let go of the throttle, the engine RPMs go down almost instantly because nothing is driving the engine. Now, try the same thing in third gear. You will notice that although the RPMs do drop, they do so slowly. This is because instead of the engine driving the rear wheel, the rear wheel is driving the engine.

To ensure that there is the least amount of load on the gears when they are placed in contact with each other, the clutch disengages the engine from the transmission before you shift gears. The first clutches were operated by a foot pedal, in combination with the suicide shifts. Having to remove a hand from the handlebar at the very moment your foot has to apply pressure to only one side of the motorcycle proved to be a bit awkward, to put it mildly.

Today, just about every motorcycle manufactured uses a clutch lever that is mounted on the left handlebar, which should be easy to remember because chances are that's the same side as the foot shift lever.

Operating Instructions

To engage the clutch, squeeze the hand lever. A cable or a hydraulic line transfers the force to the clutch arm and then to the clutch. As you squeeze, the clutch arm causes the pressure plate (the moving part of the clutch assembly) to work against the clutch spring tension and realize the clamping action of the clutch plates. At this point, the clutch plates, the power train between the engine, and the transmission are no longer connected. When you release the clutch hand lever, the pressure plate moves under the force of the clutch spring tension and sandwiches the clutch plates so that there is again a connected power train.

Using a motorcycle clutch is not much different than a car's, right? Wrong! As you might recall from the section on transmissions, most motorcycles use unitized transmissions. Almost all modern motorcycles share their oil sump with the transmission gears, crankshaft, and even clutch. In a typical automobile, if engine oil leaks past the rear main seal and gets onto the clutch, you have a problem. In a typical motorcycle, you have a problem if the engine oil does *not* get onto the clutch—hence the differences between motorcycle and automobile oil.

ALERT

Remembering what is where is easy now that the controls have become standard. Everything that is on the left is associated with changing gears. Everything on the right is associated with either going (hand throttle) or stopping (hand and foot breaks).

Automobile oil has additives that would change the friction coefficient of the motorcycle clutch. Additionally, motorcycle oil often contains baneful phosphorous additives that are not present in automobile oil because they are detrimental to the catalytic converter. Theoretically, it is possible to use automobile oil at a rating of no higher than SG, but the only rating generally found in automobile oil is SJ. Best to be safe and only use what the motorcycle manufacturer has recommended.

<h1>CHAPTER 3</h1>

Get the Most Power Out of Your Engine and Brakes

Engines determine a great deal of the characteristics of a motorcycle, but the final drive and brake system can be just as much of an influence on the all-around performance of any given bike. This chapter will address the best ways of getting the power to the ground and stopping that power once it's there.

Putting the Power on the Ground

Motorcycles have come a long way since World War I, but when you get right down to it, the basics of getting engine power to the rear wheel haven't changed a bit. They have been greatly improved, but your choices remain the same: chain, shaft, and belt. Today, each has evolved sufficiently that the real question is no longer which one is best, but which one is best for you.

1925
Harley-
Davidson

Photo courtesy of Seattle Support Group.

Chains: Old Faithful or the Weakest Link?

Chains were the first system to replace the leather belt. Most manufacturers adopted chain drives by the end of World War I. The chain system needs very little introduction because it doesn't deviate much from the single-speed bicycle. There is a sprocket in the front, a sprocket in the back, and a chain looped around both. As one sprocket rotates, it pulls one end of the chain while pushing the other end. This causes the rear sprocket to rotate with whatever is attached to it. In the case of motorcycles, that's the rear wheel. The only real difference between the modern chain-operated motorcycle and the first chain-driven bicycle is that the motorcycle has an engine.

The chain poses one significant drawback: When it snaps, it can sound like a bomb going off between your feet, and might feel like one too, if the shrapnel gets ahold of your lower legs. Chains only snap when under enough tension to fly with tremendous force. On a hard acceleration, where they stop is anyone's guess. The chain can fall on the ground underneath the bike or several lanes away.

Replacing the Chain

In the old days, replacing a chain was a very difficult task that required removal of the rear wheel and access to the primary case. Chains were continuous, so you had to get to the two sprockets that they connected, and getting to the front sprocket was no easy task. Today's chains often feature a device called the maintenance link, which lets the chain be taken apart. This facilitates ease of installation, even at the roadside, but causes its own problems. Whenever a part is designed to disassemble, it has the inherent drawback of disassembling on its own.

ALERT

If you install a maintenance link-type chain, the open part of the retaining clip always goes facing the opposite direction of chain travel when the bike is moving forward. In this configuration, momentum exerts force to keep the clip in place. In the reverse installation that same momentum serves to dislodge the retaining clip.

The bright side is that, for the most part, chains won't generally disassemble spontaneously unless they are installed improperly. Unfortunately, most people don't read the instructions. They might get the washer positions right because it's not hard to guess how they go. But when you don't know what you are doing, you only have a 50 percent chance of installing the retaining clip properly.

Modern chains are available with and without a maintenance link. The choice is up to you. If you are willing to take the time to read instructions, there is no real reason a chain equipped with a maintenance clip will fail earlier than a continuous one.

Most chains today are an improvement over the old metal-only chain. The O-ring chain is a wonderful invention. The rings in this chain actually work as seals to keep a lubricant in contact with moving parts. These improved chains last much longer than the more traditional metal-only chains, but they do require a few special considerations. Regular lubricants and cleaners can quickly break down the synthetic O-rings, leading to lightning-fast chain failure.

The chain's drawback is the mess. Even the O-ring variety requires external cleaning and lubrication. If you let gunk build up on your chain, you will shorten its life span and get that gunk splattered all over your legs and the lower portion of the motorcycle.

Getting the Shaft

Shaft-driven motorcycles are not as new as some people think. In fact, a few manufacturers have been offering the shaft-driven system since as long ago as the World War I period. A good shaft system can be extremely low-maintenance and almost bulletproof. The only regular maintenance it requires is to glance at the oil level in the differential, and topping it off or replacing it as needed. What could be easier? Well, don't get too excited just yet. It turns out that shaft-driven systems have some problems of their own.

There are three downsides to shaft-driven motorcycles. First, they are much more expensive to manufacture than other drive systems. If you are planning on keeping the bike for any length of time, you will overcome the expense with the amount of money you save on chains, belts, and labor if you are not able to do the work yourself. But there are a couple of other reasons shaft systems are not ideal.

Shaft-driven systems are extremely heavy compared to other alternatives. Making the matter worse, the additional weight is unsprung weight, weight not supported by the suspension. Unsprung weight is in more of a direct contact with the road surface, so it has a much greater effect on the way a motorcycle handles. Additional unsprung weight makes it more difficult to turn and shift weight proportionately and adds to the bike's aim to continue traveling in a straight line. This makes shaft drive systems particularly unsuited for most sporting purposes.

FACTS

Some manufacturers have successfully overcome shaft jacking with fancy geometry, but the exceptions are few. For the most part, shaft-driven systems are best left to the larger touring motorcycles, which won't see as many demands for instant acceleration.

In both chain and belt systems, the rotation of the driving force is the same direction as the rotation of the rear wheel. In a shaft system, the rotation of the drive shaft is 90 degrees different from the rotation of the rear tire. On a chain and belt driven system, the force of the drive system meets the initial resistance at the rear wheel and causes the motorcycle to dig in, effectively making it heavier. On a shaft-driven system, the effect is to twist the bike to the opposite direction of shaft rotation. This is called "shaft jacking."

Back to the Belt

So chains make a mess and shafts do funny things when you accelerate hard or turn quickly. By the middle of the 1980s motorcycles saw a gradual return to belt-drive systems. Harley-Davidson led the way, reintroducing the belt as a specialty item available only on models like the original Sturgis. Soon, improvements in materials, design, and manufacturing techniques made the belt-drive system much more viable and much less dependent on friction between contact points. Today, belt-drive systems are standard equipment on all Harley-Davidsons and many other motorcycles.

The belt-drive system offers none of the problems associated with the shaft system, and doesn't require the constant cleaning and lubricating that the chain system does. It is generally smoother and quieter, and it doesn't collect the goop that chains do. But there is one major drawback on just about every belt-driven motorcycle in production. They require a fairly large amount of work to replace.

There are no links or special pins to open a belt. This means replacement requires the full removal of the rear wheel and usually a great deal of the primary-drive system as well. You can't replace a belt by the side of the road, and many novice gearheads wouldn't want to do it themselves in their garage. If you wind up with a belt-driven motorcycle, pay particular attention to the manufacturer's specification for final drive-belt replacement. When it's time, have a professional do it after you have ridden it in, rather than after you have to tow it in.

So What Will It Be?

Like all choices in life, deciding on a final drive system will take some compromise. The real challenge is determining what is most important to you. Review the pros and cons, and decide based on your own needs and preferences.

- Chains—Easy to replace but noisy, messy, and downright dangerous when they snap
- Shafts—Quiet and dependable, but expensive and detracting from performance (shaft jacking)
- Belts—Quiet, clean, and affordable, but difficult to replace

Putting on the Brakes

Power is not only about going forward, but being able to stop. Remember Newton's law: objects in motion tend to stay in motion. To act against that law and bring a motorcycle to a stop requires a great deal of energy right where the motorcycle meets the ground, at the tires or, more specifically, at the contact patch of your wheels.

Bikers tend to forget about this second half of Newton's law. Almost every motorcycle shop offers high-performance parts for the engine, but few offer high-performance braking parts. What's the point of going faster if you can't stop faster? Plus, motorcycle mishaps happen more often while decelerating than while accelerating.

1926
Coventry
Eagle

Photo courtesy of Seattle Support Group.

The offerings for brake parts are slim strictly out of supply-and-demand issues. Bikers just don't purchase tricked-out brake rotors as often as they do tricked-out carburetors, so naturally the shops are more inclined to stock the carburetors than the brake disks. Even those bikers who insist on customizing every little thing on their bike will usually leave the brakes exactly as the factory made them, pure stock.

Brake Types

Motorcycles use two types of brakes: disks and drums. Modern motorcycles use a hand lever to actuate the front disk brakes and a foot lever to actuate the rear disk or drum brakes. Generally speaking, disk brakes are hydraulically actuated and drum brakes are manually actuated. If you've never been on a motorcycle before, you will probably prefer disk brakes all the way around. If you have gotten used to rear drum brakes, then you will probably prefer the drum rear/disk front combination even though it isn't nearly as effective as disks all the way around.

When you squeeze down on the brake lever with your hand, the lever travels a relatively long distance compared to the final travel of the brake pads. The hand lever moves a piston inside the master cylinder on the handlebar and forces brake fluid through the brake line to the caliper, which holds the brake pads. Inside the caliper is a piston that travels a much shorter distance than the one inside the master cylinder, but it is much larger. Because the laws of hydraulic motion stipulate that the pressure of fluid remains a constant at both the master cylinder and the caliper, the piston in the caliper can actually exert much more force on the brake pad than your hand can because the area of the caliper piston which the fluid acts upon is much larger than the area of the piston in the master cylinder. Pressure is measured in weight per area. In the United States this is usually expressed as psi, or pounds per square inch. The actual pressure remains the same in caliper or in the master cylinder, but the psi exerted by the fluid in the caliper to drive the piston outward is far greater than the amount of pressure exerted by the brake lever on the master cylinder. Why? Because the caliper piston has more square inches of area.

ESSENTIALS

Disk brakes have many advantages over drum brakes. They are self-cleaning, self-adjusting, and much easier to access and maintain. But they do require attention to a hydraulic system that mechanical drum brakes do without. That hydraulic system has its own set of concerns.

So how does all this stop the motorcycle? Well, the caliper is mounted to a part of the motorcycle that is not turning with the wheel. Most often this is the fork, though in some very odd rear-wheel cases it may be the frame. As the hydraulic pressure increases, the piston(s) inside the caliper move outward and exert force on the pads (also stationary), which squeeze the brake disk that is attached to the wheel. The more pressure, the tighter it squeezes and the quicker you slow down.

Drum brakes ride inside a hub or brake drum. They are typically actuated manually by a mechanical-brake foot lever. When you step down on the brake lever, the brake shoes are forced outward such that they come in contact with the brake drum, which rotates with the wheel.

There are a few exceptions to these general rules. Some manufacturers have been experimenting with proportioning valves, devices that operate much like they do in automobiles—they regulate the amount of pressure that is being distributed to any one caliper. In the case of the motorcycle, these valves control the ratio of braking power between the front and rear wheel. These new systems can confuse the seasoned rider and cause the novice rider to become overly dependent on the valve to make decisions. It's best to avoid them.

1936
Harley-
Davidson
1340CC

Photo courtesy of Seattle Support Group.

Antilock Brake Systems

Antilock brake systems (ABS) are relatively new in motorcycle engineering. ABS are computer-controlled brakes that have the ability to sense when your wheel(s) lock up and then override the operator's instructions to prevent a skid. No matter how hard a rider applies the brakes on an ABS system, the wheel(s) will not lock because the computer will interrupt the pressure momentarily and then oscillate it at tremendous speed and pressure to ensure that the maximum braking force is applied while not allowing the motorcycle's wheel to slide out of control.

As with all new arrivals, the downside to the ABS system is that it doesn't have enough motorcycle miles to have been proven or accepted. Moreover, it remains a high-ticket item and will probably find usefulness only on very large touring models. Independent control of front and rear tires as well as the ability to cause a deliberate skid are both parts of operating most other kinds of motorcycles.

Which Brake System Is Best for You?

Each has its advantages and its disadvantages. As with motorcycle style, brands, and models, there is no one right choice. You simply need to figure out which system is best for you. Proportioned brakes are never appropriate for off-road riding because there are times when you will want to operate your front and rear brakes separately.

Good first-time bikes should probably come with a chain final drive, hydraulic disk front brakes, and mechanical drum rear brakes. Let your first motorcycle be one that will advance your rider skills while remaining easy to maintain.

If you are looking for a first-time motorcycle, you need to keep it simple. First, you are probably going to put it down a time or two before you get the hang of things. Simpler usually means cheaper. Second, like a child learning math on a calculator, some of the frills may detract from your initial acquisition of skills.

CHAPTER 4

Motorcycle Categories: From Eating Bugs to Eating Mud

Before you can even consider buying a motorcycle, you have to decide what you want that motorcycle to do. Motorcycles are designed with much more than style in mind. Understanding different categories of motorcycles and their ranges of functions will help you make your purchasing decision.

What's in a Category?

If you have spent any time looking at motorcycle magazines or catalogs, you probably saw enough categories to make your head spin. The three most common categories are Supersport, Superbike, and Grand Prix. These titles are racing terms—they mean nothing when it comes to classifying production motorcycles, and appear in motorcycle catalogs for promotional purposes only. Production motorcycles might best be divided into touring, street, and off-road bikes. These categories are not based on who manufactured the motorcycle or how they choose to promote it. They are based on what the motorcycle was designed to do and what it does best.

Motorcycle categories are guidelines rather than rules, with the exception of two-stroke off-road motorcycles (environmental laws prohibit driving these bikes on city streets). However, even a motorcycle that was manufactured strictly for off-road use may be street legal if it has a four-stroke engine.

Even in situations where motorcycles share the same manufacturer, comparable construction, and similar engines, different designs are intended for different purposes. Consider the Harley-Davidson Electra Glide Ultra Classic and the 883 Hugger. Both bikes bear the Harley logo, both are powered by a v-twin engine, and both incorporate similar construction technique. But the Electra Glide is a huge touring motorcycle that pretty much fills a lane. In contrast, the 883 Hugger barely fills a doorway. For the purpose of discussion here, the Electra Glide falls into the touring category and the 883 Hugger fits into the street category.

The categories serve as a way of discussing and identifying motorcycle characteristics. They are not a way of restricting their use. Almost any motorcycle can be used outside its category, and sometimes the lines between categories blur. You could use that 883 Hugger like an Electra Glide and ride it across the country, though it won't be very comfortable because the motorcycle was not designed for that use.

You could also take a touring motorcycle off-road to your favorite fishing hole—just don't be surprised if it sinks in the first patch of mud you find.

Knees in the Breeze—the Highway (Touring) Motorcycle

The largest and heaviest motorcycles are often found in the touring class. When designing touring motorcycles, engineers keep operator's and passenger's comfort in mind. While these bikes often feature large engines, they also offer large tires, hard saddlebags, touring packs, fairings, windshields, and body panels. All that extra weight means their engines are designed and mated with transmissions for torque and pulling power. These bikes have the power to get a great deal of weight moving and then to maintain a constant speed. They are not designed for quarter-mile sprints.

Operating a motorcycle of this size requires a different mindset. Not only are they not the fastest off the line, they are also much slower to stop. Increased braking distances are in order. These are motorcycles for people who know that half the fun of a trip is getting there. After all, these bikes will get you there in the maximum amount of style and comfort that can be found on two wheels.

ESSENTIALS

If you ride long enough, you will probably find yourself owning two or more motorcycles at a time—a touring motorcycle for traveling across country, a street racer or cruiser for bopping around town, and even a strictly off-road motorcycle for serious fun. Most bikers buy motorcycles as they can afford them, one bike at a time.

If your interest lies in long-distance riding, touring motorcycles might be the best choice. Not only are they more comfortable on longer rides, they often include options that make the trip safer and more manageable. These options may include gas gauge and additional instrumentation, extra lighting, and comfort items like a stereo.

Passenger comfort is of high order for touring bikes as well. Most motorcycles offer a passenger seat, but touring models tend to offer more of a throne, with thick padding, high backrests, and even armrests. Although it is an extremely unsafe practice, passengers routinely fall asleep in the arms of this two-wheel throne.

Although they are absolutely ideal for long trips, the downsides to the touring motorcycle are many. They start slower, take longer to stop, and make horrible first-time bikes. Taking one off-road is downright foolish, and even parking one on wet grass can be a bit of a struggle. Their kickstands will sink into the grass under all that weight and the bike will tumble over. On a center stand, they will usually remain upright, but when it's time to leave, you will have to take the time to dig them out.

FACTS

The main players in the touring category are Harley-Davidson, Honda, and Kawasaki. Harley-Davidson offers its Electra Glide, Road Glide, and Road King. Honda offers its Gold Wing, Aspencade, and Pacific Coast. And Kawasaki offers the Voyager. Honda's Gold Wing and Aspencade win this category's popularity contest hands down.

Bringing Home the Bacon—the Street Motorcycle

Motorcycles in this category are made for everyday use. You can buy a motorcycle that was built for local trips and has the ability to perform well on the occasional cross-country jaunt. You can find a street bike that is able to do double duty in the dirt. It's from those varying uses that we find three distinct subcategories to the street category:

- Street cruiser
- Street racer
- Street bike

Meet the Street Cruiser

These street bikes will, on occasion, double as touring motorcycles. Because they have only mildly high handlebars, forward pegs, and forward seat, the rider position on a cruiser is comfortable for long trips. On a cruiser, the rider sits with his spine vertical to the road or leaning slightly to the rear. This tends to be much more comfortable than the forward-leaning position of other motorcycles. Although street cruisers were not invented by Harley-Davidson, they are sometimes called Harley clones (especially in the case of Japanese imports).

ALERT

People often associate these motorcycles with black leather and denim. Although the word "biker" applies to anyone with a motorcycle who has a passion for biking, when you think of bikers you probably think of this classic motorcycle style.

The cruiser's riding position reflects the rider's outlook on life—laid back. More than any other type of motorcycle, the street cruiser screams, "I do not have a type-A personality." This is why it is the perfect choice for workaholics and people who actually do have type-A personalities—this bike provides escape, release, and the nostalgic sense of a time when life didn't move so fast.

Meet the Street Racer

These are motorcycles that may, on occasion, serve as racing bikes. Street racers have low handlebars, rear pegs, and seats that force the rider to lean forward, sometimes to the point of resting on the gas tank. These bikes are also known as pocket rockets. They are light, maneuverable, and generally very fast.

People associate street racers with brightly colored riding suits and matching helmets. They just scream speed, and as a result, the owners of these motorcycles are vulnerable to being stereotyped as inconsiderate public-street daredevils.

Their speed-demon appearance may be one of the biggest reasons not to purchase a street racer. Although basing a decision on what people think about you isn't mentally healthy, these motorcycles do not make good choices for riding in heavily populated areas and in traffic, because other motorists do not give them the room that they are more likely to afford to cruisers. The bottom line is, these can make great motorcycles for people who are mostly interested in top speeds.

Meet the Street Dirt Bike

Street dirt motorcycles, also known as dual sport bikes, have limited off-road capabilities, but they generally do not make good off-road competition motorcycles. They resemble dirt bikes, but they are also street legal. In this subcategory it is especially important to remind you that these are compromise motorcycles. While they do have off-road capabilities, these capabilities are limited. If you want to participate in serious off-road riding, it is much better to purchase a serious off-road motorcycle.

FACTS

More than anything else, these street bikes beg for farm country and the open spaces of America, where public roads aren't always paved. They make great motorcycles for someone who wants to use the same bike to go fishing as well as for going to buy bait.

In the Mud—the Off-Road Motorcycle

Not to be confused with the dirt bike subcategory of street motorcycles, this category excludes any motorcycle that was built with the intention of operating on the street. Some of these motorcycles feature two-stroke engines, which make them illegal for street use. Others have four-stroke engines, but their design makes them entirely impractical for day-to-day street use.

Off-road motorcycles are always equipped with a chain final drive. Shaft systems cannot accommodate the changing drive angle that is created by the long movement of the rear wheel. Additionally, their unsprung weight detracts from the very quick direction changes an off-road motorcycle is prone to making. A belt system could be designed that would allow for rear-wheel travel, but belts need to be much wider than chains to get enough grip on the surface they are turning against. With the side area comes more opportunity for dirt and rocks to interfere. Generally speaking, off-road motorcycles have single-cylinder air-cooled engines, though there are some two-cylinder and liquid-cooled models as well.

FACTS

Two-stroke engines cannot be used on public streets or roadways because they generate large amounts of pollution. Four-stroke motorcycles intended solely for off-road use may sometimes be converted to street-legal configurations. However, this is not generally a good idea, as these motorcycles were never intended for street use.

Making the Final Decision: Compromise

Here is the word that nobody ever wants to hear but everyone must eventually deal with: compromise. Even if you have all the money you need to purchase your dream bike, chances are it was never built. With all the models in production, the chances of a manufacturer producing exactly what you want are slim.

Back in the real world where you don't always have the money you need to make those dream purchases, compromise is even more important. In this world you must address need prior to want, although you should always hope to find middle ground between the two.

SSENTIALS

Choosing a motorcycle that can fill both need and desire might seem like a compromise, but you will probably be happier with a dual-purpose motorcycle than you would be with a single-purpose one.

Maybe you want a motorcycle for your dream tour, but you also need reliable transportation when you are not touring. A street cruiser might be just your ticket. Look for a model with a smooth ride, a large-capacity gas tank, and then think about adding tour features like a windshield and hard saddlebags. Most street cruisers can be built up into very comfortable touring bikes.

So you want the ultimate cruiser. You are overwhelmingly set on a full-size Harley, but when you finally sit down on one, your feet don't reach the ground without a bit of a struggle. Or maybe your feet do hit the ground, but you won't stand a chance trying to pick the thing up. Maybe you can't afford more than $10,000 for a motorcycle, but don't want to buy it used. Consider the Harley-Davidson Hugger 883, which is substantially lighter and lower to the ground than most other Harleys and is priced at about $8,000.

1937 Harley-Davidson Flathead

Photo courtesy of Seattle Support Group.

Maybe your interest is solely in the dirt. You want to purchase a strictly off-road motorcycle because you know that street dirt bikes aren't nearly as good in the mud as those that were built for a single purpose. How are you going to get your motorcycle to the dirt track or favorite off-road location? When you figure the extra expense of a trailer, hitch, and vehicle to pull your motorcycle, it could be that the street dirt class will become much more appealing. With a street dirt bike you can ride to the track.

For First-Time Motorcycle Buyers

For some reason, owners of street motorcycles seem to think bigger is always better. Anyone who has ever ridden off-track knows that size is important, but that bigger is not always better. The larger an engine is, the harder it is to master it. The same raw power that you use to pass another motorist without downshifting can cause the bike's rear end to slip out from under you around a relatively easy turn. A larger engine adds a lot of extra weight to the motorcycle.

ALERT

Heavier motorcycles are harder to handle around the turns, take longer to bring to a stop, and have more trouble dealing with the up-and-down motion generated by bumps and potholes. You might have your heart set on a particular model, but do you really need all the complications, challenges, and expense of a large engine?

If you're looking for your first motorcycle, there is another compromise you should consider: size. It really does matter, but not in the way that most people think. Many manufacturers offer similar motorcycles with different engine sizes. The smaller sizes are generally best for anyone who is just learning. You should also be thinking cost and cost of repair, because you are going to put it down a time or two before you get it right.

The Kawasaki Ninja is the best example of this type of compromise. Maybe your dream motorcycle is a Ninja ZX12R with its 1198cc engine and reputation for being one of the fastest motorcycles in the world. A novice might look really sharp riding on top of all that machine, but he is going to look really stupid when he opens the throttle a bit too much in a turn and the bike fishtails out of control. A better idea might be to purchase the Ninja 250R. With its 248cc engine and a price tag of about

$8,000 less, the smaller motorcycle makes a great alternative and looks just about the same.

Many other manufacturers offer introductory level versions of their larger street motorcycles. Here's a list of the ones that stand out:

- Harley-Davidson Sportster, available with both 1200cc and 883cc engines
- Honda CB, available with 954cc and 599cc engines, as well as others in between
- Honda Shadow, available with 1099cc, 583cc, and other engines in between
- Honda Nighthawk, available with 747cc and 234cc engines
- Kawasaki KLR, available with 651cc and 249cc engines
- Kawasaki Vulcan, available with 1470cc, 498cc, and other engines in between
- Suzuki Bandit, available with 599cc and 1157cc engines
- Suzuki Intruder, available with 1462cc, 805cc, and other engines in between
- Yamaha YZF, available with 998cc and 558cc engines

Additionally, virtually all road and street dirt models have a range of engine sizes for each model.

CHAPTER 5

Buying Your First Motorcycle

If you know what you want and you are reasonably sure you can afford it, you have to determine where you can find it. If it's a new motorcycle, the answer is simple, a local dealership. But are you all that sure you want to purchase a new bike? This chapter will outline your options for buying a motorcycle.

New or Used

There is an exception to every rule. When it comes to the price difference between new and used motorcycles, the rule is that new motorcycles cost more than used motorcycles. Harley-Davidson is the biggest exception. The HD assembly line is so far behind the demand for motorcycles that buying a used Harley is often more expensive than buying a new one—people just don't want to wait for the assembly line to catch up with demand.

FACTS

Deciding to spend the extra money on a new motorcycle instead of going the more economic route is a choice each consumer must make. New higher-priced motorcycles come with a great deal of benefits that you won't typically find while shopping for used machines.

Once you take Harley-Davidsons out of the discussion, you are left with a very competitive market. Yet, despite the competition, which generally keeps new motorcycle prices low, not everyone can afford a brand-new motorcycle. Even when purchasing a bargain-priced new bike, you can expect to spend between $3,000 and $5,000 for a machine you'll be using as a learning tool. Used motorcycles can be had for a fraction of that price. If you aren't picky about specific models, you can purchase decent running motorcycles for less than $500 in a booming economy. When the economy slips, you might be able to do even better. If you don't want to buy one in the middle of the winter and want more of a selection, you can expect to find used motorcycles in good condition for between about $1,000 and $2,000. At the lower end of that range, you might have a bit of a fixer-upper, but that can be fun, too.

Investing in a New Bike

Let's say you have read everything you can get your hands on. You have compared the ups and downs of several models and you have found the one motorcycle that just screams your name. If you are looking for a new one, chances are a trip to the right dealership with cash in hand will yield exactly what you want. Again, the exception to this rule is Harley-Davidson. At the Harley dealership, you either take what they have or spend time waiting for the right model to arrive from the factory.

1937
Harley-
Davidson
Flathead

Photo courtesy of Seattle Support Group.

Warranty

What happens when something goes wrong? How much money will you save if you spend $1,000 on a used motorcycle with a new list price of $3,000, and then spend $2,000 on transmission repairs? Yes, these numbers are a bit impractical, but they do illustrate a point. When you buy a new motorcycle with a good warranty, the mechanically unexpected is usually someone else's problem. When you buy a used motorcycle with no warranty, you could be in for an unpleasant surprise. You can improve your odds in this department by purchasing used motorcycles from reputable dealerships, but generally they will charge for that reputation by pricing their used bikes higher than you will find from a private seller.

You can sometimes find a warranty for 50 percent of parts and labor on used motorcycles by shopping at motorcycle dealerships. Other times, an additional warranty can be purchased at a premium.

Ease of Repair

It is the nature of all mechanical things that parts wear and break. When it comes to new motorcycles, replacement parts are usually at hand, or at least you can order them to be delivered in a matter of a few days. In the case of used motorcycles, which have not been in production for years, you might not be so lucky.

Furthermore, buying a new motorcycle from a local dealership might be the first step in a good preventative maintenance program. Many dealerships offer discounted scheduled services and programs to help customers who have purchased their motorcycles.

1938
Harley-
Davidson

Photo courtesy of Seattle Support Group.

The Advantages of Buying a Used Bike

On the other hand, modern motorcycles are built well and you can always find used motorcycles with low mileage and in very good condition. The practical aspect of this decision isn't what's at the heart of the matter. Motorcycles are more than transportation—they are an expression of the soul. When buying your first motorcycle, your soul should be part of the decision-making process.

Remember the general rule of thumb: The older a motorcycle is, the harder it can be to find parts for it. If you buy a motorcycle that is more than ten years old, expect to do a little hunting whenever a part that is unique to that motorcycle needs to be replaced.

Some people just don't like getting dirty. If you are one of these people, you shouldn't buy a used motorcycle. If you are the type of person who likes taking things apart just to see how they work, then buying a used motorcycle might not be a bad idea—especially if you are also the type of person who can put them back together again. Look at it this way: If you buy a new motorcycle, it will come with new brake pads. If you buy a used motorcycle, it will probably come with used brake pads. So if you like changing brake pads, you should probably buy a used motorcycle. If you don't like changing brake pads, you should buy a new car and skip ahead to the following section on motorcycle prices.

Still reading? Well, the next task is deciding just how used a motorcycle you are looking for. Some bikers won't take a used bike around the block until they have stripped it to its frame and then put it back together piece by piece. This is often the case with AMF-built Harleys, which many believe were never put together right in the first place. Others insist that you should only fix those things that are broken. Most are comfortable with replacing brakes, batteries, oil, and lights, but leave the engine, transmission, and even tires in the hands of professionals.

There is something deeply spiritual about working on your own motorcycle. If you don't think so, get one up to highway speed and look down at the road. Imagine what would happen if just the right part failed due to poor maintenance and your body struck that road. You might survive the impact. But would you survive the truck that was tailgating you a moment before? Working on your own motorcycle is like packing your own parachute. You don't want to do it if you don't know how, but if you do know—why would you trust anyone else?

How to Find Good Deals on Good Motorcycles

Finding a good price on a used motorcycle isn't always about where you look. Sometimes it's *how* you look. But don't go slapping motor oil on your favorite pair of jeans just yet—how you look is all about who you are, and what the potential seller sees when he or she meets you. Ask yourself the following:

- What impression will I make on the seller?
- What type of motorcycle will I be looking at?
- Why should the seller help me buy a motorcycle?

If this is your first motorcycle, don't act as if you have been riding for years—the seller will see through your dishonesty. If money is an object, don't act as if it is not. The seller will see you as pompous.

ESSENTIALS Be honest about who you are, what your skill level is, and what you can afford. Most people respect honesty and will give you the best deal if you present them a realistic view of the person that you are.

If you have been honest about how much you can spend and your bottom line is still far from the seller's bottom line, let it be. Shake the seller's hand and wish him luck with the next potential buyer. Also, ask him to let you know if he hears of a motorcycle in your price range and leave him your phone number. This way he can take your phone number without any sense of shame. If the seller isn't in the business of buying and selling used bikes, chances are there is a reason he is selling. His family could have come on hard times and he needs to feed his children or pay off his work truck so the bank won't have it repossessed. Buying a motorcycle is part of the social experience of being a biker. Some of your best friends may come from the motorcycles that you don't buy.

Where the Sellers Roam

So, where do you find sellers? The obvious place is the dealership, which represents specific motorcycle manufacturers. Most dealers take used motorcycles as trade-ins, and don't seem to like having those used motorcycles in their show rooms if they were not built by the manufacturer that dealer represents. You could find a good deal if, for example, you buy a used Honda at a new Yamaha dealership.

Bulletin boards, long part of Harley shops, have been popping up in other motorcycle shops recently. In the past, shops might keep a photo collection of the bikes that their customers had for sale and then collect a commission upon sale. Nowadays, shops and other biker hangouts have figured out what Harley-Davidson knew all along—that keeping loyal customers means keeping them happy. Many now feature commission-free bulletin boards in the hopes that after you find a used motorcycle you will be back for new parts.

Motorcycle clubs usually know which members have put their bikes up for sale, or consider doing so. Chances are, you won't find the deal of a lifetime through a motorcycle club, but you are likely to find fair market value and a square deal. To find clubs in your area, check at the local dealerships, call the AMA, or look at Appendix C in the back of this book. Often, clubs sponsor swap meets—fantastic opportunities to find good motorcycles and parts for sale.

Newspapers are a great way to find used motorcycles. This is especially the case with specialty newspapers. Supermarkets and gas stations usually have specialty newspapers at the checkout counter. Unfortunately, if you see a good deal on a motorcycle, the rest of the world probably saw it, too, so stay sharp. An inexperienced buyer will let the seller get the best price every time.

By far the best deals that you will ever find will be just that—deals that you find. They won't be listed in a newspaper or pinned to a bulletin board at the local dealerships. If you see a motorcycle that hasn't moved in a season or two, you are probably looking at a motorcycle whose owner simply does not value it enough to maintain and ride. The ideal situation for the buyer is when the buyer values what is offered for sale more than the seller.

1942
Harley-
Davidson

Photo courtesy of Seattle Support Group.

When approaching someone in a situation like this, let the first words out of your mouth be "I'm sorry," because the owner is probably going to wonder why you were snooping. "I'm sorry, I didn't mean to snoop but I saw your motorcycle . . ." Explain how you happened to be driving by and saw the garage door open.

No matter how you find a used motorcycle, the most important thing to remember is to be patient.

What to Look For and What to Look Out For

Starting with the outside of the motorcycle, how does it look to you? Is everything straight? Does the right and left side look symmetrical? Plastic and fiberglass panels may be your friends and they may be your enemies. They do scratch and break quickly when a motorcycle hits the ground, but they also cover up more serious problems. Ask the owner to remove anything that might hinder your decision. Broken frames as well as repair welds will show themselves readily behind flaking paint, so look for new paint as well.

When you arrived, was the motorcycle sitting where it was probably stored or was it wheeled into position fifteen minutes before you arrived? Major fluid leaks will show themselves quickly, but sometimes not nearly as quickly as a deal is made. Start the motorcycle and let it idle while you watch the pavement beneath. This will give the engine time to display any problems as you walk around the motorcycle and inspect other items. It's a bad sign if the owner seems nervous while she stands there. Chances are, she has something to be nervous about.

FACTS

Cracks in the frame are serious problems, but you can find a good welder to repair them. Noticing these kinds of defects could drive down the price of the motorcycle.

Even if the bike looks like an absolute cherry, there is a really good chance it has been laid down a time or two. This is especially likely if you are looking for a beginner's motorcycle. Remember, you might not be the only beginner in the negotiations. Look for scratches, dents, and anything that looks like the motorcycle hit the pavement with something other than its tires. Look at the tires themselves. Roll the motorcycle forward so you can examine the entire tread. Flat spots from panic stops and plugs from nails mean you should be prepared to buy new tires, just as if they were bald. Also look for spongy and dry or severely cracked spots. Tires should show uniform wear. If a motorcycle has been stored on its tires for a long time, it's likely that the tires are shot.

Is the motorcycle complete with all of its covers, brackets, and cosmetics? Has there been any custom work performed? If the owner has changed the windshield, fairings, exhaust, mirrors, or other factory features in favor of after-market parts, does he still have the factory parts? If he does, chances are he will have no use for them. Even if it is as simple as a missing side cover, you might be looking at a very expensive part that might be next to impossible to find.

ESSENTIALS

A motorcycle that has hit the ground doesn't necessarily have serious problems. There's hardly a bike out there that won't hit the pavement a few times in its lifetime. But just like missing teeth make it harder to sell yourself at the local pub, deep gouges in the chrome will make it harder for you to sell your motorcycle when you trade up.

Even seemingly desirous modifications can do serious damage to your pocketbook. There is a saying that "loud pipes save lives." While that may be true, loud pipes also attract muffler violations. If the motorcycle you are looking at doesn't meet state and local codes, you will probably have to either bring it up to code or pay the fines again and again.

When you ask for a test ride, be prepared to leave your car keys with the seller as collateral. If dealing with an individual rather than a dealer, you can put the seller at further ease by typing up a statement of financial responsibility before you arrive and offering to sign it in front of him or her. If you are talking with a dealer, don't bother typing one up yourself because the dealership will probably provide the form.

The Inside Scoop

That brings us to the inside of the bike. Modern motorcycles are relatively solid machines. If nothing hit the ground while the engine ran idle and you didn't notice anything as you traveled through each gear, then most likely everything inside is running fine.

But before you determine that all is well, ask yourself the following question: *Does clean oil and low miles mean you are looking at a cherry or a recent oil change and a new odometer?* Sometimes perfect oil means the cooling system is leaking into the oil and the owner didn't want you to see the froth. Or the engine is ripping itself apart and the owner didn't want you to see the metal grit. If the oil is new, and the price seems far too good to be true, you might want to do a little detective work. Buy the owner a new oil filter and offer to trade it for the one on his bike; then cut open the old filter and see what you can see and feel what you can feel. If there is a great deal of metal grit in the oil filter, that could be a very bad thing. If there is a great deal of metal grit on the dipstick, that is definitely a very bad thing. If there is a milky froth in the oil of a liquid-cooled engine, that is also a very bad thing.

Foam in the engine oil can indicate a costly engine repair. If this is your first motorcycle, steer clear of unknown engine maintenance costs. Unlike obvious repairs, engine problems can be tricky to spot and even trickier to price.

Different engines and drive systems have unique problems. If you are looking at a belt-driven motorcycle, turn off the engine and check the belt. Missing or excessively worn teeth will lead to a costly repair. If you are looking at a chain-drive system, ask the owner how long ago the last chain was installed. If you are looking at a Harley, ask the owner how long it's been since the primary was serviced. You'll have to take the owner's word for it, but if the owner is reliable, all you will have to do is check the recommended service specs in a repair manual and determine how long it will be before that service is again required.

If the Price Is Right

Buying a new motorcycle is no different than buying a new car. Once you have decided on a model, you go to as many dealerships as possible and get as many prices as possible. Then you play dealerships against each other. No, it doesn't sound like a nice thing to do, but if you are like most people, you don't have a soft spot for the average dealer. Half the time, they don't have a drop of biker blood in them and were selling cars just last month. This is especially true of Honda dealers—Honda motorcycle dealerships sometimes trade salespeople with their car dealerships.

Keep in mind that even when dealers show you their cost, there is also a game of incentive programs, which obscure the dealer's real bottom line. While some dealers will take manufacturer's incentives into consideration, others won't. When you think you have found your best deal, take a business card and return to a dealership that you feel comfortable with. Even if they gave you a higher price previously, offer them the chance to beat the price that you finagled elsewhere. If they won't beat it on the cash price of the motorcycle, see if they might be willing to beat the deal by adding accessories, a better warranty, or a couple of free bits of service like oil changes. If they already offer the first oil change free, ask for the second.

In this case, Harley-Davidson is not an exception. Although you probably won't be able to play dealerships against each other when it comes to price, service and hospitality are a completely different story. No matter where you go, you will probably wind up on a waiting list and pay more or less the same price, but what type of service will you receive once your motorcycle arrives? If you are buying a new Harley, it is probably going to be with you for the long haul, so you might as well have a leg up on the maintenance costs.

ESSENTIALS

If you are talking cash with a dealership, then let the dealer know exactly what you mean. If you are planning on putting the purchase on a credit card or even a debit card, you are not going to get as good a deal because the dealer has to pay a premium on the transaction.

Some will pass that premium on to you over the counter, but most won't mention their extra cost and just not deal as well. If you are worried about bringing cash, offer to bring a certified check from your bank.

If you plan to finance your purchase, your own bank is the best place to start. If you have your purchase tentatively financed before you talk money, the dealer is more likely to be willing to work with you than if you are going through their finance company. This is because they see payment programs declined again and again. The longer a salesperson talks to you, the more chance you have to determine his or her bottom line.

Pricing Used Bikes

Buying a used motorcycle is an entirely different story. Used motorcycle prices vary widely from region to region and seller to seller. Worse yet, even local guides and trading papers will offer a range of prices without any conceivable reason for the discrepancy. This is because motorcycle owners more so than automobile owners tend to place their own value on their machines. Still, there are a few things that you can be sure of.

Waiting also gives you the chance to save a little more money. If you have to buy now, you might wind up with a horrible deal, when you could have had a great deal around the corner if you just had another hundred dollars.

If you think that the right price is the price you can afford, you probably haven't thought the issue through entirely. Ask yourself if you really want the best motorcycle for your money. The amount of time you have spent looking at other used motorcycles is a good way to judge how important getting the best deal is for you. Never buy the first one you see unless your heart just won't let you do anything else.

When comparing bikes that are the same model, keep track of what a bike will need to bring it up to standard. If the tires are balding, show flat spots, or are plugged on one motorcycle, and only slightly worn on the other, figure the model with the bad tires is worth about $300 less than the model with good tires. If you are looking at a belt-driven Harley, pay very close attention to the drive belt. Remember, the belt itself might not cost an arm and a leg, but if you can't do the work yourself, the labor cost should definitely drive the price of the motorcycle down.

Noncritical parts are critical for a fair price. If there is a missing side cover, price that side cover and figure it into any comparison you are making even if you don't care about cosmetics. Remember that you are not purchasing a new motorcycle with clear starting prices. The seller may already have considered that missing side cover or new tires into the asking price. The only way you can be sure is to shop around.

Comparing years and mileage: Generally, the older the motorcycle, the less it is worth. So if you find two models that seem identical in every way except age, the older one should be less expensive (unless the mileage is wildly different). Mileage and maintenance play a more important role than age in wearing down a motorcycle, especially when it comes to sport bikes. A pocket rocket is more likely to have been pushed to its limits than a touring or cruising model. Try not to compare the two equally.

Crossing model barriers: So you've found a Kawasaki Ninja 500R and a 250R. Naturally the 500R should cost a bit more. But what should you think when these motorcycles are only a couple hundred dollars apart? After all, the new prices were a couple of thousand dollars apart. Either the 500R is a really good deal or the 250R isn't such a good deal. Keep on looking until you can assess such matters against still further examples.

Crossing manufacturer lines: Let's say you find a used Honda VT600D Shadow Deluxe and a Yamaha V-Star Classic of the same year. If they are in about the same condition, they should be priced about the same, because they originally sold for about the same price. Sure, there were a lot of "abouts" in that last sentence—in the realm of SWAG, there are more "abouts" than anything else. New, the Yamaha probably cost the original owner about a hundred bucks more than the Honda, but there is that word "about" again.

Choosing among sellers: Which sellers gave you a handshake when you met? Would you feel comfortable closing a deal with any of these people? Did they try to put pressure on you to close the deal? Did they seem nervous? If you have any reason to feel like there is something you don't know, ask. When buying a motorcycle, it is more than just your money on the line. If you have any reason to think everything isn't on the table, get it on the table or walk away.

CHAPTER 6

Accessories and Chrome

Whether you love the open highway or steep hills and mud puddles, you also love your bike. Bikers may deny it until hell freezes over, but the truth is, they love gadgets and gizmos that help make their rides look just a little bit different from everybody else's. Motorcycle accessories express the rider's personality and make your bike more unique and interesting.

The Options Are Almost Limitless

Today, motorcycle accessory options seem less radical than in the chopper days gone by. Fortunately, they are also safer. High handlebars and extended forks destabilized motorcycles at even the lowest of freeway speeds. Even those extra-high sissy bars tended to make a bike wobble in some of the most unpredictable ways. Gone are the days when you could get away with just about anything. The new rule of thumb is: If it's relatively safe, someone is probably manufacturing it.

Windshields and Fairings

You don't need bugs in your teeth to put your knees in the breeze. Windshields and fairings can improve just about any street motorcycle. But before you know what to ask for, you have to know what you are talking about.

Windshields

On a motorcycle, a windshield is used to deflect the flow of air and bugs from the driver's face and upper body. Riders don't look through the windshield, except at very close objects. When sitting on your motorcycle, your field of view should be above the windshield, and its edge line should not obstruct your view. That way, the onrushing air, rain, and bugs will fall into the stream created by the windshield and float safely over your head.

Most bikers who spend time on the highway consider windshields necessities. Besides keeping bugs out of your teeth, your lower back will thank you for installing a windshield on any cruiser. Without the windshield, you will find yourself in a constant struggle to remain in a comfortable position because the wind will constantly try to move you backwards.

You should not have any problems finding a windshield that will fit your motorcycle, while providing the style that you are looking for. Although "universal" windshields generally don't fit nearly as many motorcycles as their manufacturer would like you to believe, you will be able to find windshields that fit a very wide variety of bikes (because the front end of many motorcycles is similar).

Fairings

Fairings, which often incorporate windshields, are generally opaque and usually protect a great deal more than your upper body. They range from simple handlebar-mounted units, which protect both the upper and lower body, to fully incorporated shields, which cover the front half of the motorcycle while channeling airflow to the cooling system and/or engine. Finding a fairing that will fit your motorcycle is a bit more difficult than finding a windshield, because they generally cover a much larger amount of the bike. This means more mounting points, and more mounting points means greater diversity of design. You are more likely to find a properly fitting fairing by consulting a dealer that represents your particular make of motorcycle.

Never believe a windshield or fairing offers a universal fit for all motorcycles. Motorcycle design is much too diverse, and you are likely to find that it almost fits—but not quite. Almost-fitting accessories can cause highway mishaps.

Soft Saddlebags

Saddlebags are almost a necessity for any trip, and are also useful when you ride around town. You might make it to the grocery store and back without a windshield, but without saddlebags you'll have a hard time bringing home so much as a gallon of milk. Saddlebags transform a motorcycle from a purely recreational vehicle to a viable mode of transportation.

The most common saddlebags are made of leather, nylon, and vinyl. Of these, leather is the most durable, but also the most expensive. Leather saddlebags are generally available in either black (most common) or brown, though you can usually special order other colors. Nylon and vinyl bags are much more affordable and can be purchased in just about any color.

Saddlebags, or "soft bags," mount over the seat. They might be the most common and most affordable, but they tend to be the most annoying as well. Typically, they don't lock so it's easy to steal what's inside—and someone can just as easily walk off with the saddlebags themselves.

Most soft bags are sold as universal-fitting bags or bags intended for an almost never-ending list of motorcycles. Sometimes these bags interfere with the wheel; as a result, the bags will quickly wear out, or, even worse, they may damage your rear tire. To compensate for this, some soft saddlebags require metal frames to keep them off the rear tire and hot engine parts. When shopping for bags, remember that the price of the frame isn't usually covered by the price of the saddlebags.

Other Bike Bags

Kin to the soft saddlebag is the tank bag. Although not nearly as common or stylish as saddlebags, tank bags do offer a convenient storage system and actually offer a bit of safety if you back them right. Think of tank bags as having two purposes: They offer you another place to pack clothing for a trip, and they provide a safety pillow, should your chest violently come in contact with the gas tank.

ALERT

Never carry tools or anything hard in a tank bag. If you should get into an accident, it is likely your chest will strike the bag. What you've packed in it could mean the difference between a mild bump and a broken rib.

The alternative to a soft saddlebag is just what you thought it would be—a hard saddlebag. Hard bags are infinitely more useful than soft ones, but they are also a great deal more expensive. They offer better weather protection, can't be removed from a motorcycle without tools, come in factory colors, and usually lock. Even better, a great number of them are bolted to the motorcycle in such a way that you have to unlock them to get to the retaining bolts. A final benefit is that no matter how you pack a hard bag, it retains the same shape. Pack a soft bag differently from side to side, and you might experience some strangely off-center pulling at high speeds or when the wind kicks up.

You also have the option of getting a tour pack. Typically, tour packs are capable of holding much more than saddlebags, which is why they are excellent for touring. With the design of the average motorcycle, their size means there is just one place to mount them—center stage, behind the passenger seat. If you have a factory paint job, you will be happy to know that most dealerships can provide tour packs to match. Unfortunately, between the price of the pack and the price of the mounting parts, this option tends to be a bit pricey.

Tool Bags and Boxes

One of the most useful accessories that you will ever purchase is a little sealed box that you bolt high on the frame, and which carries nothing but two dry spark plugs. That spark plug box and a wrench will pull you out of more jams than you can imagine.

After-market tool bags and boxes come in a variety of sizes and styles. Usually they are made of leather, and mount just below the headlight or behind the rear seat. Make sure you mount your tool bag or box away from everything else you will be packing or unpacking. And don't reach for your emergency tools and parts if you are working in your garage. Otherwise, they won't be there when the real emergency strikes. Tools you should keep in your toolbox include:

- **Tire pressure gauge:** Make sure it matches the pressure stamped into your tires. Most will be calibrated in pounds per square inch (psi), but there are metric calibrations out there as well.
- **Extra spark plugs and spark-plug wrench:** Spark-plug wrenches come in two sizes, so make sure you buy the right one.

When it comes to extra spark plugs, read your operator's manual to find out what kind you need. Don't just look at the type of plug that is in the motorcycle, because if you bought it used, the previous owner could have installed the wrong spark plugs into the motorcycle.

- **Spark-plug gap setter:** It is really tempting to trust that the plugs are gapped properly. It is also tempting to believe that if you gap them before putting them in the tool bag, they will be right when you need them. Both are wishful thinking. Plugs are never gapped right at the factory and they always get banged around in your tool bag.

- **Vise grips:** This tool has no official use when it comes to motorcycle repair, but (much like duct tape) it does amazingly well at the tasks it was not intended to do.
- **Adjustable wrench:** This is another tool that supposedly has no place in a mechanic's toolset, but that no mechanic would ever work without.
- **Needle-nose pliers:** These are good for working on small parts and removing those light bulbs that you broke trying to remove them with your fingers.
- **Tape:** Include electrical tape, friction tape, and, of course, duct tape.
- **Flashlight:** It's a good idea to carry flashlight and batteries separately, so they have no chance of discharging and so that corrosion does not have as much of an opportunity to set in.
- **Ratchet:** Make sure you find one with sockets that fit common parts on your particular motorcycle.
- **Medical emergency supplies:** For quick repairs of a different kind, it is also a good idea to include Band-Aids, gauze bandages, adhesive tape, and a topical antibiotic. These items should be bundled into a heavy Ziploc bag and saved for an emergency.
- **Other items:** It is also a good idea to pack a cigarette lighter, a handful of nuts and bolts, and some insulated wire. Usually you will only use the wire to keep a broken side panel in place after a mishap, but you never know what else could go wrong—so it might as well be insulated.

Gadgets and Gizmos

Okay, you have the saddlebags, so you can fetch a gallon of milk for your sweet aging mother. You bought the fairing and windshield to be practical and save money on the chiropractor, and you even purchased a combination tool and first-aid kit. You have been an upstanding, responsible adult. Now it's time to talk about your reward—the toys.

The first toy that comes to mind is chrome. Unlike the old days, this does not usually involve removing pieces from your motorcycle and sending them out to a chroming service. Today, you can purchase brand-new chrome parts for a fraction of what it would cost you to custom-order. But accessories are much more than just chrome.

If you can imagine a motorcycle accessory, chances are someone else has beaten you to it—and is now selling it. As a result, you need only think of a motorcycle accessory and, like magic, it will be available at your local custom-motorcycle shop. Having trouble finding exactly what you want there? Browse the Web—you will find practically anything you look for. The following is a brief list of accessories to start you on your way.

Highway bars: Also called leg guards, highway bars are U-shaped bars that bolt to the front of the frame and offer some level of leg protection when the motorcycle hits the ground. They also make good places to mount extra lights or highway pegs.

Some highway bars provide absolutely no protection in an accident. The worst of these can actually bend and trap your legs. Always purchase bars that are designed for crash protection as well as good looks.

Highway pegs: These are little more than footrests, but after a couple of hours at a steady speed, you will wish you had a pair. Generally speaking, they bolt to highway bars, but there are a few that you can attach directly to the frame.

Forward controls: Most often seen as add-on features for Harley-Davidsons, forward controls are foot controls placed further forward than one might expect. This allows the driver to put his or her feet in a more comfortable position without sacrificing quick access to controls. Forward controls are convenient when you ride on the freeway, but they tend to be awkward in the city. They should only be purchased from a dealer; be sure to check that they are factory-certified.

Intercom systems: Sometimes intercom systems are built into high-end helmets, but more often they are add-on devices. Typically, they are great for operator/passenger communication, but don't work all that well between motorcycles. More often than not, other motorcyclists do not have them and even when they do, they are on different frequencies. Avoid the ones that use wires to connect driver to passenger. They might cost a bit less than wireless models, but they can be downright annoying.

Stereo and CB systems: Imagine tooling down the highway at 60 mph. The wind is rushing by your face and your engine is humming along. Over all that racket, you can still hear "Born to Be Wild," just like you do in biker movies. It's not a fantasy. A plethora of very loud stereo systems are available both from motorcycle manufacturers and as a separate purchase. Some, believe it or not, are connected to the engine's throttle and turn the tunes down when you come to a stoplight. Citizen-band radios don't seem to have come as far as stereos, but they are still a good idea.

Camper trailers: Did you know that there are motorcycles that comfortably seat three people? Maybe it's not hard to believe when you think sidecars, but would you believe a motorcycle that sleeps three adults? Motorcycle camping has become very popular, and you can now purchase camper trailers for some of the larger bikes.

ALERT

Adding the trailer hitch to a motorcycle should be done only by someone who has the training to know what the particular motorcycle can and cannot tow. Always check with a manufacturer representative before adding a hitch or trailer.

Running lights, log lights, and other lights: Every light on your motorcycle is one more chance that you will be seen at night, but some enthusiasts have gone so far as to turn their motorcycles into rolling Christmas trees. You can even buy glowing spark plug wires, spark plug boots that flash with each firing of their cylinder, and even ultra-tall CB and radio antennas with illuminated tips. And if you become addicted to accessory lighting, you may have to upgrade your battery and charging system to accommodate your addiction.

1942 Indian (front view)

Be careful when it comes to extra headlights. Many states have regulations against more than two clear lights on the front of a motorcycle, so if you are going to mount fog lights on the leg guards, make sure they comply with state laws. Likewise, even the best safety ideas might ruffle some feathers. Brake-light oscillator regulations vary from state to state. The idea behind brake-light oscillators is that if you are sitting still in traffic, the person behind you might confuse your brake light with a running light. The oscillator flashes the brake light so fast that it is hard to tell it is flashing, but still manages to fool the mind into looking at it and thus realizing you and your motorcycle are there.

1942 Indian (side view)

Photos courtesy of Seattle Support Group.

Where to Shop?

You have decided that you just can't live without neon running board lights, or that new satellite-powered global positioning system (GPS). So, where do you go?

By far the most entertaining places to shop for motorcycle accessories are motorcycle shows and swap meets. You will find these listed in major city newspapers every spring. Some of them are shows only, with no merchants, others offer row after row of new merchandise, and still others offer used and collectible parts for sale and trade. Motorcycle shows and swap meets are fun, and can offer some of the best prices. However, if you have to return an item, you might have trouble finding the merchant once the show is over.

Mail-order catalogs and Internet shops can offer a much better variety of accessories from which to choose, and their products are usually much more affordable than those at bike shops. The only downside is that you can't see and examine the accessory before buying it. Often, what looks like a quality part in a catalog or on a Web site is actually a flimsy piece of sheet metal. Returns can be problematic or an inconvenience, depending on the outfit you are dealing with.

Local shops don't offer the volume of selection found in mail-order catalogs, but they generally do offer a much better return policy. Besides, it's always a good idea to keep money flowing in your own local community. If you have to choose between a local shop and a mail-order company, ask yourself what each has done for the local motorcycle community.

CHAPTER 7

Biker Fashion from the Bottom Up

Motorcycle fashion is more function than form. Leather is one of the best defenses against road rash. Tall boots protect the feet and ankles from road debris. Safety glasses and sunglasses with safety lenses protect the eyes from bugs and the odd piece of gravel. Even when a helmet isn't worn, a bandanna keeps road grime off the hair.

The Birth of Biker Fashion

Until relatively recently, most people thought of biker fashion as scruffy blue jeans and a heavy leather jacket, and maybe even leather chaps and tall boots. It wasn't until very recently that the color-coordinated helmet and riding suit appeared on the market.

The earlier black and brown leather stereotype was born in a mixture of nostalgia, necessity, and a sense of style. When the Hell's Angels first started riding together, many of them wore the same leather jackets that they were issued during World War II. That's nostalgia. When a biker refuses to leave home without his trusted leather boots, that's necessity. With new motorcycles came new fashion. In the way that black leather complemented chrome and black parts, new brighter colors hit the scene to complement the new breed of brightly colored motorcycles. Much of this fashion was provided by the manufacturer, which always knew what color the next season's motorcycles were going to be. As a result, you can now find a jacket and helmet that will match the paint on your motorcycle right down to the racing stripe.

ALERT

Consider your budget, but also consider your body. If you wind up being that squid with flip-flops on his feet and nothing else but a bathing suit, tank top, and color-coordinated helmet, you probably won't keep your knees in the breeze very long.

The realization that people were buying factory fashion fueled the business. Before long, each of the large motorcycle manufacturers offered a wide range of licensed fashion products in addition to their motorcycles and accessories. Because bikers tend to be immensely brand-loyal, many became walking talking billboards with their favorite manufacturer's logo on everything from their boots to their helmets.

Safety First

In that mad dash to advertise a particular motorcycle, a lot of people seem to have forgotten that in motorcycle fashion, safety must come first.

There are an amazing number of motorcycle enthusiasts out there who seem to think that spending an enormous amount of money on a helmet that matches their motorcycle is more important than a good pair of boots. A matching helmet won't do a thing for you if the rest of your body is missing.

You see, biker fashion might be a mixture of nostalgia, necessity, and a sense of style, but it is all-functional. Boots are safety gear. Sandals are not.

Protecting the Feet and Ankles

When it comes to footwear, nothing but boots will do. At a very minimum, these should completely cover the ankle to protect from both exhaust temperatures and road debris, like the gravel your front tire will toss at you.

Cowboy boots just won't do if they have slick leather soles. What you are looking for is usually leather uppers and rubber or rubberlike soles. When you come to a stop, the bottoms of your boots work like additional wheels to support the motorcycle. Make those wheels smooth and put them on an oily surface (which every intersection offers)—and you are headed for disaster. One leg will go one way, the other leg will go the other way, and the weight of your motorcycle will rip at the tendons in your groin. Needless to say, this does not feel good.

If you have the option, go for boots with a zipper in the center or on the outside, and no loose lacing. If laces are flapping in the wind, they can become loose or bang against paint and chrome. If they are very long, they might also come undone and get trapped in moving parts. The zipper on the outside or center is so that it doesn't scratch your paint or chrome as you get on and off your motorcycle.

Full-sized lineman's boots work great and provide protection almost to the knee, but they will cost you an arm and a leg. This is especially the case if your feet are larger than size 13. But even with the extra expense of being built like a yeti, you can find boots that will fit if you are willing to take the extra time of ordering them.

When it comes to economy boots, consider how long they will last. Chances are better that you will save more money in the long run with a quality pair of boots because they will last upwards of ten years. Buy economy boots and you are probably going to have to replace them season after season. If you can't afford more than $65 on a pair of boots, take a trip to the local Army-Navy discount store. Most offer a selection of military style combat boots with zippers on the outside.

1947
Harley-
Davidson

Photo courtesy of Seattle Support Group.

Protecting the Lower Body

At a very minimum, you should never ride a motorcycle without blue jeans. Although it might not seem like a great deal of protection, denim is often the difference between an embarrassing slide and a serious injury. Leather is a better option. The problem with leather pants is that they don't breathe. They keep you nice and warm while you are riding, but when you get to where you are going you have to find someplace to change out of them or saturate them with sweat. If that happens, you will be even colder during the ride home.

This brings us to chaps and your fear of looking like an idiot. Chaps do look funny as everyday clothing, but if you wear them as everyday clothing you aren't using them as they were intended. Chaps serve one purpose and one purpose only: They protect you from rashes. That's right, road rash and wind rash (or frostbite). The road rash part is easy to explain—with an extra layer on your legs there is an extra layer for the road to grind off before it gets to your legs when you and your bike go down.

ESSENTIALS   When purchasing riding leathers, don't forget to ask for recommendations for cleaning and waterproofing products. Often merchants will throw in a free sample.

But there is something else. When used properly, they protect against wind rash. Blue jeans might keep you perfectly warm on a late fall day while you are sitting still, but on that same day the wind-chill factor temperature that you generate by traveling at highway speeds can be incredibly low. Here is where chaps come in. Once you've come to a stop, you can take chaps off easily, and without concerns for modesty. This prevents your clothes from becoming damp with sweat and keeps citizens from thinking you are a rogue member of the Village People.

A word of advice on purchasing chaps: Because there really are people out there who think it is a good thing to look like one of the Village People, it is always best to purchase chaps from motorcycle shops. At least then you have a better chance of buying something that was made more out of a desire to protect your legs rather than draw attention to them on a dance floor. But even when shopping at your local motorcycle shop, make sure you are buying competition-weight leather that is at least 1.3 millimeters thick.

Protecting the Upper Body

To find a good motorcycle jacket, avoid department stores like the plague. What they offer might look like something that will protect you in a spill, but they are usually much too soft and poorly designed to do the trick.

Like chaps, your jacket should be 1.3-millimeter competition-weight leather at the very minimum. It should also feature reinforced and padded elbows and shoulders. Its pockets should have zippers to prevent things from falling out, but not in such places or angles as to scratch your motorcycle's paint or chrome. Interior pockets are also a good idea. Look for fully lined jackets or ones with removable lining if you are planning on riding in cold weather.

There are alternatives to the tried and true. Synthetic jackets and entire riding suits are available at a premium. Usually these outfits are made of either Kevlar or Cordura nylon, and feature extra protection in areas where you need it most. Most of these provide excellent protection and require a lot less attention than more traditional leather. They tend to be machine-washable and either waterproof or water-repellent. If you have to wear a suit and tie to work, these things are great because you can wear them over your regular clothing. Incredibly, some riding suits even feature their own heating units, air conditioning, and running water. European riders love these things.

Those fingerless driving gloves might look really cool, but they only protect half of your hand. Full-finger gloves are the better way to go. Again, competition-grade leather is the more traditional way to go, but here Kevlar is a great alternative in warm weather. Hands have a tendency to sweat, and Kevlar breathes more than leather, allowing your hands to remain dry.

Protecting Your Eyes

There are fools out there who think that windshields offer enough eye protection by themselves. Unfortunately, a few states support their opinions and do not mandate eye protection for riders with windshields. You should never operate a motorcycle without proper eye protection. Regular sunglasses you might purchase at the gas station are not enough. They simply were not designed to protect your eyes from anything other than ultraviolet rays. Some of them don't even do that.

Purchase only shatter-resistant eye protection and check to make sure they are indeed shatter-resistant. You'll be able to find both tinted and untinted glasses at your local motorcycle shop. For the ultimate in protection, consider padded goggles. You also have the option of wearing a full-face shield or one of the flip-down kinds that often come with helmets or that you can purchase separately. The best is the snap-on kind rather than the flip-down because you can easily substitute a clear one for a tinted one when it gets dark.

Cheap sunglasses can be more dangerous than no eye protection. If a large bug or piece of debris strikes a poorly made pair of sunglasses, it might cause them to shatter and cause further eye damage. Always use shatter-resistant eye protection.

Helmets

You've made sure to protect your lower and upper body, arms and legs, and hands and feet. Now, what about your head? Many states prohibit motorcycle riders from riding without a helmet, but in other states, the choice is up to you.

If you live in one of the states that trusts you with this decision, consider this one statistic: In a motorcycle accident, the chance of you receiving serious head injuries is five times greater if you don't wear a helmet. Head injuries are not always fatal, but how much are you going to enjoy your newfound biker lifestyle if you can't remember the difference between a motorcycle and a light bulb, or can no longer see your bike (or anything else, for that matter)? It is common knowledge that emergency room workers call motorcycles "donor cycles."

Warning

So, any helmet is better than no helmet—right? Well, sort of. A properly designed and fitted helmet can save not only your life, but your ability to tell the difference between a pizza and a Frisbee. A poorly designed and/or fitted helmet, however, might actually cause additional damage. Worst of all, the very organization that the government depends on to approve the safety of motorcycle helmets is just about useless when it comes to doing so.

Motorcycle helmet laws are not a simple matter. Some states require helmets for anyone under eighteen years of age. Other states require anyone who has been riding for under a year to wear a helmet. Others only mandate them during the learner permit stage.

It appears that the Department of Transportation (DOT) awards certification to any helmets that won't break in half when you drop them on the ground. Many of these certified buckets obstruct peripheral vision to such an extent that you couldn't pass the vision part of your driver's test with the thing on. Even if you drive in a straight line and never change lanes, you are going to have trouble hearing approaching vehicles because most of these helmets block your hearing better than ear plugs. Worse yet, after you crash because you couldn't see or hear the rest of the traffic, if you were traveling at a speed in excess of about ten miles an hour, there is no guarantee the thing will offer any protection whatsoever. To make matters even worse, you can buy DOT helmet certification stickers at almost any swap meet or from the back of magazines, and affix them to anything you like. Doing so is illegal, but this doesn't stop unethical merchants from slapping them on their uncertified helmets before they try to sell them to unsuspecting customers.

ESSENTIALS

Look for the DOT sticker on the outside of the motorcycle, then look for the permanent one inside the helmet. If the helmet was actually certified by the Department of Transportation, then you will find a permanent label on the inside with the date of manufacture and other information.

What Else to Look For

The DOT certification is just the bare minimum a motorcycle helmet needs to be sold in the United States. You should also look for certification from the Snell Memorial Foundation. Once you've found a helmet that is both DOT and Snell certified, you are on the right track.

You do not want a helmet that rides past the point where your spinal cord meets the brain stem (at the rear base of your head). If the ridge of the helmet rides any lower than the ridge on the back of your head, it can provide a dangerous lever action, which might cause permanent injury to your spine on impact.

Look for a helmet that has made provisions for hearing. Even if there are no channels in the hard shell, look for recesses that will allow for air pockets around your ears.

ALERT

Don't go looking for a bargain when it's time to buy a helmet. A proper, well-fitting helmet is an important investment—it will save you money on motorcycle repairs, as well as medical bills. And, of course, it will help keep your head in one piece!

Make sure the helmet fits you properly. Put the helmet on your head and look straight forward. Can you see the helmet out of the corner of your eyes? If you can, do you wonder what's on the other side of that portion of the helmet? Seeing something on the periphery and responding in time could mean avoiding a serious accident.

Finally, there is your particular head. Head shapes vary from person to person, so pay attention to pressure spots and loose spots. If a helmet feels right everywhere except one particular spot, the helmet doesn't fit. A properly sized helmet will fit your head evenly and snugly.

Biker Fashion Faux Pas

Now that you know all about biker fashion, find out what you should avoid. One good rule of thumb is staying away from the biker look as portrayed by Hollywood. Much of what is seen in the movies is downright impractical on the street.

Chains: Connecting a wallet to the belt by a chain might seem like a good way to keep your wallet from falling out of your pocket, but a better way is to put your wallet in a place where it won't fall out. Chains that dangle from the belt are quick to scratch paint and chrome.

Fringes: Those fancy fringes on a leather jacket just flop around in the wind until they eventually break off.

Studs: These are just more metal to scratch paint and chrome.

Spurs: They are extremely dangerous in a crash, and a constant threat to paint and chrome.

Long hair: Pull it back, cover it, or tie it up. If long hair is allowed to flap in the wind, it will just break off at shoulder length.

CHAPTER 8

Riding Instructions

The following chapter will provide some guidelines on riding a motorcycle. However, remember that it is impossible to learn how to ride a motorcycle from a book. Oh, you can learn the basics, but really learning how to ride means getting to know your motorcycle.

Breaking It Down

Operating a motorcycle requires moving both feet and both hands in harmony, and may be broken down into two distinct categories: primary and secondary controls. The primary controls allow you to go and stop. The secondary controls make going and stopping easier and safer.

Each limb is responsible for at least one primary control (your right hand is responsible for two). After years of struggling to decide the best location for each of the controls, the industry has pretty much settled on the standards that are presented here.

FACTS

In addition, each hand is generally responsible for a selection of secondary controls, but these controls are not subject to industry standards. Give the motorcycle makers a couple decades, and they might catch up.

Your Right Hand

The primary controls operated by your right hand are the throttle and the front brake lever. You twist the grip (throttle) toward you to accelerate. The twisting action causes a cable to move within a sleeve, which is connected to either a throttle body (fuel-injected engines) or a carburetor. In both systems, the movement opens a throttle plate. In a carburetor, the movement also operates a device called the accelerator pump, which provides a bit of extra fuel.

ALERT

Some motorcycles feature cruise control, which amounts to nothing more than a throttle lock. Others have had the throttle spring adjusted in such a way that the throttle stays in position once it has been moved there. Both of these practices are foolish. When you release the throttle, it should spring back to the closed position without any assistance. Anything less is dangerous.

The Brake Lever

The brake lever is a simple device. When you squeeze it toward the throttle, you force a rod or connector into the master cylinder. This causes the piston in the master cylinder to move forward and displace the brake fluid in the cylinder. That fluid travels from the master cylinder to the front brake caliper(s), where it pushes the disk brakes to squeeze against a portion of the wheel that is rotating. The friction slows and stops the rotation. The more you squeeze, the more pressure is applied to stopping the motorcycle at the front wheel.

1949
Harley-
Davidson

Photo courtesy of Seattle Support Group.

Like in an automobile, you could apply the brake at the same time you apply the accelerator, but doing so is clumsy, so the design helps prevent acts of stupidity. Unlike an automobile, one action does not usually apply all of the vehicle brakes evenly. If equipped with a hand brake lever, chances are that lever only applies the front brake, an important thing to remember when you get to the next chapter.

Starter Button/Kill Switch

The secondary controls operated by your right hand will vary depending on your motorcycle. Generally, they include the electric start button (if so equipped) and the engine kill switch (also called the cutoff switch). In an absolutely ideal situation, if you are sure you are about to hit the pavement, you should hit the kill switch. The problem is, in an absolutely ideal situation you wouldn't be worried about hitting the pavement. In the real world you won't have time to worry about it. This safety device, despite its good intentions, ended up being the cause of many a failed start. If you can't get your motorcycle to start, check this switch before checking anything else.

Your Left Hand

The primary control at your left hand is the clutch lever. On most motorcycles, when you squeeze the clutch toward the grip, it will cause a cable to move within a sleeve. At the other end of the sleeve, that movement causes the cable to pull an arm, which in turn separates friction surfaces that otherwise connect engine and transmission. Some unusual motorcycles accomplish this with a hydraulic system.

Choke/Enrichment

The secondary controls at your left hand are numerous. Like the secondary controls operated by your right hand, these will differ from motorcycle to motorcycle. Generally, the left hand controls the choke (on motorcycles with carburetors) or enrichment (on motorcycles with fuel injection). Sometimes, however, this device is located closer to the carburetor/fuel-injection system. The idea behind putting it on the handlebar is that you should never have to move your hand from the handlebars while the motorcycle is moving. Generally speaking, a properly running motorcycle will never need this adjustment once it is warmed up, and you should not ride it until it is.

ESSENTIALS When starting a motorcycle, it's better to give it too little choke than too much. If you give it too little, it won't start, but you can adjust the choke. If you give it too much, you may saturate the spark plugs. If your plugs are saturated, you will have to dry them, replace them, or wait until they dry on their own.

Headlight and Dimmer Switch

The headlight switch is also generally located on the left portion of the handlebars. On most modern motorcycles, the headlights are always on when the engine is running, so this is really just a dimmer switch.

Turn Signals

The turn signal switch (if your bike is so equipped) is mounted here as well. All street motorcycles manufactured in the last twenty years are factory-equipped with turn signals. Unlike automobiles, these are not often of the self-canceling variety.

To activate the turn signals, you push the switch left to signal "left" and right to signal "right." The method of canceling the signal differs. With most switches, you either push it straight or push it in, but some require sliding the lever back to the center position. Still others have a ratchet function similar to the gear shift: From the center position, click left to turn left; then click right once to cancel, or twice to signal a turn right. Play with it just a bit, and you will figure it out.

The Horn

The horn is the final secondary control that is usually located on the left side of the handlebar. The device can reportedly save your life, but more often than not the motorcycle will have a horn that won't get anyone's attention. Automobile drivers just don't seem to be able to hear motorcycle horns. Use it when you want to make some extra noise, but don't bet your life that anyone is going to hear it.

Your Right Foot

Your right foot's primary responsibility and primary control is to bring your motorcycle to a stop. This is where the rear brake lever is found. On most motorcycles, when you step down on the foot lever you cause a series of mechanical connections to move the brake shoes to contact the inside of the rear brake drum. This causes friction to slow and stop the drum. On some motorcycles, the rear brake functions in the same way the front brake does. This is usually the case when a motorcycle has two-wheel disk brakes. Recently, a few manufacturers have attempted to eliminate the dual brake system by installing two-wheel disk brakes with a proportioning valve. The operation of the brakes on systems equipped with proportioning valves is similar to the one found on modern automobiles.

1949
Panhead
Harley-
Davidson

Photo courtesy of Seattle Support Group.

This might seem to be a very good idea for people who are just learning to ride motorcycles and who never intend on riding anything but similarly equipped bikes. But it is very limiting—it's like handing a child a calculator but never teaching him or her how to do math without it. In the hands of someone who has never ridden a motorcycle before, the mono-brake lever seems like a disabling crutch. In the hands of someone who has spent any time on the more conventional hand-and-foot braking system, it can be downright dangerous, as the more traditional controls provide a much wider range of functions.

Kick Starter

If your motorcycle is equipped with a kick starter, you'll probably find it next to the right foot peg. In some rare cases, the kick starter is mounted on the left.

Make sure your foot is firmly planted on the kick starter, and be ready for it to kick back hard. Most motorcycles will not cause physical injury during this procedure, but be ready for the unexpected, especially when starting an older motorcycle.

Your Left Foot

Fortunately, your left foot only controls the shift lever, because shifting a motorcycle may be a challenge if you haven't had much practice. Different transmissions have different numbers of gears, and the ratcheting motion might not seem as easy as the rather straightforward shift pattern of an automobile.

The ratcheting motion and gear patterns might seem odd, but once you get used to them, they make more sense than anything else that has come along. The only real problem with the design is that it is not universal. Not only do different motorcycles have different numbers of gears, they also have different shift patterns. The most common is one down and three (in a four speed) or four (in a five speed) up. So what about neutral? Well, it differs from motorcycle to motorcycle.

What follows is a description of the gear pattern that is most common, but it is important to remember that this is only a discussion of the gear pattern itself. (How to shift a motorcycle will be covered in the next chapter.)

1. Starting at neutral, push down to find first gear.
2. From first to second, lift the lever up with your toes one solid click. On some motorcycles, the difference between finding second and finding neutral on an upshift is the amount of force you kick the lever with.
3. From second to third, third to fourth, and fourth to fifth, lift the lever up with your toes one click.

With the exception of the way different motorcycles handle neutral, it is generally difficult to accidentally miss one of the gears due to the ratcheting motion. If you are in second and kick up to go to third, the lever will stop at third and will allow you to shift to fourth only once you have let up on the lever.

When you downshift, follow these steps:

1. From fifth to fourth, fourth to third, or third to second, just step down on the lever one click.
2. From second to neutral, some motorcycles will put you in neutral just by stepping down with any amount of force. Others will put you in first if you step down hard, or in neutral if you step down lightly. With either shift pattern, once you have done it a time or two, you will recognize what shifting into neutral feels like, and will be able to choose between first, neutral, and second easily.

Again, it is important to stress that this shift pattern is nowhere near universal. Check with the manufacturer or manuals on specific shift patterns for specific motorcycles.

ALERT

Be aware of "false neutral"—when you shift between gears and the motorcycle acts as if it is in neutral, though it is really in between gears. If this happens between first and second, you might think that it is safe to let up on the clutch and rest at a stoplight. If it is not really in neutral, it could drop back into gear with little warning.

The Rest of the Story

The last primary control isn't associated with an individual hand or foot. The handlebars control the direction of travel, and rely on both hands, both feet, and the entire body to make the motorcycle move in a particular direction.

Fuel Petcock

The fuel petcock is usually located on the left side of the motorcycle, lower than the gas tank, and generally opposite the air intake. The fuel petcock usually has four positions; on, off, reserve, and prime. On and off are self-explanatory. Reserve is the position that will get you to the gas station when you run out of fuel. If your bike doesn't have a gas gauge, you will praise the designers for including the reserve position. The "prime" on the petcock allows fuel to flow much quicker than the "on" position, and is used to fill carburetor float bowls quickly when the motorcycle has been at rest for some time. The prime position should be used only for this purpose, and may cause complications if used incorrectly.

ESSENTIALS

If you run out of gas while the fuel petcock is set at "on," you can move it to "reserve" to conserve enough fuel to get to the gas station. If you forget to turn it back to "on" after filling up, you won't be nearly as lucky the next time you run out of gas.

The Gas Gauge

If your motorcycle sports a gas gauge, it is usually found on the gas tank. Even if you have one of those luxury devices, don't depend on it. Motorcycle gas gauges are notoriously inaccurate due to a delicate float mechanism and the nature of how motorcycles vibrate and respond to road conditions.

The Tachometer

The tachometer displays the speed of the engine (not the motorcycle) in revolutions per minute. When learning how to shift, the tachometer is your first indicator of when you should do so. Motorcycles perform best when the engine is operating within a certain range of RPMs, known as the "power band." When you are below the power band and the motorcycle doesn't want to respond quickly to the throttle, it is time to downshift. When you are in gear and above it, it's time to upshift. As you get to know your particular motorcycle, you will develop a feel and an ear for this, but it is always nice to be able to double-check by glancing at the tachometer.

The Speedometer and Odometer

Never leave home without it. Not only does the speedometer keep you from getting tickets, its built-in odometer will keep you from pushing your motorcycle to the closest gas station. Sure, if you are in a city you can just ride until you hit reserve and then stop at a gas station, but what about riding cross-country in the middle of the night? To use the odometer to determine range, fill your gas tank and then write down the mileage. Ride until you run out of gas and have to switch to the reserve. Then fill it up again and write down the amount of gas you used to fill the tank as well as the mileage.

1949
Triumph

Photo courtesy of Seattle Support Group.

Now for some math: Subtract the original mileage from the new mileage, and divide that into the amount of gas you used to get the miles-per-gallon figure. Now you have two figures you can work with—the brute-force way of figuring out your cruise distance, which was determined by running out of gas, and you have the miles-per-gallon estimate, which you can apply to total gas tank volume (see owner's manual). Because conditions and fuel economy vary, you can make an educated guess and decide that your actual cruise distance is about halfway between these two numbers.

Idiot Lights and Additional Gauges

If you see a green light on the instrument panel, it probably just means you are in neutral, but don't trust the thing. Even if that green light is on, ease off your clutch gradually, expecting it to be in gear. Otherwise, you might launch yourself into oncoming traffic due to an electrical error. If one of the lights is a red (the "idiot light"), that usually means there is a rather serious problem. With the right instrumentation to determine what that problem is, you might be able to make it home. But if you don't, your best bet is to shut down your engine immediately to avoid damaging it further. The problem is, without full instruments, you cannot be sure if the problem is a "ride it home" problem or a "stop instantly" problem, so better play it safe than sorry.

If you do have gauges to further explain why the idiot light is on, look at the gauges to determine your best response:

- **Oil pressure low or gone:** Stop immediately. If you fail to do so, you will probably destroy your engine and potentially your transmission right along with it.
- **Temperature too high:** Stop immediately. If you fail to do so, you will probably destroy your engine.
- **Battery not charging:** Don't panic. Chances are, you have enough in your battery to keep you going for a while, but as your battery dies so do your lights, and eventually your engine will stop running. Fortunately, this does not generally damage the engine. It is your call on this one.

Finding Help

A book can give you the basics and point you in the right direction, but when it comes to learning how to ride a motorcycle, there is no better direction to turn than toward the Motorcycle Safety Foundation (MSF). Established in March of 1973, the MSF is a 501c nonprofit educational organization that, among other things, offers classes in motorcycling. More than twenty states are now willing to waive their motorcycle endorsement test for those who successfully complete the MSF Rider Course. Other states have modeled their licensing procedure on MSF courses. If that is not good enough, many insurance companies will give you lifetime rate reductions for passing one of these courses just once.

FACTS

Still not enough to get you interested? If you are buying a new motorcycle, the MSF course could be free. Many dealers offer to reimburse either part or all of the cost of the program once you have successfully completed it. On top of all this, the phone call to find out more is toll-free: 1-800-447-4700.

Chapter 9
Putting It All Together

So you think it's finally time to get out there and ride your bike. Before you get on the highway, put in some hours practicing in an empty parking lot. That way when you feel ready to hit the road, you won't actually do so—literally.

Starting the Engine

Even getting on a motorcycle requires a bit of knowledge that might not always come instinctively. Always mount a motorcycle from the left. This is because the kickstand is on the left, so that is the direction the motorcycle will be leaning toward. Even if it is on a center stand, mounting from the left is a good practice because as your right leg swings the motorcycle, an accidental tap on the rear break lever won't change a thing. If you mount the motorcycle from the right, you might accidentally knock the gear shift lever into an undesired position as you swing your left leg over.

ESSENTIALS

The starting procedure for each motorcycle will vary from manufacturer to manufacturer and even model to model. The best place to look for the specific procedure for your bike is in the operator's manual. However, there are enough commonalities for a general procedure provided here.

Standing to the left of the motorcycle, grab the handlebars at both grips and swing your right leg over the seat so that your foot touches the ground. Lift the motorcycle upright and retract the kickstand before sitting down on it. If your motorcycle has a center stand, squeeze the clutch (in case it is in gear), be ready at the hand brake (right hand) in case it rolls too far, and gently rock the motorcycle forward before sitting down on it. Once a motorcycle is off the center stand, it is a good idea to make sure the kickstand is also retracted.

If your motorcycle is equipped with a fuel petcock, turn it to the "on" position. If you can't find the fuel petcock, your motorcycle probably has a vacuum-operated petcock that opens the moment the engine starts and closes the moment it stops. This is either a great idea or another part to break, depending on how you look at it.

Make absolutely sure that you are in neutral. Once you are absolutely sure, check again by attempting to roll the motorcycle forward without using the clutch. If you should try to start a motorcycle while in gear, you will be lunged forward and might lose control. A full-size motorcycle is heavy enough to break your leg even when falling from a standstill.

Make sure the kill switch is in run position and then turn the ignition switch on. Now it's time for a Zen experience: setting the choke. No matter how long you have been riding motorcycles, you will never get the choke setting perfect on an unfamiliar motorcycle the first time. There are just too many variables, so take your best guess. If your motorcycle fails to start, let your nose guide you. If you smell too much raw gas in the exhaust, you are giving it too much choke. If you aren't getting even the hint that the engine is turning under anything other than the power of the starter, chances are you aren't giving it enough choke. With practice, you will become much more proficient at this almost magical art.

ALERT

On a hot day, the extra weight of a rider is oftentimes enough to drive both kickstand and center stand into the pavement, so never put your weight on a motorcycle until it is suspended by its wheels alone.

Even if you are absolutely sure you are in neutral, the neutral light is on, and God has sent a special angel to assure you that you don't have to pull in the clutch lever, ignore all of these signs and pull in the clutch lever.

Electric Start

With both feet firmly on the ground, the clutch lever pulled tight, and your right hand ready at the brake, push the starter button. You will first hear a slight grinding noise. Don't panic. This is just the starter making contact with the flywheel on the engine. A moment later, you should hear the beginnings of internal combustion as the ignition takes over turning the engine. If you do not hear this noise within a few seconds, release the button and double-check the starting procedures listed previously. You probably just forgot to open the fuel petcock or move the kill switch to "on." If you do hear the sound of internal combustion, release the starter button immediately. Failing to do so will cause internal damage.

Kick Start

Fold out the kick start lever. With the motorcycle leaned a little bit to the left, your left foot firmly on the ground, and your left hand squeezing the clutch and your right hand ready at the brake, drive the kick start lever down with as much force as you can muster. The engine may kick the lever back against your foot, so make sure it is planted securely on the lever. If it fails to start on the first try, and it will, invoke the only word worse than *compromise—repeat*. You will soon be convinced that the Fonz was a purely fictional character.

Getting It Rolling

So, you are on top of your motorcycle with your engine running and the clutch lever squeezed. Now, it's time to learn how to move forward in a straight line. The trick here is remembering that timing is everything.

Shift into first gear and place both feet firmly on the ground. Now slowly release the clutch until the engine starts to slow down and the bike nudges forward. Then squeeze the clutch back in again. What you have just done is found the point where the engine and transmission meet. This is the point where the clutch plates have contacted enough to transfer power, but they are still slipping because not enough force is being applied to sandwich them together.

Now try again, only this time when you reach the point where the engine slows down, give it a little bit of throttle to compensate. After traveling for about ten feet, squeeze the clutch and release the throttle. If you have to, apply a little rear brake to bring the bike to a stop. Practice this several times before actually letting the motorcycle take off. Although it might seem tough right now, once you have learned it, it will be such a normal operation that you will barely have to think about it.

The next step is learning how to stop your motorcycle. Stopping a motorcycle is even harder than starting it. You will need to use both hands and both feet in harmony. In almost the same moment, you must squeeze the clutch with your left hand, squeeze the front brake with your right hand, apply the rear break with your right foot, and in all but panic stopping you will need to downshift with your left foot.

Due to factors like weight shift, your front brake does most of the real work. It is responsible for about 75 percent of your stopping power. This number becomes larger on lighter (sport) motorcycles and smaller on heavier (cruiser) motorcycles, but it is always responsible for more than the rear. But the front brake cannot work alone. When any vehicle is brought to a stop, the vehicle's mass remains the same but its weight becomes disproportionately greater because the energy of inertia must go somewhere.

1951
Harley-
Davidson

Photo courtesy of Seattle Support Group.

Remember, objects in motion tend to stay in motion. Well, making matters a bit worse is the difference between sprung and unsprung weight. Without going too deep into physics, the rear unsprung weight of the motorcycle becomes lighter and the front unsprung weight of the motorcycle becomes heavier. Although the wheels generally stay put on the ground, if you use only the front brake, the rear portion of the motorcycle will rise and the front portion of the motorcycle will sink. Wheels *generally* stay put on the ground, but there is a point when the motorcycle's sprung weight becomes so disproportionate between front and back that the rear wheel will lift off the ground and the motorcycle will do a cartwheel.

No matter how fast you are going and how hard you hit your front brake, chances are you are not going to cause a motorcycle to cartwheel, unless you run into a stationary object. Motorcycles simply do not have the traction necessary to turn that much inertia into disproportional weight. The majority of motorcycle accidents that do not involve striking that stationary object do not come from overloading the front brakes—they come from overcompensating with the rear brake.

The rear brake not only slows the motorcycle down, it does so in conjunction with the front brake, so that the motorcycle does not shift too much weight to the front. The problem is, the more front brake you use, the less effective the rear brake becomes, because its ability to maintain traction decreases as the weight is shifted to the front of the motorcycle.

FACTS

The laws of physics work both ways. The same principle that causes the rear of the motorcycle to become lighter during a very fast stop also causes the front of the motorcycle to become lighter during a very fast start. This is called a wheelie.

The solution is finding a happy medium. To do so will require a great deal of practice before you even get it out of first gear, and then more practice once you have mastered shifting. Generally speaking, ideal stopping means applying the front and rear brake in a ratio that keeps the motorcycle from either leaning forward or back.

Remember, you will not always be the one in charge of when you are going to stop, so practice panic stopping as well, and keep these three ideas in mind:

- Your motorcycle always wants to travel in a straight line.
- If either of your tires locks up, you won't have the ability to overcome your motorcycle's tendency toward traveling in a straight line.
- If you brake, it's probably because you don't want to go where your motorcycle wants to go.

Keeping It Rolling

Now that you know how to get your motorcycle rolling and—more importantly—how to stop, it's time to learn how to keep it rolling. That means learning how to shift into gears other than first and neutral.

First, get on your motorcycle, start the engine in neutral, and squeeze the clutch lever as explained in the previous sections. Place your left foot on the shift lever and drive the lever down into first gear.

As you release the clutch, throttle up enough to prevent the engine from stalling as the clutch makes contact. Slowly release the clutch until it is fully released. You are now traveling in first gear. If you feel the engine sputter, give it more throttle, but don't race the engine. If at any point you become concerned about balance, release the throttle and squeeze the clutch at the same time, bring your motorcycle to a halt, and try again.

If you are comfortably touring the parking lot in first gear and think you are ready to graduate to second, put your left foot under the gearshift lever. Squeeze the clutch and let off the accelerator for a moment. Kick the shifter upward sharply with your foot—you are now in second gear. Release the clutch smoothly while at the same time twisting the accelerator a bit. As you gain speed, upshifting further is just a matter of repeating these seemingly simple steps.

ESSENTIALS

Downshifting to slow down is silly. No matter what you do to slow a motorcycle, you are going to cause friction, which harms parts. Better to use the brakes to slow a motorcycle because brakes are much easier and less expensive to replace.

Downshifting is done in the exact opposite way as road conditions warrant. Do not downshift to slow your motorcycle, but do downshift as your motorcycle slows down for a stop. Try to time it so that you are in first gear as you reach the stop. That way you will be ready to leave when the light changes. If your engine stalls, try to keep the front wheel straight. Otherwise you run a good chance of taking a spill.

Around Your First Corner

Have you ever noticed how some people need everything explained to death? Other people just seem to take naturally to something, even though they might never understand how it works. Steering a motorcycle is like that. If you have already mastered this art instinctively, you might want to skip this section entirely. Some people just instinctively know how to steer a motorcycle; other people try and try, but it never seems to work right.

FACTS

At all but the slowest speeds (less than five miles per hour), steering a motorcycle is exactly opposite of what it appears. When you want to turn left, you turn the handlebar to the right. But don't run right out and try this—if you do this consciously, you are going to turn too hard and land face-first in the gravel.

Unless you travel at the lowest possible speeds, you do not steer a motorcycle, you countersteer it. You do this by leaning into the turn. If you want to turn left, your body leans to the left. If you want to turn sharply left, your body leans sharply left. Your hands counter this action (countersteer) by turning the handlebar to the right. Now, if you think about this too hard, it is going to hurt your head; if you think about it while you are riding, it might hurt something else. You see, after years of driving an automobile you have probably been conditioned to turn the wheel to the left when you want to go left. But when that conditioning runs into the laws of physics, bad things can happen—the laws of physics always win.

When you turn your front wheel even slightly to the right, you put inertia back to work. Remember, inertia tries to keep your motorcycle moving in a straight line. With the wheel trying to move to the right and the rest of the motorcycle trying to move forward, the motorcycle leans. When the motorcycle leans far enough, the part of the tire that contacts the ground will no longer be centered on the crown of the tire. Instead, it will choose the left side and—presto!—you are turning left, because that is the direction of the tire tread that is in contact with the road.

QUESTIONS?

Why aren't motorcycle tires flat where they contact the road? Motorcycle tires are not flat where they contact the road because the tire itself is more responsible for steering the motorcycle than the handlebars.

Under normal street conditions, you might not even notice this is all happening. The speed at which it is safe to take turns in normal traffic is low enough that if you are riding safely, you will probably never even notice that you are indeed countersteering, because the handlebar moves only slightly. It will just feel as if you are more or less keeping your front wheel straight and steering entirely with the lean. Moreover, if you make no conscious decision to move the handlebar but learn to make the turn, the bar will move on its own because the wheel will move out of the turn with the lean. If you want to see a situation where this countersteering is obvious, watch a motorcycle race with a lot of high-speed turns.

Parking a Motorcycle

After you have brought your motorcycle to a stop and shut off the engine, you should gently lower the kickstand. Place both feet on the ground and stand up so that none of your body weight is on the motorcycle. Then gently lower the motorcycle onto the kickstand. Once the motorcycle is firmly resting on the kickstand, exit by standing on your left leg and swinging your right leg up over the seat.

If you do not have a center stand, you should also consider where you choose to leave your bike. Generally speaking, parking lots are made of asphalt and sidewalks are made of concrete. Concrete is much harder than asphalt (especially on a sunny day). Many a motorcycle parked on asphalt falls over, because the surface area of the kickstand that comes in contact with the asphalt is much too small, and the kickstand sinks into the asphalt.

If you are parking on a surface that might not be entirely solid (wet grass or hot asphalt being prime examples) via kickstand only, you should try to carry a thin piece of wood or metal with you to place under the kickstand. If you didn't think about it and aren't comfortable with the surface on which you parked, see if you can't find an empty can of soda or beer lying around. If you do, stomp it flat—it will work just fine in a pinch.

If you do have a center stand, always use it to park your bike. To do this, stand with both feet on the left side of the motorcycle. Grab both sides of the handlebars, and use your right foot to lower the center stand until it contacts the ground.

Keep your right foot on the center stand and your left hand on the handlebar. Move your right hand to the frame just below the driver's seat. Some larger motorcycles feature a handle for this procedure; others require you to grab the frame.

Now push the center stand tang down and back with your right leg while rolling the motorcycle backwards with both hands and lifting slightly with your right arm. Some motorcycles will pop right up onto their center stands. Others will require a bit more work, depending on their size and design. Even the lightest biker can get the heaviest motorcycle on its center stand by following this technique.

CHAPTER 10

Close Encounters of the Worst Kind

Motorcycles once outnumbered automobiles on our city streets. Now, the designers of those streets care so little about two-wheelers that they practically build motorcycle deathtraps into their roads. Expecting these traps and knowing how to successfully negotiate them will make riding your bike a safer experience.

Negotiating Intersections

The most dangerous place for a motorcycle rider is an intersection, a concentration of traffic and road hazards. If you live in an area that uses sand every winter, you can rest assured that sand will be there every spring. It tends to accumulate at intersections and especially around the road's shoulder. You may be able to avoid the sandy patch altogether by making a wider turn. If not, negotiate it by keeping your motorcycle as vertical as possible. Shift your weight from the seat to the foot pegs—this will help lower the center of gravity.

ESSENTIALS

Intersections are a favorite place for sand and debris to collect. Always follow other motorists with enough distance to avoid what comes out from under leading vehicles unexpectedly.

Streetcar Tracks

Streetcar tracks at intersections are particularly dangerous. Where all other traffic may cut the intersection at right angles, streetcar tracks arch their way along, making sweeping turns. Automobiles don't have much of a problem going over these tracks, but depending on their height and angle, motorcyclists can find themselves trapped and unable to steer. If you can, cross these hazards at a 45- to 90-degree angle.

Railroad Crossings

Railroad crossings present their own challenges. Usually their angle to the road is about 90 degrees, so there is little worry about getting trapped by an uneven surface. But with every blessing comes a curse. Sometimes it is hard to tell which is slicker, the railroad track itself or the rotted wood plank to either side of it. To make matters worse, many of these planks have come loose and tend to seesaw as traffic passes. If the vehicle next to you should push its side of the seesaw down right before you reach the other end, it could spell disaster. Always try to cross railroad tracks alone and at a steady speed.

Railroad and streetcar tracks both tend to become shinny-slick with age. Motorcycles were never designed to operate on such surfaces. These slick rails can easily cause your front tire to slide sideways, and motorcycles have tremendous difficulty maintaining balance when the wheels are not turning. In both situations, try to stay off the brakes. Cross at an angle of 45 degrees or greater, and maintain a steady speed. If you lose control due to a slip, you will recover almost instantly, because the slick surface is very narrow, so don't panic.

Automobiles

To make intersections even more of a challenge, you have to remember that you are not alone. Automobiles are by far the majority of motor vehicles on the road, and although they might not always have the legal right of way, they should be given as much—what might amount to a moving violation for the automobile operator could amount to serious injury for the biker.

FACTS

The most common cause of motorcycle accidents is a motorist turning left in front of the motorcycle. It doesn't matter who has the right of way—the car will always win this battle.

When you need to stop at an intersection, make sure you are aware of the vehicles behind you as well as the ones in front of you. This is especially the case when you will be the first one to stop. Some drivers think that the yellow light means they should go really fast. If you are not one of those drivers but the person behind you is, you had better make your intentions clear, or else start driving the same way until you can get out of this car's way.

Try to position yourself for a quick exit. More often than not, this will mean staying in the right-most part of the right-most lane, as far from oncoming traffic as possible. That way if you need to avoid being rear-ended, you can move off the road instead of into oncoming traffic. When you stop behind other motorists, leave enough wiggle room to get out if something goes wrong.

ALERT

When leaving an intersection, always take a moment after the light turns green to make sure someone hasn't been waiting for that last left-hand turn or last-second streak through the red light. Even my seventy-one-year-old mother seems to think that red means "stop," green means "go," and yellow means "go really fast."

The most common intersection accident is the left-hander. This is when a vehicle from oncoming traffic makes a left-hand turn right in front of you. They always have the same excuse, "I didn't see him." When riding in heavy traffic, some very experienced riders advocate riding through intersections with a car to your left, which will shield you from the left-hander. Others recommend that you do what you can to see and be seen. Ride on the left-hand side of your lane and never follow behind a large vehicle that might prevent the potential left-hander from seeing you.

1955
Harley-
Davidson

Photo courtesy of Seattle Support Group.

Changing Lanes and Merging on Highways

Because you travel at much greater speeds on highways than on city streets, you might think that highways are more dangerous, but they are not. Statistically speaking, highways are much less dangerous because they remove the biggest threat to the motorcycle: the left-hander. On a highway, everyone is traveling in the same direction.

Now, make no mistake: Highways are *safer*, but they are not safe. Faster travel means things happen faster, so less reaction time will be available. To compensate, you need to be aware of what is going on even further ahead. Be aware of not only what the car in front of you is doing, but also the cars in front of that car, and beyond. As your speed increases, so should your scanning distance.

FACTS

The advantage of riding on the freeway is that everyone is going in the same direction. The disadvantage is that they are all moving a lot faster. Increased speed means less time for decision-making. Your responses to highway threats must be instantaneous.

On-Ramps

On-ramps often present very tight turns that require steep leaning. Even if you have mastered countersteering and are ready for the lean, you will find that on-ramps are some of the slickest areas on the highway. When vehicles accelerate, they put more of a strain on their engines. This causes vehicles that leak oil to leak more. The result is that while you are trying to take the turn slowly due to its slippery nature, the automobiles behind you will pile up, tailgate, and even try to pass. This causes you to go even slower, fearing what will happen if you hit the pavement, which in turn will cause the automobile drivers behind you to become even more frustrated.

Fortunately, when you get to the straight road, you will distance yourself from those frustrated motorists. Once you have reached the merge lane, you will have to reach safe merging speeds. This is where you have the advantage, because motorcycles almost always out-accelerate automobiles. As you prepare to reach merging speed, watch the traffic to your left for a good slot into which you can merge in order to safely join traffic. Be aware that other merging cars might dart out in an attempt to overtake you and merge first. If that happens, let them. You should not accelerate until you have cleared the turn and your motorcycle is no longer leaning. Once you passed the turn, identified a safe spot to join traffic, and are sure no one is trying to overtake you, accelerate to highway speed and slip into position.

When and if you can, get out of the right-hand lane. Don't hog the fast lane if you can avoid it, but try to avoid the right lane because that is where other vehicles will try to enter and exit the freeway. The right-hand lane is to the highway what the intersection is to city traffic.

Changing lanes on a motorcycle is not as easy as changing lanes in an automobile, because other drivers cannot see you as easily as they see other cars. Do signal and try to make your intentions known, but never assume the other motorists have seen your signal. Many motorcycle books advise you to slow down before changing lanes, but this recommendation seems ridiculous. Slowing down only causes the vehicle behind you to become frustrated and to accelerate into the lane you are about to move to. Instead, maintain speed as long as you are not in another driver's blind spot, make absolutely sure there is no sign that either the driver behind you or in another lane intends to move into the lane you have chosen, and then switch into the desired lane.

Off-Ramps

Off-ramps, like on-ramps, have a tendency to contain sharp turns. But just getting to them can be problematic on a motorcycle. Prior to leaving the highway via an off-ramp, you have to be in the lane closest to that off-ramp, which happens to be the most dangerous place to be. Scan for drivers who might dart for the off-ramp from another lane. Be aware that neither your headlight nor your taillight is visible to drivers who are abreast. Even if you don't think the driver to your left is planning on exiting, do not allow yourself to be in his or her blind spot. As you are exiting anyway, slow down and make sure he sees you before you find out that he doesn't.

Make sure you signal your exit long before committing to it. This will let the drivers behind you know that you are slowing down for the exit and make them less likely to become frustrated and pass just to cut you off in a race to make the same exit. In general, off-ramps to the right will turn to the right, and off-ramps to the left will turn to the left, but there are many exceptions. Be ready for those exceptions and remember that the slower you are moving the more time you will have to compensate for false assumptions and unseen obstacles.

1955
Vincent

Photo courtesy of Seattle Support Group.

Passing and Overtaking

Traveling closely behind automobiles is dangerous. Without the ability to see the road surface ahead, you will have no response time to deal with obstacles that might not present a threat to the automobile. Traveling closely behind a truck, van, or other larger vehicle is even worse. In addition to blocking your view, trucks tend to push the air aside in all sorts of strange ways. This causes a wake behind them, which is just as strange and unpredictable.

The first rule of passing is not to do so from directly behind the vehicle in front of you. Fall back a little before you change lanes. If there is not enough room to do so, then don't attempt to pass. Once you are well behind the vehicle you want to overtake, scan for oncoming traffic, obstacles on the road, and uneven road surfaces. Finally, assess the automobile that you hope to overtake.

Motorists won't always make sense. Sometimes they respond to being passed as if they were deeply insulted or even worse, challenged. In ideal highway conditions, every driver keeps a safe distance, maintains the speed limit, and there are always at least two lanes in every direction, so that passing may be conducted as safely as lane changes.

ESSENTIALS

Unfortunately, you will rarely see either ideal highways or ideal operators. Moreover, when the road conditions are horrible, the temperament of other operators tends to get worse. This is because road conditions generally add rage to drivers who shouldn't be on the road in the first place.

Be alert to the drivers in front of you—they might not be as well-rested or even-tempered as you. How are they driving? Are they staying in their lane or swerving like they have been drinking? If the vehicle seems to be going too slow for road conditions and especially if the interior light is on, maybe the driver is looking for an address. If this car should turn left just as you are passing, you might have to demonstrate that quick-stop ability you have learned about earlier. Better to avoid the situation entirely and only pass someone who looks safe, sane, and sober.

If the driver you plan to overtake seems okay, and you see nothing that will impede your travel, signal your intent to both the folk behind you and the vehicles in front of you. It's a good idea to blink your brights two or three times to give the drivers in front of you an extra clue.

ALERT

The actual mechanics of passing are not as hard to understand as how people act and react to your passing them. Remember, always assess the driver you are overtaking before and after you pass.

Do not accelerate until you have left your lane, and your motorcycle is pointed straight ahead. Not only can road surfaces differ between lanes, but the painted line that divides lanes is often slick. As you begin to pass larger vehicles, you will first feel a lot of turbulence. After you pass that first layer of violent airflow, you will hit a kind of draft or backdraft that will either try to pull you toward the vehicle or push you away from it. This will last only a few seconds, so stay calm and ride it out. If you feel it is necessary, lean against the force just a little—you don't want to overcompensate. When you come around the other side, the last bit of air pressure that you feel will probably be the strongest.

Once you have succeeded in overtaking the slower-moving traffic, make absolutely sure the overtaken vehicle was not blocking your view of another vehicle in front of it. Also make sure that this vehicle hasn't decided to speed up suddenly. If it is safer to return to your original lane, do so. If there is trouble, fall back and re-enter your original position rather than pressing on and pressing your luck. Every moment you are left of center is a moment you are in danger.

If all has gone well and you have successfully overtaken the other vehicle, don't assume that you are finished. Keep an eye on the vehicle you passed in your rearview mirror. If the vehicle does not fall behind, there is a good chance you might have ruffled some feathers. If that is the case, maybe it is a good time to take a break and fill up the tank.

Standing Still—Always Know Your Out

Most riders never give a thought to sitting still at an intersection or stop sign. But think about that for a moment. You are at a complete stop, your motorcycle is in neutral, and both your feet are down on the road. What is your brake light doing? Absolutely nothing. As the next vehicle approaches the intersection, the vehicle's driver has absolutely no indication of your intent. Are you stopped? Are you about to move forward? If the driver gets the least bit distracted, what is there to get their attention back to you?

Even if you know that a particular traffic light is a long one and you decide to put your bike in neutral, always be aware of what is going on behind you. Driving has become so routine to some people that they often arrive at work with no conscious memory of how they got there. It is not normal for an automobile operator to see a vehicle stopped at an intersection without a brake light, and the running lights just blur with the lights of the traffic on the other side of the intersection. Stay on that rear brake or at least be aware of what is going on behind you. Unless a car behind you has already come to a full stop, apply and release the brake to cause the light to flash on and off to get the driver's attention.

Always know your out and be ready to point your motorcycle in that direction. Sometimes your out might not be the best place to be, but it is better than where you are. Consider the potential situation in which you could find yourself before you are in it. If the car that is approaching from behind does not stop, what are you going to do? Where are you going to go? What is your out?

Be aware of more than what is going on behind you. Unlike automobiles, motorcycles offer almost no protection from the actions of other motorists. If you are at an intersection and someone from oncoming traffic makes a left-hand turn too fast, you are in danger. If you are stopped in the left-turn lane and someone cuts the corner a bit too sharp, you are in danger. If someone turns right too fast onto your road, you are in danger. If an accident takes place in front, on the sides, or behind you, you are in danger. Always know your out.

CHAPTER 11

Four-Wheel Hazards and Other Assassins

The single most dangerous thing the biker will encounter on the road is the operator of an automobile or truck. Recognizing this danger is the first step to avoiding it. Although they don't generally act with malicious intent, motorists may become motorcycle-rider assassins.

As Large As a Car and Completely Invisible

The laws of man do not hold authority over the laws of nature. If you ride in traffic for any length of time, you are going to run into actions that are simply against the law, and there is only one thing you can do about it: Accept it. If you have the right of way and a car cuts you off, the driver's actions might be unacceptable according to the laws of man, but according to the laws of physics you will accept it and yield, or face the consequences. When you consider the difference in weight and size between a motorcycle and a car, you will realize those consequences are far too great to allow you to take a stand on the moral high ground.

1956
Goldstar

Photo courtesy of Seattle Support Group.

Splitting Lanes

Some states have laws that allow motorcyclists to "split lanes." This is a practice where motorcycles can move between the lanes of stopped traffic. Don't do it! Forget the fact that a frustrated motorist might fling open his car door right as you pass. Just remember that you are as large as a car. Automobile operators will never look for you in a position in which a car would not fit, so don't go there. It doesn't matter if you have every legal right to be there—the law doesn't matter much when you are dead. Never ride where a car won't fit.

Also remember that you are as quiet as a mouse, because automobile operators will not always hear you. When you lay on your horn because you think the driver is about to cut you off, it will do you no good. The driver won't hear you because no matter how much noise you make, you are as quiet as a mouse. Some bikers have considered turning that little mouse squeak into a roar. "Loud pipes save lives," as a popular expression goes, and for the most part, police officers tend to look the other way as long as you aren't really flaunting your noncompliance with muffler laws. But be that as it may, selective enforcement of the law doesn't matter much when you are dead. You can make all the noise you want, but automobile operators will not always hear you.

ALERT

If you take nothing else from this book, always remember this little bit of advice: Whenever you put a motorcycle in traffic, remember that you are as large as a car, as quiet as a mouse, and completely invisible.

There must be a strange function of light that renders a motorcycle and its operator completely invisible. That's the only explanation for why automobile operators continue to say the same thing after striking a motorcycle: "I didn't see it." So remember, it might be a violation of the laws of sanity to think you are completely invisible, but those laws don't matter when you are dead.

To Improve Your Chances

Of course there are a few things that might improve your odds of being seen or heard. You can replace that quiet factory horn with a real honker. Some motorcycles have been equipped with after-market horns that sound like a ship trapped in a fog bank.

Then there is the exhaust system, which some swear can save lives. In the right situation, loud pipes do save lives. But what about the other situations when you want to hear traffic yourself? You can't always be looking to either side, but you can be listening to both sides at the same time.

All modern motorcycles come from the factory with both front and rear lights, but very few come with sidelights. A couple of marker lights on either side are a great addition to any motorcycle. Some motorcycles come equipped with headlight oscillators. These devices modulate the front headlight so fast that they appear to be slightly brighter. They also seem to work subconsciously to generate more attention than even brighter lights. Similar devices are available to the aftermarket for both headlights and brake lights.

Even something as simple as the color of your motorcycle could be a contributing factor. It has long been held that green is an unlucky color for motorcycles. You probably can't find a study that supports this idea, but it seems to make sense. After all, motorcycles are usually operated where the sides of the road are covered in grass and other green plants.

Don't Turn Road Rage into Road Rash

For some reason, some drivers just hate motorcycles. They are probably jealous. Other drivers just hate everyone. They probably don't much like themselves. In the movie *Easy Rider*, Captain America (Peter Fonda) and Billy the Kid (Dennis Hopper) had it explained by George Hanson (Jack Nicholson). People don't hate you because you are bikers, they hate you because you represent the freedom that the rest of the country is craving.

QUESTIONS?

What do you do when you encounter dangerous drivers?
Just get out of their way. Sure, it is frustrating when someone cuts you off, but it isn't nearly as frustrating as the grief you will get at the airport when the pins in your leg set off the metal detector. Don't let others' road rage turn into your road rash.

That movie ended with a couple of shotgun blasts from a passing motorist. Chances are, there is nothing that extreme waiting for you.

The thing to remember is that most people do not consider automobiles to be lethal weapons. There is no waiting period for purchasing an automobile, you don't have to be twenty-one, and you are allowed to do so even without a criminal background check. This represents a clear and present danger, because people are much more casual about using an automobile in a threatening manner than a firearm. Most people will go through life without ever having a warning shot fired in front of them. Few people will go a year without experiencing another motorist using their vehicle in a similarly threatening manner.

The average motorist does not realize that an automobile traveling at a relatively slow speed has tremendously more destructive power than a bullet traveling at a very high speed. If you have ever looked down at the highway from atop a motorcycle, you can probably imagine what will happen if you should come into contact with that road surface at high speed. This means that when the operator of an automobile thinks that he is just being assertive, you might feel as if he is trying to kill you. It is your responsibility to fight the instinct to become enraged, and to see things in perspective: The problem is more of ignorance than of malice.

ESSENTIALS

If you find yourself playing tag with an outraged automobile driver, get off at the next town. If he follows, see if you can't find a place where other motorcycles are parked and take a break. Bullies normally respond to fear, so if you have been singled out because you are on a motorcycle, the problem will probably go away when you are no longer alone.

Usually, avoiding an accident involves a choice of either accelerating or decelerating sharply. When you suspect that road rage has caused the other driver to act dangerously (road conditions not being a factor and everything else being equal), decelerating is probably the better of the two choices. Only a complete idiot doesn't know that most motorcycles can easily out-accelerate most automobiles, so you have absolutely nothing to prove. Let those drivers have their way, because trying to prove that they are idiots might cause a rather unpleasant reaction.

Road rage tends to be contagious. Worse yet, it grows exponentially. Maybe you do something innocently or maybe you do nothing at all. Another driver becomes furious with you, or maybe it's just misplaced aggression. Who knows, maybe his wife left him for a biker and now he is just looking for anyone to vent on. If you become that person, you will act in a way that will cause his anger to keep growing, until someone gets hurt.

Road Rage among Bikers

Idiots don't always come on four wheels. Spend some time on a motorcycle, and you will meet a number of two-wheeling idiots. More often than not, these are young males with egos disproportionately larger than their engines. They think they are indestructible and beg for someone to demonstrate how they are not. Instead of letting them get under your skin, just remember that you don't have to remind them of their own mortality—the road will take care of that in due time.

Two-wheel idiots are normally speed freaks who can't cut it in the proper environment for drag racing. Sure, their bikes can outperform the average cruiser, but they present no real competition at the track. Instead, they demonstrate how fast they can go from one stoplight to the next. Experienced riders without a death wish simply do not conduct themselves this way, so once you have mastered cornering, you can pretty much bet you can lay waste to them in the turns.

If you take them up on their little challenge, you are allowing road rage to become contagious. Instead, tell them that you will take them up on the race and agree to meet on the same day, at the same time, and at the same intersection, but make it about twenty years later. Chances are, their zippy little motorcycle will be long gone, and they will have moved on to other equally annoying practices.

Nature of the Road

Because roads are made wide enough for cars and trucks, motorcycles have a lot of wiggle room within the confines of their lanes. Deciding where to position yourself for the safest experience means finding a balance between the nature of the road and the traffic on that road at the time. You may pick to ride on either the left or right edge of your lane, but try to avoid the middle: that is where the oil line is.

1958
AJS 7R

Photo courtesy of Seattle Support Group.

The oil line is the patch of darker pavement that runs right down the center of a lane. It was built up over years of leaky automobiles and trucks, and is more pronounced at intersections and places where automobiles sit for a period of time and then accelerate hard. The problem gets much greater during the first hour of rain, because the water brings all of the oil and muck to the surface.

Another reason to avoid the center section of a lane is painted instructions. The stop signs that are painted on the ground in parking lots and the arrows that are painted at intersections, as well as other painted road surfaces, are often much slicker than the rest of the road.

Debris also tends to find its way to the center of a lane. It is where dead animals tend to remain intact for longer periods of time. And it is the most likely place to find a crowned spot. Crowned spots are elevated areas that sometimes appear on one-lane roads. They are there to allow rainwater to cascade to the right and to the left. The problem is, they also tend to cause a motorcycle to cascade to the right and to the left; you can never seem to ride right on top of a crowned spot, and end up moving from side to side.

When traffic dictates, travel between the left edge of the lane and the oil line. This forces drivers to fully leave your lane when they pass, and it gives you the best chance to see and be seen by traffic. Moving over just a couple of feet can tremendously change the angle at which merging or turning automobiles can see you. Keep in mind that this is just a guideline. If traffic dictates that you will be better off on the right side of the oil line, then ride right of the oil line.

Warning: Challenging Road Conditions

Other road conditions you should watch for as you ride include:

Steel plates: Steel plates over construction holes are not only slick, they can move. Because the pavement is dark and there is nothing to illuminate the hole under the plate, small gaps might not be easily distinguished from the road surface. Watch these things carefully—a gap that the automobile in front of you might roll right over can engulf your smaller front tire and cause your motorcycle to come to a sudden stop.

Deer crossings: A sign indicating deer crossings doesn't just mean that deer might be crossing at that location. It means they have crossed at that location. How do they know? Someone hit them before and someone will hit them again. Don't be that someone. Some of the most enjoyable roads are littered with deer crossing signs; when you see one of these signs, slow down and be ready to stop.

Farm country: The countryside landscape offers its own little challenge. Whenever farm equipment moves from field to pavement, there is a trail of mud, clay, and goop that can send you sliding. If those clumps survive long enough to dry, you can probably plow right through them without much of a problem, but why risk it? One might be a rock large enough to give you one hell of a stir. Instead, go around.

Tar snakes: Tar snakes are those lines that are left behind from quick road-crack patches rather than repairs. These things can be really slick when new, and iffy even after a couple of months. If you can't get around them, treat them as you would any road during the rain. Slow down and decrease your inertia, because the available friction to stop your motorcycle decreases due to the slick spots. Dark patches in the road can be freshly repaired or sealed potholes. Often, these are soft on hot, sunny days.

Traction grooves: The grooves that cross your path right before a bridge or other potential hazard are known as traction grooves. The idea behind them is twofold. First, they cause your tires to make a lot of noise. This can alert a driver to a pending road condition that may require special attention. The second purpose is to help clean your tires a bit before hitting a potentially slick area. By alternating the pressure that the road places on the tires, the tires flex just enough to knock loose some of the debris they tend to carry. These grooves tend to give motorcycle operators the willies. When crossing one, you bike feels just a bit out of control because with each grove, a shock wave is transmitted through the handlebars. Don't worry, this is normal. Just continue moving forward and try to avoid changing the direction of travel while on top of one.

FACTS

Of course, it is impossible to mention every possible road hazard, but there are entire books dedicated to the subject. One of the best is David L. Hough's *Street Strategies* (Bowtie Press, 2001). Others you will have to discover on your own, but with a quick and level head you will be fine.

All Things Are Not Equal

It is hard to imagine that just a small difference in pavement height is enough to bring a motorcycle tumbling to the ground. If you should happen to find yourself trapped by uneven pavement, the most important thing to remember is not to panic. To break free, you are going to have to do something that feels incredibly unnatural. You are going to have to steer further off the surface that you wish to return to.

Easing back up to the surface just isn't going to work. The rounded edge of your tire will hit the edge of the road and it will jump, bounce, and do everything except go where you want it to go. Instead, steer away from the edge until both front and rear tire are on the same surface and your front tire can be aimed right back at that edge but with an angle of no less than 45 degrees.

Road Surfaces That Pose Problems

Uneven road surfaces can be found in many locations. Watch out for grooves in the road, which can rip the handlebars right out of your hand. Avoid them like the plague because there is no sure-fire way to get out of them and you might not want to go where the groove leads you.

New pavement is sometimes applied lane by lane, to keep traffic moving. One night they might pave the center lane, then open the whole road back up for daytime traffic. The next night they close down the portion they didn't finish previously. As a result, lanes become uneven. Although you should always be aware of traffic as you change lanes, you have to be aware of the road as well. Best to avoid changing lanes that are of different height, but if you absolutely have to, do so with the magic number, mentioned earlier, in mind: 45 degrees.

ESSENTIALS

A shift in the color of lanes may also indicate a change in height. Always consider the possibility that color changes in road surfaces may mean that the heights of the lanes vary.

You know those long white lines that look like they might be curbs? Well, there is a good chance they are. Perhaps in an attempt to cause less damage when a car crosses such a section of a road, they are much lower than curbs, but that also makes them much harder to see, especially at night.

On-ramps and off-ramps can present some of the most challenging of all the uneven road surfaces, because you simply cannot avoid them. These usually occur when a highway has been recently repaved, but the on- and off-ramp haven't been attended to. If the ramp has a gradual merge, you will have to move from one corner of your lane to the next to hit the proper angle; this is not always practical because drivers behind you will have no idea what the maneuver is for.

ALERT

"Warning: No edge line" usually means "Warning: The edge drops an inch or two and we are not going to show you exactly where, because we are not done fixing the road."

Over Bridges and Under Passes

If sudden bad weather catches you and there is no place else to hide, bridges and underpasses will see you through, as long as you are well off the road and aware of traffic that might be inadvertently traveling in the breakdown lane due to the weather. However, bridges and underpasses also present some real challenges, in even the best of weather conditions.

Because bridges and overpasses have nothing underneath them to maintain heat, they are the first to ice up. And because there is no sunlight to hit the road inside an underpass, they are the last to thaw out. This information is more or less important, depending on your location, time of the year, and even time of day. Bridges and overpasses are generally worse than the rest of the road in the early evenings. Underpasses are generally worse than the rest of the road in the early mornings.

Fog Forms Quickly in Low-Lying Areas

Because underpasses tend to be constructed in low-lying areas, they are generally good places to worry about fog and slick roads (condensation on the road raises old oil, making it slicker).

During the best of weather, underpasses tend to be slicker than sections of the road exposed to the elements. They don't experience as much of the cleansing effect of rain, but they certainly do experience the same amount of oil leaking onto them.

Bridges

Bridges offer their own particular challenges depending on the material from which they have been constructed. If the bridge is old, it might be made of bricks or cobblestones, or even of wood. These relics have been preserved more out of a sense of antiquity rather than function. Be aware that wood can be one of the slickest surfaces you will encounter, especially when wet. Brick and cobblestone vie for a close second.

The more open the bridge is to the elements, the more you may have to contend with wind shear, which can alternate from side to side seemingly at whim. Remember, when the wind tosses you in a direction you do not want to travel, the distance that you move in an unwanted direction is dependent on your speed. The faster you are traveling in such conditions the further you will travel before you can compensate for the wind shear.

You may find that an unexpected gust blows you into an unsafe position and you will have to countersteer with force rather than just lean into it. Be prepared to push against the wind by steering into it (thus countersteering out of it). If the wind pushes you hard to the left, push your right grip forward—your front wheel will be steered left, thus countersteering into the wind at the right. Be careful not to overcompensate, especially on slick surfaces.

CHAPTER 12
Riding in Bad Weather

No matter how well you plan a trip or how often you listen to the weather reports on the radio, you are going to find yourself trapped in a storm. You will have to decide to either go on or dig in. Better to know how to respond prior to that eventuality rather than try to figure out what to do when it does occur. This chapter will help get you ready to make and cope with those decisions.

"Riders on the Storm"

Ever since Jim Morrison's song, there has been something unexplainably romantic about traveling during a storm, but, once again, reality is radically different from the way it is presented in popular culture. With even the slightest hint of dampness your clothes act like a wick to draw every little bit of body heat into the wind. The best thing to do when encountering an unexpected storm is to find a nice warm spot and let the storm pass entirely.

If you can't stop for the duration of the storm, try to stop for the first half-hour, especially if it hasn't rained in a month or so. The first half-hour of a rainstorm is when the oil and goop that has been working its way into the pavement does a U-turn and works its way back up. This causes road surfaces to be incredibly slick. As the road saturates with rainwater, oil is gradually washed away. You will still have to slow down due to the decrease in traction, so take it easy even hours after the storm has begun.

Rain can cause marginal final-drive belts to start to slip. If you know you are going to face bad weather conditions, it's a good idea to double-check belt-drive systems to make sure the belt is in good condition. Once it starts to slip, it will wear itself out very quickly.

With rain, much of what you have become used to will change. Stopping distances will increase as friction decreases. Your depth of vision decreases as the rain and mist build up on your eye protection. You won't be able to lean as hard or ride as fast, so just figure that it is going to take you a great deal longer to get where you want to go.

With extra care for decreased traction and visibility, riding in the rain can be a relatively safe procedure as long as you are prepared for it. Do not respond to anything suddenly. Use brake, throttle, and clutch smoothly. The only tool you have against inertia is friction. With decreased friction, rapid changes in steering, acceleration, or braking can have disastrous results. Remember to avoid the oil line—in fact, take that warning twice as seriously when it rains.

Preparing for Bad Weather

Being ready means training, proper maintenance, and packing. Worn tires just don't cut it in the rain. In ideal conditions, the best traction for forward motion is achieved with an absolutely flat tire surface. With more tire coming into contact with the road, there is more of a friction area for the road to grip. This is why drag racers tend to have tires with zero tread. Motorcycles can't operate this way because they are expected to go both forward and around turns in less than perfect weather.

1959
Harley-
Davidson

Photo courtesy of Seattle Support Group.

Part of the reason for the groove in your tread is so the tire can channel water out of its way to prevent hydroplaning. When a tire wears, that groove becomes shallow. If it's too shallow to do its job, you have a problem. With worn tires, motorcycles can easily hydroplane. When they do, they ride on a thin layer of water rather than the road, and steering becomes impossible unless you happen to have a motorcycle equipped with a rudder.

If you are planning on riding the storm out, be sure you have prepared your gear. Nothing says miserable like riding through a storm only to arrive and realize that all of the dry clothes that you had packed are wet because water leaked into your saddlebags. Soft bags leak. Hard bags tend to leak. The solution? Wrap your goodies in heavy plastic garbage bags. If you can find them, yellow is the best color. If not yellow, then white. To prevent tools and extra spark plugs from rusting, freezer Ziploc bags work the best.

Then there is the banana suit. Some might argue that bikers should always wear extremely bright colors so other motorists can see us. On the other hand, it's quite possible that some bikers out there just can't stand the idea of somebody mistaking them for a giant banana on roller-skates. When it comes to riding in a rainstorm, you have to take safety into consideration. Not only should you be worried about the hypothermia that might set in during cold weather, there is also the diminished vision of other motorists. Those bright yellow banana suits have saved many lives.

ESSENTIALS

Sometimes, the unexpected happens. If you find yourself without a banana suit and you just can't stop to let the storm pass, those extra garbage bags can come in handy. Cut a hole for your head and arms and then pull them over like a poncho. At least you will have a little bit of protection against the rain, wind, and the cold.

Riding in Cold Weather

Your absolute favorite season to ride will probably be middle to late fall. It's not too hot, not too cold, and the road isn't filled with the spring-born commandos that zip from one stoplight to the next. The only problem with fall is that a nice day for a ride can turn into a bitter nighttime ride home. Hypothermia and frostbite are a major threat to any biker who ventures out in anything but steamy weather.

Even if it seems like a perfectly comfortable temperature when you are sitting still, cold-weather injuries can strike any part of your body that is exposed to the air at a rate proportionate to your relative speed. If it is 35 degrees outside, it might seem warm enough when you are sitting still, but at 40 miles per hour, it will seem like 3 degrees. To make matters even worse, the ratio is not 1:1. If the ambient temperature drops from 35 to 30 degrees, the wind chill drops to –5 degrees (an 8-degree difference); if it drops to 25 degrees outside, you are looking at a wind-chill factor of –13 degrees at 40 miles per hour.

To calculate the wind-chill factor, use the following formula:

$$\text{Wind Chill} = 35.74 + 0.6215T - 35.75(V^{0.16}) + 0.4275T(V^{0.16})$$

V= Velocity
T= Temperature

The Right Clothing

One-piece thermal underwear is the best way to go. If you are really lucky, you will be able to find one with that butt flap that makes a great conversation piece, should you ever show someone your underwear. Nylon stockings are a good bet. You might not think it is all that necessary at 65 degrees, but even on warmer days the wind-chill can hit freezing at highway speeds. High-tech bikers will be happy to know that a few manufacturers offer electrically heated jackets, but they are very expensive. On the budget side of high tech, you can find electrically heated vests to wear under your regular jacket. Rain suits also help keep the cold out by keeping body warmth in and preventing the wind from stealing it away.

Your face and eyes are a major concern in cold weather. Scarves are a tremendous benefit at keeping air off your neck and throat. If you use a full helmet with a face shield, pulling your scarf up over your face will help keep the moisture in your breath from condensing on the transparent shield. Most safety glasses are no good at all in cold weather. Even if you can wrap that scarf or bandanna around your face so no skin is exposed, the wind will whip right around them. If you don't wear a face shield, it's better to go with goggles.

Another way to keep warm is by beefing up your bike. You can purchase electrically heated grips and windshields. The things look like they were made in outer space, but you would be amazed at how far keeping the wind from your hands will go toward keeping your whole body warm. Some of the largest touring motorcycles even offer electric blowers to force engine heat toward the rider, but you will only find these offered on the most expensive models.

Riding Through Snow

You are soaking wet from the rain that has just turned to snow, 20 miles from home with no shelter for an equal distance in either direction. There is no sign of other traffic on the old country road, and it will probably be the last road to see salt, sand, or a snowplow. What do you do?

ESSENTIALS   The citizen band radio (CB) allows two-way radio communication between all motorists and even base stations. The CB is a popular motorcycle accessory, but the emergency channel (channel 9) is just about useless in real emergencies. The range of most CBs is only a few miles. Although there are plenty of blank spots where cell phones do not work, they are currently the best bet for acquiring emergency roadside assistance.

You should never try to operate a motorcycle in the snow. However, there are times when you simply have no other choice. Cold-weather injuries and even loss of limb or life can happen very quickly. If you are wet from a preceding rain, those injuries can start to attack your body in less than ten minutes. Knowing the limitations of the human body is essential for making proper decisions when you find yourself in these potentially fatal situations. Sometimes the choice you have to make is one in which doing something that is normally considered very unsafe is actually the safer of the available choices.

If you find yourself suddenly trapped in a snowstorm and there is a place to stay that isn't more than a healthy walk away, abandon your motorcycle, go to that place, and retrieve your bike after the storm has passed and the roads have been adequately cleared. Don't like leaving your motorcycle there? Then call a tow truck from the hotel or rest area. Have it brought home, and if the driver can pick you up on the way—even better.

If you find yourself trapped in a snowstorm and there is no place to stay within a reasonable distance, consider your physical condition. Are you dry? Do you have adequate clothing for the weather? With a military-issue extreme cold-weather sleeping bag (available at any Army-Navy surplus store) you can sleep comfortably in snowbanks and wake up to clean roads and a safe ride home. If you can safely dig in, then do so.

If you are wet, do not have dry clothing or adequate protection from the cold, and do not think there is shelter within safe walking distance, then bite the bullet and flag down a motorist. Semitrailer drivers seem to have the most rules against picking up a hitchhiker, but they also seem to have the biggest hearts for bikers. Even in a day when carjacking incidents make the evening news on a regular basis, many people have retained enough humanity to risk picking you up rather than letting you freeze to death.

1972
Triumph

Photo courtesy of Seattle Support Group.

But what if none of these is an option? You are cold, wet, unable to reach shelter, and you haven't seen another vehicle in a half-hour? That is when you might have to make the decision to ride in the sleet and snow, and that is the only time when it might be a good idea. Once you start riding, and see a vehicle approaching from the rear, pull far off the side of the road and try to hitch a ride. That's right, abandoning your pride and joy makes more sense than risking life and limb.

1972
Yamaha

Photo courtesy of Seattle Support Group.

Motorcycles just aren't snowmobiles, so the first thing you are going to have to look for is a set of skis. Fortunately, you have followed the advice given in Chapter 7, so you are wearing a thick pair of high-top leather boots. Think of your feet as outriggers. Don't drag them, but have them ready to keep you and your motorcycle upright.

If you can, decrease the idle on your bike to a point where it is just able to keep itself going in first gear. The normal setting for the idle will probably cause your rear wheel to break contact due to the tremendously low friction between you and the road.

Turn on your bright lights and, if you have them, your hazards. The brights will actually decrease your vision, because they will illuminate the falling snow, but you won't be traveling fast, so better that you see a little less to ensure that others see you a little more. Do everything possible to be seen, including putting that banana suit on. If you don't have one but do have a brightly colored T-shirt, put it over your dark clothing.

Squeeze the clutch, kick it in first, and put both feet flat on the ground. Release the clutch much slower than normal. Yes, this will cause it to burn out quickly, but remember, this is an emergency situation. Balance the clutch with as little throttle as you can. Once the clutch is completely released and you are idling, you are done. Do not accelerate, do not shift, and do not brake. Probably the most you can hope to do is idle in first gear.

ALERT

Remember, these guidelines are for snow emergencies only. The first car or truck to be seen in your rearview mirror is a potential end to the emergency. If you come upon a motorist that has pulled off to the side, ask if he or she will share their shelter. If you come upon a rest area, truck stop, hotel, or other warm place, your emergency has ended as well.

Countersteering is right out. In fact, steering at all will be just about impossible, but you might manage to get a bit of control by using both the front tire and your feet. When you have to stop, pull in on the clutch and drag your feet a bit, because the brakes will be useless.

Night Moves

When you were young, your mother probably told you that if you can't see it, it can't hurt you. If she did, she probably never rode a motorcycle after sunset. Bikers should fear the dark because it does offer the perfect hiding place for obstructions, animals, and other threats to hide.

The dark also detracts from your ability to see color and shade differences. Oil and wet spots on the road become invisible. Without shadows, potholes will be undetectable until the very last moment. Dissimilar road surfaces seem smooth.

If it isn't enough that your visibility is reduced tremendously, the things that you have to watch for increase. Over 50 percent of the people on the road after midnight are driving under the influence of drugs and/or alcohol. Animals tend to be active in the night and routinely cross streets and roads in search of food. The number of bugs will increase wildly, especially near water, where the flying insects can make riding a motorcycle akin to swimming in pea soup.

FACTS

Motorcycle headlights simply are not as good as automobile headlights at lighting up the road. When making fast turns, they are even worse. Most motorcycles have their headlights mounted to the front fork. Because motorcycles are countersteered, this means that when you are turning left, your headlight is turned slightly to the right.

If there are automobiles on the road whose drivers seem safe, sane, and sober, learn to read their headlights. If they bounce up and down, expect a bump. If they turn to the left, prepare to turn to the left. Always give yourself enough room behind them to respond to their many signals. If there are automobiles on the road that do not seem safe, sane, and sober, avoid them.

Quick Advice

Before you go on to the next chapter, take a look and commit to memory these last few road rules for motorcycle riders:

1. If you can follow an automobile, do so from a safe distance.
2. If you see matching reflectors light up along the side of the road, they are probably the eyes of our furry little friends out for a night walk.
3. Always make sure your headlight is aimed properly (check owner's manual).
4. Remember to read the headlights of other vehicles.
5. Pack a cell phone even if you don't plan to use it.

CHAPTER 13

When You Have to Hit Something

When no escape is in sight, choose the lesser of two evils: It's better to hit a highway gator (tire scrap) than an oncoming eighteen-wheeler—if the object is small, you can probably deal with it and receive little damage. In such cases, panic can mean the difference between a mild bump and a major case of road rash, or worse.

Hitting Something Small

So you are riding along the highway in the center lane. There is a car on your right and a car in front of you. You are comfortable knowing your out is one lane to your left. You see something move out of the corner of your left eye, so you glance over your left shoulder for just a second to see a car speeding into your only out. Not a problem, it will move on past you. You turn your attention back to the road in front of you just in time to see a big nasty road gator emerging from beneath the car that you are following. What do you do?

ESSENTIALS

The disposition of the operator can mean the difference between a serious crash and a minor bump, so it is imperative to keep your emotions under control. Remain calm even when everything tells you to panic.

Your instincts will tell you to put on your brake, but that can be the worst thing you can do when you are about to hit something. Doing so will shift weight to the front tire and make it want to stay planted. The goal when hitting small hazards is to make your front tire as light as possible. Instead of braking, you should try to accelerate right before you hit. At the same time, pull back hard on the handlebars and shift your weight to the rear of the motorcycle. With any luck, this will lighten the front end, and you will be able to go up and over that gator.

When your heart starts beating again, you should pull off to the side of the road at your first safe opportunity. You might have made it safely over the gator, but you are going to have to inspect your motorcycle to make sure it did. Start a quick inspection with the tires. Roll the motorcycle forward and inspect every portion of the tread. If the object you struck was a board, make sure there are no punctures in your tires from stray nails. If it was an animal, make sure the critter didn't leave any bone matter stuck in the tread. Sometimes puncturing objects are not yet driven deep enough into your tread to strike air. Spotting something early can mean the difference between simply pulling it out and a blowout while you ride in traffic.

Next, check your drive train. There are very few things that will hurt a shaft in this situation, but belts are especially susceptible to certain types of road debris. The metal cords on chunks of tires can whip around and slice a belt in half. Chains are less susceptible to this, but should also be inspected before getting back on the road. With either chains or belts, check to make sure proper tension is still maintained.

Not noticing tire damage after a near spill can cause a spill down the road, which would mean more damage to your motorcycle. Always check for damage, even after minor mishaps.

Check the underside for fresh oil and broken cases. The difference between replacing the lower-end case and the entire engine is often the difference between running an engine without sufficient oil and stopping when you develop a serious leak. Brick, rocks, and other solid debris can do serious damage to the lower end at sufficient speed. But even low-speed collisions with relatively soft materials can damage the oil cooler, oil lines, and spin on oil filters. If you don't spot a leak with the engine off, start it up and see if you have an oil leak while running. The same goes for liquid-cooled engines, including the radiator and cooling hoses.

If everything seems okay, pay extra attention to handling and noise when you get back out on the road. It doesn't take much to throw a wheel out of round, but this problem is easily identifiable. If you feel a vibration that wasn't there prior to the collision, one of your wheels could be out of round or out of balance. If you seem to be veering to one side or the other, you may have thrown your rear wheel out of alignment.

Hitting Something Big

Hitting larger objects may include hitting the pavement. To make the best of such an event, you are going to have to be ready for it: how and where you hit the pavement can mean the difference between a two-strike and a three-strike (or more) accident. A two-strike spill is the simplest and least dangerous. In this type of accident, the first hit is between your motorcycle and some other object. Maybe it's another car, curb, traffic cone, or some other object—the list goes on. That first strike causes a second impact: you hitting the ground.

FACTS

Severe injury and even loss of life can occur at any speed, but two-strike spills at relatively slow speeds are the least likely to cause serious damage. More often than not, the rider can walk or even ride away from such spills.

Three Strikes and You're Out

It is the third impact that usually does the majority of the damage. This is when a two-strike spill turns into a three-strike tragedy. The third strike is the one that occurs after something strikes your motorcycle (or your motorcycle strikes something), and after you strike the ground. This third strike is when something else hits you. The third strike can lead to a fourth and a fifth, and with each the chances of survival decrease rapidly. To keep yourself away from the third (and subsequent) strikes, you are going to have to keep a level head even when it is particularly hard to do so.

When you are alert to the events preceding a collision, you will realize that most often you have a clear choice of what you are going to hit and how you are going to hit it. For instance, you are riding down a road when a parked motorist flings open the car door. If you move right, you hit a parked car. Move left and you hit oncoming traffic. There is no time to stop, so what do you do? You choose what to hit. Oncoming traffic is probably the worse choice. If you can rear-end the car, you will probably fare better than if you hit that car door. If you can't rear-end the car, you are going to have to hit the door.

So why does rear-ending that car seem like the preferable idea? After all, the door might give and cushion your impact as it does. Well, when you hit the rear bumper of the car, only one life is in immediate danger: yours. If you hit the car door, you and the driver of that car are in immediate danger. The second reason is what happens after the first impact.

Doors ride higher than bumpers. If you hit the bumper, your motorcycle will probably stop almost instantly and you will probably be thrown forward by your own inertia. It will hurt like hell and you will probably sustain serious injury, but there is a good chance you are going to come to a stop on top of the car where there is no traffic. If you choose that route, you have kept a potential three-strike accident to a two-strike accident. First your motorcycle struck the parked car; then you struck the parked car.

1975
Norton

Photo courtesy of Seattle Support Group.

Hit the door and you have a good chance of a three-impact crash, or worse. Your motorcycle hits the door, and you are deflected to the left, where you hit the ground, and oncoming traffic hits you. Do you know what's following behind you? If the door doesn't deflect you, the strike could be just as bad. Your motorcycle hits the door, you are thrown from your motorcycle into the same door, then the traffic that you didn't see behind you runs into you, your motorcycle, and the door—again, three impacts. Of course, you could fly up and over the door and hit the ground where the third hit will be from another car as well as the fourth, fifth, and so on—you get the idea. It is so much safer to hit that parked car and land on the trunk where, with any luck, no other motorists will be.

It might not seem like the brightest idea in the world, but sometimes you just have to abandon ship. Motorcycles simply do not offer the crash protection that automobiles do, so your best bet is to avoid being where the accident is occurring. When you are absolutely sure you are going to hit something that will cause your motorcycle to come to a sudden stop, remember that you are not attached to that motorcycle. Although it might stop all forward motion, if you are not deflected inertia will force you to travel in the same direction as your motorcycle before the collision. Do what you can to control what direction that is, and you might be able to turn a three-strike accident into a two-strike accident.

1989
BMW

Photo courtesy of Seattle Support Group.

On the Road Again—Literally

The only thing more dangerous than hitting another vehicle is being hit by another vehicle. If you did the hitting, chances are you had a split second that you might have used to decide what you were going to hit and how. Use that small moment in time to change the future. Decide where and how you are going to hit. If, on the other hand, you are the one being hit, you will probably have no warning whatsoever. One minute you are on your motorcycle and the next you are in the air.

Even in this extreme situation, there is time to take action. That time is the few seconds between falling off the motorcycle and hitting the ground. What you do during that time may well save life or limb. If you can, try to bring your arms in, crossing them at your chest with your hands closed in fists to either side of your neck. If you can twist so that you will land on your side, do so. When you feel contact, roll, roll, and roll. The more you roll, the more you will disperse energy slowly and decrease friction. Road rash might not sound like a horrible thing, but it can rip your flesh right off your body. It's not so much the flight that will cause the damage, it is the sudden stop at the end of the flight.

ALERT

Fingers are easily broken, especially if you use your hands to try and stop your fall. Fight the urge to put your hands out. Instead, hold your fists to your upper chest/neck area and protect both fingers and throat from the impact.

If you come to a stop and are still in the road, get up immediately. Do not assess personal injuries until you are off the road. Do not check on your motorcycle until you have determined your own state of repair. Do not even try to figure out what happened until you are sure that it is done happening. Just move off the road as fast as humanly possible. If this means walking on a broken leg, so be it. Risk the chance of doing further damage to yourself by moving to avoid having further damage done by other vehicles. This is different from getting into an accident while driving an automobile—in that case, you might do better to stay put. However, when you find yourself completely unprotected in the middle of the road, you have more of a chance of sustaining further injuries by not moving. The majority of serious injuries received in a motorcycle accident do not come from the initial impact, they come from impact number two and three.

Do not, under any circumstances, remove your helmet after an accident of this type. Once you are safely off the road (though not so far off that emergency vehicles won't find you), assess your injuries. First, look back at where the accident was. Did you leave a blood trail? If you did, you are bleeding severely and will need to identify the injury and stop the bleeding first. A human can bleed to death in a very short time.

1990 BMW
(front view)

If you do not observe a blood trail, then lie completely still while you make sure you do not suffer any form of paralysis. Try moving your fingers and your toes. If there is any sign of paralysis, don't panic. Just stay completely still. There is a very good chance that you will be fine as long as you do not aggravate the injury by removing your helmet or trying to move. The spinal cord is subject to shock and can shut down temporarily, with no permanent injuries.

If, on the other hand, there is absolutely no sign of paralysis, check for blood loss. Many serious injuries will bleed into the fabric of your clothing and not leave a blood trail, but they still need immediate care. Once you address possible bleeding, you must assess the situation further to determine the next course of action.

1990 BMW
(side view)

Photos courtesy of Seattle Support Group.

Unless you are in a remote area where help simply won't find you, your best bet is to remain absolutely still until help arrives. You may have received physical injury that will be aggravated by movement. But what about your passenger and other people who were involved in the accident? Could someone else need help? What happens if you are in a remote area where help won't come on its own? Does anyone have a cell phone? Are you well enough to walk to the closest house to call for help?

ESSENTIALS

Quick thinking and proper training can save lives; knowing how to act in emergency situations is essential. For basic first aid courses, call your local chapter of the Red Cross.

Righting a Wrong

If you can't lift your motorcycle on your own, you shouldn't be riding something that heavy. It's just common sense. The other bit of common sense is that if you can find someone to help, by all means use his or her additional strength. This is especially the case if you just put your bike down. You'd feel really stupid calling that ambulance back after you dislocate a disk or pop a hernia trying to lift your bike back up. When your body undergoes a stressful event, such as a motorcycle crash, it will often flood your blood stream with chemicals that mask pain and seem to give you inhuman strength. If you try to lift a motorcycle with these chemicals coursing through your veins, it is entirely possible you will further aggravate what could have been a minor injury and not notice it until the damage is much greater.

How to Pick Up Your Motorcycle

Go to the side of the motorcycle that would normally be the top. Grab the handle bar that is under the motorcycle and turn the front wheel toward you. This will force the tire down and the motorcycle up. At the same time, grab at a solid portion of the frame or other solid location. Avoid holding on to the carburetor, air filter, or body panels, as these items damage easily. When you are sure you have a firm grip, lift with both of your legs. Do not lift with your back.

If you find that you simply do not have the strength for this method to work, you can try doing the same while sliding your knee further and further under the motorcycle as you lift. That way you can lift a bit, rest a bit, lift a bit, rest a bit, and eventually work it back to being upright.

ALERT

Be aware that many fluids can leak out of a motorcycle during a spill. Oil can cause you to slip while trying to right the bike. Fuel can burn your eyes and presents a fire hazard. Battery acid can eat at your paint, clothing, and skin. Checking all fluid levels before starting the bike might save the engine.

Usually, this will be the sum of the damage: A little oil here, a little gas there, and a few scratches both on the motorcycle and yourself. But before you ride the bike again, you should go through it in search for greater damage. In particular, look at the brake lever, shifter lever, chain, belt, wheels, and anything that either moves in close proximity to a nonmoving part or any place that protrudes from the frame (levers and knobs).

Good Body Work Is No Accident

The best way to survive an accident is not to be involved in one. If you have to choose between rear-ending another motorist and riding off the road, then ride off the road. Be aware of what is going on behind you. If someone looks like they might rear-end you, take that same way out.

When you stop, consider the direction of your front tire. It should point to where you would want to go, should you have to. Be ready at the brake to warn drivers who approach from the rear that you are stopped, but also be ready at the clutch, in case they don't take notice of your warning.

CHAPTER 14

Preventative Maintenance

Individual abilities and willingness to learn new procedures will determine just how much time you spend working on your bike and how dirty you get. Presented here are general procedures for motorcycle maintenance, but keep in mind that every motorcycle is different, so buy the service manual for your particular motorcycle before attempting any procedure.

Motorcycle Tools

Most new motorcycles come with a cheap set of tools. The exceptions are Harley-Davidsons and BMWs. Harley provides no tools whatsoever, and BMW provides a very nice toolset. In the case of the Harley-Davidson, buy a cheap set, mount it somewhere on the bike, and then forget it's there. In the case of all other motorcycles, make sure the tools are there and then forget they are there. These are not tools for the garage—they are tools for the road. The minute you confuse the two, you are going to find something that you desperately need in one place back in the other place.

Air-Pressure Gauge

If you can, buy a good-quality combination metric/standard air-pressure gauge. If you can't find one marked with the metric ratings, then check your tires and see what they say. Even on imports, chances are they will be listed in psi (pounds per square inch), and you will be fine with a standard air-pressure gauge. But if you see a metric rating only, you will have to go back to the store for another gauge.

Motorcycle tires are much smaller than automobile tires. They fill very quickly and can become overinflated easily, so check the air pressure of your tires frequently.

Wrenches

You should have combination-set wrenches, Allen wrenches, and torque wrenches. The word "combination" refers to both open-ended (crescent) and box-ended (enclosed) wrenches. Whenever possible, you will use the box end because it provides better grip, but there are many areas on a motorcycle where it is impossible to do so, so use the open end on that part.

Most Allen wrenches are cheap flimsy hexagonal pieces of metal that you will never keep organized. There are a few sets that keep all the wrenches connected like a Swiss Army knife—reserve these for the road-tool set. For the garage, purchase Allen wrench sockets and screwdrivers.

Torque wrenches are socket wrenches that are used to measure the amount of twisting power placed on a particular bolt. This device is essential when installing critical parts.

Brass Drift and Hammers

A brass drift is a device used for striking. It is much softer than the metal used to build motorcycle parts, so it is much less likely to cause damage. The drift rests against the part on one end and is struck lightly on the other end with a ball-peen hammer.

Motorcycle hammers are sometimes called Harley wrenches. You will want a rubber-face hammer and a ball-peen hammer. Claw hammers should never be used. They were not designed for striking hardened metal, so they can chip and splinter when using a center drift or while conducting other metal-striking procedures.

Oil-Filter Wrenches

You will want at least two of these. The first is the one you will hope to use. It slides on the end of the oil filter and then you use a ratchet to turn it. But this one will not always be effective. For situations where you just can't get it to work, there is the belt-type wrench. A belt-type oil-filter wrench wraps around the filter and tightens its grip as you loosen the filter. It tends to crush the old filter while taking it off.

Screwdrivers

You will need the standard regular and Phillips screwdrivers. As you work on your bike, you will probably find that you need additional screwdrivers for your particular model. Sometimes it is necessary to buy these oddball screwdrivers from a dealer; other times they have been around long enough that other tool manufacturers have caught on.

ESSENTIALS   Examine your motorcycle to see if you need any of those oddball screwdrivers, because you will need to have them for roadside repairs. Make sure to look at the light covers to see what type of screwdriver you will need to unscrew them.

Ratchet and Socket Set

Ratchets come in three different drive sizes. It is best to get one with a ⅜-inch drive if you can afford only one set. You will have a love/hate relationship with this tool. It will be love whenever you find the right socket and hate when you start losing sockets. Buy a set that comes with a carrying case and always return the sockets to the case when you are done.

Tires—First and Last

Tires are the first thing you want to inspect every time your motorcycle leaves the garage and even at pit stops. Your life depends on them.

Check both pressure and tread. If you don't have enough experience to check the tread, purchase a tread-depth gauge from your local dealer. They are relatively inexpensive and very easy to use.

Tires are also the last thing you should think about repairing on your own. They can be plugged or patched, but only to allow you to limp to a repair facility. They are also the last thing to replace yourself. Tire replacement requires specialized equipment, but that doesn't mean you have to take the whole motorcycle to the shop. Just the wheel will do (see Chapter 15 for instructions on wheel removal).

Final-Drive System Maintenance

Whether your bike's final drive is a chain, belt, or shaft system, you will need to pay particular attention to it as well as spend some time on preventive maintenance. The following sections will help you figure out what you need to watch out for.

Chain System

To check the chain for proper tension, you can buy a special chain-deflection gauge and then check specifications in the owner's manual. Or you could just SWAG it. If you choose to SWAG it, just grab the chain on the bottom, midway between front and rear, with the motorcycle's full weight on its tires (not on a center stand). Move it up and down to see how far it will deflect. More than about an inch means it's too loose. Less than about an inch means it's too tight.

E **SSENTIALS** After you have checked one spot, roll the motorcycle to check at each six-inch interval. If the deflection is different, you probably have a tight spot in the chain. If you do, have the chain replaced.

To adjust the chain, put it on a center stand or secure lift. If you are using a deflection gauge, follow the procedure in the operator's or service manual. If not, then take another look at the deflection, as it will have changed when you shifted weight onto the center stand or lift. Note the difference and adjust accordingly. The goal is about an inch of deflection when the full weight of the motorcycle is on the wheels, not on the center stand. Loosen the axle nuts (see Chapter 15 for instructions), but do not remove them.

You will be able to find the adjusting bolts on the swing arm—there is one on either side. You will have to adjust these identically; otherwise the rear wheel will become misaligned. Usually the adjusting bolt on each side has a locking nut at the end. Loosen the locking nut and then turn the adjusting bolts an equal number of turns. Generally speaking, clockwise will tighten and counterclockwise will loosen the chain.

When you think you have gotten it to the right spot, retighten everything to factory torque specifications and put the bike back on the ground. Measure deflection again and then repeat the procedure as necessary.

There are many variations on this theme. Most swing arms come in the shape of a Y, with the rear wheel between the arms of the Y. Other swing arms go to only one side of the wheel. If you have a single-side swing arm, you are likely to run into an offset cam system; if you are dealing with an exotic adjustment system, you might even run into a worm-screw design. These all serve roughly the same purpose—to increase and decrease the distance of the rear wheel from the drive system. A glance at each will usually tell you how it works.

Cleaning the Chain

Older motorcycles use a metal-only chain. It's best to have these chains replaced with a modern O-ring chain as soon as you can. The more modern O-ring chain lasts longer, rides quieter, and requires less attention. But it does require special cleaning and lubricating materials. Never use standard chain products on O-ring chains.

1990
Enfield

Photo courtesy of Seattle Support Group.

Clean chains with a soft brush and approved cleansers. If you can get your rear tire off the ground with a stand, then do so and rotate the tire to get every spot of the chain. If not, then walk the motorcycle forward so you can get to every last spot. Then dry it completely and let it stand for a half an hour or so to ensure that it is completely dry.

Lubricate with approved lubricants. With the rear tire off the ground, you can aim the spray bottle at the inside of the chain and rotate the tire to get an even coat. If not, you will have to walk it the way you did during cleaning.

Remove excess lubricant from the chain, clean away the lubricant that you accidentally sprayed on other parts of the motorcycle (particularly painted surfaces), and then go for a ride with an old pair of blue jeans. When you get back, wash down the bike as well as the jeans, because your bike will always splash lubricant for the first mile or two.

Belt Service

Belt services vary widely from manufacturer to manufacturer. Some can be as simple as adjustments similar to the ones done with the chain. Some manufacturers insist that nothing should ever be used to lubricate the belt, while others maintain that factory-only cleaners and lubricants (preservatives) should be used. When it comes to belt-drive systems, it is best to consult the operator's manual for specifics.

Shaft Service

Shaft systems require less maintenance, but for some reason they are more likely to be ignored by novice riders. You may not have to constantly adjust the tension (as in a belt or chain), but you will have to remember to replace its lubricant at least once a year. See your operator's manual for scheduled maintenance.

There is no easier maintenance procedure than this one. To drain the oil in the rear end, unscrew the drain plug in the bottom of the differential. Then unscrew the one in the top. The oil will rush out of the one in the bottom. When it has finished, replace the one in the bottom, fill with approved lubricant, and then replace the top plug. The proper level is generally the amount of oil that will fit with the top plug open and the motorcycle level.

Oil Service

There is no oil to change in a two-stroke engine. It enters the crankcase with the air/fuel mixture and then leaves via the exhaust pipe after having been burned with that mixture in the combustion process. You could say that whenever you run a two-stroke engine, you are changing the oil. But you do usually have to check it on a daily basis because two-stroke engines do not recycle oil as four-stroke engines do. Just like fuel, they burn it as they go. This is why they are generally banned from street use.

ESSENTIALS

Checking the oil on these motorcycles is simply a matter of finding the oil tank and then looking at its side for a sight glass that allows you to see the level. If it does not have a sight glass, there will be a dipstick that you can pull to check the oil the same way you do with an automobile. Sometimes this dipstick is affixed to the cap.

Four-Stroke Engines: Changing Oil

Engines fail permanently primarily because their operators never change the oil. Even if you change the oil occasionally, but not as often as stipulated by factory specifications, you will take valuable years away from your engine. Always use the grade of oil specified by the manufacturer. Generally, this will be 10w40 on air-cooled motorcycles and 10w30 on liquid-cooled motorcycles.

Be on the safe side. Change your oil every 1,200 miles, even when the manufacturer says every 6,000 miles. It's probably not possible to replace oil too often, as it starts to break down after just 1,000 or so miles. Manufacturers lie to make the service schedule sound better. In so doing, they make recommendations based on the warranty period and the estimated life expectancy of a motorcycle.

Oil-Change Instructions

Warm your engine before draining the oil. Place a pan underneath the bottom end and remove the plug that you will find there. (Be ready for the oil to gush out.) Leave the plug out until you are ready to add the new oil.

Remove the filter (except prior to winter storage). There are two types of oil filters: canisters (messy) and beer cans (spin-ons, like automotive-oil filters). In either case, clean the area around the oil filter.

In the case of a beer can, spin it off with an oil-filter wrench. Check to see if the large rubber O-ring that rides in a groove on the top of the oil filter is present on the old filter. If it is not, check the place where the oil filter met the engine housing. If you accidentally leave the thing in place, it will cause a severe oil leak down the road. Once you have found the O-ring, discard it and the old oil filter. The new filter will come with its own O-ring.

In the case of a canister type, there will be a bolt in the center area that runs the length of the filter. This bolt is usually made of steel, but the case that it screws into is aluminum. If you have any doubt that it will strip, then leave it where it is, replace the oil, and have a service department deal with it. If you should happen to snap or strip it, you will have to trailer or truck your ride into the shop. If it does come loose, carefully remove the filter insert and note the position of any retaining clips or springs. Discard the filter insert and O-ring. Clean both contact surfaces (canister and engine case).

Do not rev the engine any more than is needed to start, because it will take a moment or two for oil pressure to build and lubricate the internal parts. When you are done, recheck the oil level with the engine off.

Both types of filters have an O-ring. On the canister types, make sure the new filter insert comes with the O-ring; otherwise, make sure to purchase it separately. Coat the O-ring with oil. If it's a beer can you are replacing, and if you can do so without creating too much of a mess, it's not a bad idea to fill the filter with oil prior to installation. Spin the filter on and tighten only by hand.

If it is a canister type, place the filter insert in the canister and make sure all the clips and springs are as they were when you removed them. Then very carefully set the filter in place and tighten the bolt only by hand at first. If there is any sign that something is not lining up right, stop and correct before moving on. After the canister is in place and finger-tight, tighten lightly with a wrench.

Clean the oil pan plug. Most of these are magnetic and will accumulate the tiny bits of metal that wear off the engine while it runs. Clean well. If you notice a metal washer on the plug, it is a good idea to replace it, because its seal is based on initial compression. In either case, clean both plug and the portion of the engine that contacts it to ensure a good seal, then replace the plug and fill the engine with fresh oil.

Start your engine and let it run for two minutes while observing the oil pressure gauge (if your motorcycle is so equipped), and checking the lower half for leaks.

Air Filters

Running a motorcycle without an air filter will make it sound a bit more throaty and might even increase performance a bit. But any desired enhancements will come to a screeching halt when the engine sputters and dies due to the damage even tiny specks of dirt and sand can cause.

To stop that dirt and grit from getting into the engine, motorcycles use one of two primary kinds of air filters. Paper filters, which you will replace as needed, and foam, which you can either replace or clean in a special solution. Check the price of new foam filters before attempting to clean one.

ESSENTIALS

Original air filters are often overly restrictive, and cause the engine to run leaner and hotter. While it might be tempting to switch to a performance air filter, in so doing you will be making modifications that could result in steep fines based on increased emissions. Many states now conduct scheduled and spot inspections for emission-control devices.

Air filters are found in different locations, but they all somehow connect the airflow to the intake system. If you follow the flow backwards, you will most likely find the air filter either bolted right onto the carburetors or in an air box mounted somewhere else with a hose or other method of getting air from the filter to the engine.

The removal process varies significantly from bike to bike. The filter may be held in place with a single screw, or have an Allen wrench in the center. This is most likely the case in the ones that bolt onto the carburetor. Or, the filter may be attached to the air box with a set of spring-loaded clips, or with a combination of clips and screws. If you don't want to explore, see your operator's manual.

Once you have removed the air filter, either discard or clean it. If you have a foam-type filter, soak it in an approved cleaner and squeeze out the grunge. Repeat this process until the filter is clean.

Take the cleaned-out or new filter, and apply the recommended oil in accordance with the owner's manual. Some manuals call for only slight oiling, while others will advise you to soak the filter. To install it, simply follow the instructions for removing it—but in reverse order.

Batteries

You should check the electrolyte level every couple of weeks. Some battery manufacturers have blessed the biker with translucent cases. If that's the case, you can just glance at the level to know whether the battery needs to be topped off. With other types of batteries, you have to pull or screw the tops off each cell to check. If they are only mildly low, you can use distilled water. If they are more than one-third down, you should use battery acid.

Why Was It Low?

Make sure your battery is not leaking. Check for cracks in the case, and jog your memory. You could have forgotten a minor spill that caused battery damage. If you lay a bike down even for a moment, you can lose battery acid. It will also evaporate over time. If you check regularly, you will notice a sudden change. If you do and there haven't been any spills and you see no cracks, have the charging system checked. An over-charging of the battery can boil fluid away.

Check the terminals and clean with a solution of baking soda and water. If you notice any sign of corrosion, take a wire brush to the terminals while they are removed, so that you can clean the contacting surfaces as well.

Keep the following six guidelines in mind while you work on your battery:

1. Never smoke around a battery or do anything else that may cause a spark. You may cause an explosion.
2. Always wear eye protection.
3. Don't touch your face or other sensitive parts of your body when you work with a battery; clean your hands with water and baking soda right afterward.
4. Avoid inhaling while close to a battery compartment.
5. If the battery has a vent/down tube, make sure it is not blocked and is properly seated.
6. Always disconnect the negative post first and never wear jewelry when working on batteries, to prevent shorting the ground.

The Clutch

Unless you have proper training, the only thing on a clutch you should try to adjust is the free travel. Go any further, and you will burn out one clutch after the next.

Ideally, the clutch lever will have enough free travel to ensure that it does not prevent the clutch from making full contact between disks. That exact distance will depend on what the manufacturer recommends.

Methods of adjusting the clutch-lever free play vary. Often, a series of nuts and threaded sleeves around the clutch cable are played with to effectively lengthen and shorten the cable housing, thus taking up the slack in the cable itself. The only way you can be sure how your particular motorcycle works is to either check your operator's manual or tinker until you get it right.

Front and Rear Brakes

Manufacturers frequently mount a brake-lever adjuster with the brake lever, a practice that is becoming more and more popular. You adjust these brakes by rotating the brake lever by hand. With other models, you would achieve travel adjustment by rotating the rod that connects the brake lever to the master cylinder. Some motorcycles have no provision for adjusting the brake-lever travel. Check your operator's manual.

If you can adjust the free play in your front brakes, doing so will lower reaction time and increase the chances of avoiding an accident. Ideally, the lever will have the least amount of play while not engaging the master cylinder and dragging the brakes.

Pads themselves do not need to be adjusted, but they do need to be checked. To remove the pads, you may have to remove the caliper cover and even the caliper itself. If you have to remove the caliper, follow the procedures outlined in the next chapter. If you just have to remove the cover, you can usually figure out how to do it by looking at the thing. They are usually held in place with clips or screws.

Replace pads if they look thin. They can also become glazed, but you can't see the glazing unless you remove them (see next chapter). If you noticed a decrease in stopping power, just assume they are glazed and replace them.

The rear-brake foot lever requires much more play than does the front brake, because, typically, there is a physical connection between the brake and the rear wheel. The length of that connection has to change as the rear wheel moves up and down.

On drum rear brakes, the free play is usually adjusted at the rear of the brake lever with a bolt and lock nut. There is no way to check the brake shoes of a drum system without removing the rear wheel (see next chapter). On rear disk systems, the rod that connects the lever to the master cylinder is typically twisted to make the adjustment. Checking rear disk pads is very similar to checking front disk pads.

Keeping It Cool

You should check coolant level every couple of weeks. Usually, this procedure involves nothing more than looking at the transparent overflow tank, which is sometimes marked with a hot and a cold line. If your engine has been running, it should be at the hot line. If it has not, it should be at the cold line. If you need to add coolant, make sure to mix the proper ratio of water and motorcycle-approved coolant.

SSENTIALS

Additionally, check all hoses to ensure that there is no seepage or cracking. Check the radiator and oil coolers to make sure they are not blocked or leaking.

CHAPTER 15

Motorcycle Repairs

I t is spiritually rewarding to take responsibility for your own bike within your
own limits. You can enjoy working on
your motorcycle, and use the money you
would have spent at the garage to pay for
accessories. On the other hand, beware of
attempts to do repairs outside of your abilities—they will prove costly in the long run.

What You Should and Shouldn't Attempt

With that service manual in hand and a little help from your friends, you can successfully accomplish much of the work yourself. Some bikers won't so much as change their own brakes. Others insist that rebuilding the engine is part of a regular schedule of preventative maintenance.

This chapter will outline the repairs that may be done by an average motorcycle owner, including regularly expected repairs and replacements, as well as unexpected work due to some type of failure or accident. Think about how much you are willing to do, and set your limit for work that you find reasonable to do on your own.

ESSENTIALS It's not recommended to try a new procedure when you work alone. Find other bikers who may be willing to help you learn. Don't rely on this book to give you everything that you need—the intention here is to provide you with an overview. Professional mechanics with a lifetime of experience rely on the service manuals for individual models, and so should you.

Working on the Brakes

Bikers choose motorcycles for a variety of reasons and use them in a variety of riding conditions. The engine, accessories, and overall style top the list of priorities, and often bikers address them first when it comes to general maintenance. However, it is important to make a conscious effort to remember the parts that do not add to either speed or appearance, but are essential for safety reasons. Keeping your brake system in a good state of repair might not make the motorcycle look better or go faster, but it will go a long way toward making it—and your life—last longer.

Replacing Front-Brake Pads

All modern motorcycles have front disk brakes, which use a device called the caliper to squeeze brake pads against the rotor (disk). The caliper and brake shoes are mounted stationary and the rotor spins with the wheel, so when the caliper squeezes the brake pads against the rotor, it creates friction and slows the wheel.

The exact procedure for replacing pads depends more on the caliper design than it does on the motorcycle itself. Some calipers must be removed in order for you to replace the pads. Others require that one bolt be removed. Still others require both bolts and the caliper itself to be removed from its mount. If this is the case, don't be tempted to dangle the caliper by the brake line.

BMW
L85S

Photo courtesy of Seattle Support Group.

The pads are held in place on the caliper by either a pin or a clip. Note how this device is situated. Here is where a digital camera makes a great addition to a tool set. Failing that, drawing diagrams can be a great aid. When you are certain you can repeat the procedure of removal in reverse order, remove the pads and discard them. You may need to use a pair of pliers.

Clean the caliper well. As the caliper is used, it actually slides on two surfaces. Identify those surfaces and take extra care to make sure that they are clean. If a caliper should seize, braking power will diminish sharply. Check the rubber around the piston. It is there to prevent dirt from contacting the piston and causing failure at a later date.

Disk brakes are self-adjusting. As the pad wears down, the piston just keeps moving forward. During normal use, there is no mechanism to pull the pads away from the rotor. It just happens on its own because no rotor is 100 percent flat. The tiny amount of warp that is inherent to any metal surface is enough to kick the piston back so the pads do not rub.

New Brake-Pad Installation

New pads are thicker than used pads. As the piston has no mechanism to draw it back with use, you will have to do it manually. There are specialty tools for this procedure, but if you don't have them you can usually use a screwdriver with a plastic or wooden handle. Press the handle (not the tip) onto the piston, and lightly drive the piston backwards into the caliper, moving it enough to give you the clearance you need for the new pads.

ALERT

It is a good idea to wrap the master cylinder with a towel or unwanted rag when compressing the caliper piston. The internal pressure that you generate in the brake hydraulics can cause the returning volume to exit the system at the master cylinder. Brake fluid eats paint rather quickly.

To install the new pads, reverse the procedure. If your brake system uses a split or cotter pin, always get a new one. If it uses clips to retain the pads, it is a very good idea to replace these as well. They are inexpensive and will prevent problems down the road.

Bleeding the Brakes

Brake fluid is one of the most disgusting liquids you will find in a motor vehicle. If it gets on your skin, it will feel slippery slimy, and it's hard to wash away. If it gets on a motorcycle's painted part, it will leave spots and can corrode and ruin even old paint jobs. If you leave the stuff sitting around with the top open for more than a short time, it will soak up water and become almost useless. If you use the wrong kind, you can destroy your hydraulic system. Even if you use a type that is safe for your motorcycle, it might not mix well with another kind of brake fluid that is also safe for your motorcycle.

ESSENTIALS   Whenever you bleed or top off brakes, use new brake fluid in accordance with the operator's manual or the stamp on the master cylinder. Once the seal on a can of brake fluid is opened, the fluid will begin to degrade—don't save it to be used later on.

The good news is, you do not have to bleed your brakes just because you replaced the pads. The bad news is, you will have to bleed them if any repair procedure requires that you open the hydraulic brake system. This includes replacing calipers, hoses, and the master cylinder. It also includes any situation where the brake fluid in the reserve on the master cylinder became low enough that air was pumped into the system.

Furthermore, you also need to replace the brake fluid every couple of years or so, because every time you open the master cylinder to check fluid level, you let some moisture into the system. Eventually, the fluid has enough moisture in it that the heat generated upon braking will cause air pockets (steam bubbles) in the fluid. When this happens, the fluid becomes spongy and stopping distances increase wildly. But don't worry: Bleeding the brakes might be a pain, but it is a relatively small procedure that you can accomplish quickly.

Bleeding Instructions

Clean the top of the master cylinder to make sure no dirt or debris will fall in once you open it. Take the reservoir top off the master cylinder, which is usually done by removing the screws that hold it down (on some motorcycles, the top itself screws off). There is a rubber diaphragm between the reservoir and the cover. This will sometimes stay with the cover and sometimes stay with the reservoir. Either way, remove it to expose the brake fluid. Fill the reservoir and replace the diaphragm and cover.

At each caliper, you will find a device called a bleeder valve. Place a box-ended wrench on this valve and make absolutely sure it seats perfectly. If you have six-sided box-ended wrenches, they work best. Place a clear plastic tube on the valve. Put the other end of the plastic tube in a container of brake fluid. This container should be clear so that you can see bubbles rise from the tube. Remember to discard this brake fluid later as it will become tainted as you bleed the brakes into it.

ESSENTIALS

Instead of searching for the right-sized plastic tube, you can always buy a tube made specifically for bleeding brakes. These tubes are readily available and are relatively inexpensive.

Turn the wrench a half turn and squeeze the brake lever. Observe what moves through the tube. If you see bubbles or liquid that is different in color from the fresh fluid, you are not even close to being done. Close the bleeder valve by turning it in the opposite direction and release the brake lever. Wait a moment and then repeat, until you can do this at least three times and see nothing but bubble-free new brake fluid coming out of the tube. It may be necessary to refill the master cylinder during the bleeding process. This depends on how many times you repeat the procedure. It will certainly be necessary to do it after you are done.

Removing the Front-Wheel Assembly

Usually, it's not really necessary to remove the front wheel in order to replace the brakes or perform any of the maintenance routines that most bikers will be comfortable with. However, the procedure is fairly straightforward and can save a ton of money when it comes to replacing the front tire. Not only will removing your front wheel lower the maintenance costs of having a tire replaced, it can be the difference between paying to have your motorcycle towed into the shop and just bringing it in yourself using a different vehicle.

Before you begin the wheel-removal procedure, place the motorcycle on a proper stand. A center stand does not count. Both wheels should be suspended off the ground and the motorcycle should be cradled firmly to prevent it from tipping.

1. **Remove the speedometer cable.** The vast majority of motorcycles have a speedometer cable attached to the front wheel.
2. **Remove the brake caliper(s).** This step is not required for all motorcycles. Generally speaking, once the wheel is loose you can just wiggle it free. The wiggling will push the pads against the caliper and usually make enough clearance. If you do have to remove the brake caliper, wire it to the fork so that it doesn't hang by the brake line.
3. **Remove the axle.** On most bikes, this is just a matter of removing the end caps at the bottom of the fork. Generally, this will cause the wheel with the axle to drop straight down. You might have to wiggle a bit if the brake pads are tight.

More on How to Remove the Axle

On some motorcycles, you will have to remove the axle bolts before lowering the wheel assembly. To do so will require removing the axle pin or cotter pin, a bent piece of metal that resembles a bobby pin. It slides through a hole in the threaded portion of the axle and prevents the crown-topped axle bolt from turning; to prevent it from slipping out, the axle pin is generally bent at the end.

The axle pin or cotter pin is a one-time use item. Throw it away after you are done and replace it with another.

With the pin removed, it is time to unscrew the axle nuts. The axle may be held in place with axle nuts only, or an axle nut and a pinch nut; both remove the same way. If an axle nut covers a crown nut, take off the axle nut first. Once you remove all of the retaining nuts and pins, you should be able to remove the axle with your fingers. If not, tap the threaded side with a rubber-faced hammer. Note the position of spacers and washers, as they will fall off when the axle is removed.

If your front-wheel assembly comes off in one piece with the axle in place, bring it to a repair facility in one piece for the replacement of the tire. They are sure to have the proper replacement pin.

To reinstall the front-wheel assembly, simply reverse the procedure. However, be sure to use the proper amount of torque listed in the individual service manual, and always use a new cotter pin.

Removing the Rear-Wheel Assembly

Many motorcycles require the removal of body parts, panels, and even shock absorbers before removing the rear wheel. Still other special procedures need to be followed for different belt, chain, and shaft configurations. Check your service manual before you begin.

FACTS

The procedure for replacing rear disk brakes is much the same as for front disk brakes. You do not have to remove the rear wheel unless you have drum brakes.

On some motorcycles you will have to remove the rear-brake caliper. If you do, the procedure is about the same as removing the front-brake caliper. If you don't have rear disk brakes, you will have to determine how to remove the mechanical connection between the foot brake lever and the rear brakes—it is typically exposed and easy to discover.

Unbolt and Take Out the Axle

Remove the axle pin and throw it away. Then loosen and remove the axle nuts. Just as with the front-wheel assembly, some will have an additional pinch nut or cover.

Once you are absolutely 100 percent sure you have removed all nuts and retaining devices, use a rubber-faced hammer to tap the axle through while wiggling from the other side. Gently tapping from one side while turning from the other usually works. If you note too much resistance, you missed something. If it requires an extra tap or two after you can no longer reach it with the rubber-faced hammer, use a brass drift against the axle and tap on the other end of the drift with a ball-peen hammer.

You may meet resistance after the axle slides through only one side of the swing arm. In this case, the tire has fallen a bit, either causing the final drive to pull it forward or creating an awkward angle. It may be necessary to loosen the final drive on a chain or belt system, but usually you can just lift the wheel into a level position and proceed with the removal of the axle.

Be very careful to note the location of spacers and washers, because they will probably fall out the minute you remove the axle. If not, they will let loose when you remove the wheel assembly itself.

Push the wheel forward to slack the chain or belt. Swing the chain or belt out of the way and remove the wheel. If you have a shaft-driven motorcycle, pull the wheel backwards to disengage it from the drive system and then remove the wheel.

To reinstall the rear-wheel assembly, reverse the procedure. However, be sure to use the proper amount of torque listed in your particular service manual, and don't forget to use a new cotter pin.

Rear Brake Shoes

With the wheel assembly removed from the motorcycle, pull the back plate from the hub assembly. If you have ever worked on automobiles, this will seem exactly backwards. On an automobile, the back plate remains with the vehicle when you pull the hub off.

At this point, you could try looking up the specification for brake-shoe thickness. But why bother? Shoes are cheap and you have already done a lot of work to get you this far, so just plan on replacing them rather than deciding they will last another month and having to remove the wheel again.

The shoes are held in place by a combination of clips and springs. If you haven't put safety glasses on yet, now is a good time. Here you will have to become almost ambidextrous. You will have to compress the brake shoes toward each other and remove the clips and springs. (Note: Using a screwdriver as a lever will make your task easier, but also more dangerous.) Reverse the procedure to install the new shoes.

The Missing Link: Final-Drive Chain Replacement

Replacing either a belt or a continuous chain is far beyond the scope of this book because they do not disassemble, and the procedure for removing them varies tremendously from motorcycle to motorcycle. However, replacing a chain that contains a "repair link" is not as difficult. A repair link is a special link in your chain that can be disassembled to facilitate replacement. When you purchase either the chain or a repair link, it will come with instructions.

FACTS

The argument on the benefits and shortcomings of the repair-link chain will continue for years. On one hand, they give the average motorcycle owner the ability to replace the chain in the garage—or even on the side of the road. On the other hand, they are more likely to fail due to improper installation.

If you decide you want a chain with a repair link, you have made a wise choice. You can even go to a local shop to install a repair-link chain on a motorcycle that came factory-equipped with a continual chain. Then, when it's time to replace the chain due to scheduled maintenance or road happenstance, you will be ready.

Remove everything that blocks the rear sprocket. If you are making this repair by the side of the road, you will not be replacing the rear sprocket, as that requires the removal of the rear-wheel assembly. If you are replacing the chain as an in-garage service, remove the rear wheel.

If you lost your chain going down the road, look for remnants and remove the pieces. You will be amazed at where links can fly and how deep they can embed themselves when they do. If the old chain is still attached to the motorcycle, find the old repair link and use a pair of needle-nose pliers to remove the retaining clip. Discard the link and chain. It is not a good idea to reuse a repair link.

If you are working in your garage, remove the rear sprocket. If you are not, skip this step for now, but do so when you can. You should always replace the rear sprocket with the chain. The sprocket is held on by bolts, which will have to be loosened and removed. If you find them difficult to turn, stand the tire up between your legs and squat on it. Your weight is generally enough to hold the assembly in place. Remember, if you haven't removed the brake plate, it will easily fall from the hub, so you might want to set it aside before rocking on the wheel for leverage. Once the bolts are out, the old sprocket will easily lift off. Replace the sprocket and remount the rear-wheel assembly.

Harley-
Davidson
Chopper

Photo courtesy of Seattle Support Group.

This is where the procedure becomes the same for roadside and garage repair. The wheel is back on, but the chain is still off. The old chain will have stretched over time. To compensate for this, follow the procedure for adjusting the chain (refer to the previous chapter for detailed instructions), but instead of adjusting the chain move the adjusters to full slack.

Feed the chain over the top of the front sprocket until you can see it dangling out the other side. Then place the other end of the chain over the rear sprocket so that there is an almost straight line of chain from the top of the front sprocket to the top of the rear sprocket. Lace the chain all the way around the rear socket and up front to join the other end. As you do, be extremely careful not to drag it on the ground. If you do, make sure it is still clean.

Assemble both ends of the chain with the repair link in accordance with the chain manufacturer's instructions and make sure that the closed end of the retaining clip faces the direction the chain travels. This causes inertia to retain the clip rather than remove it. Finally, adjust the chain (as described in the previous chapter) and reattach all of the covers that you removed.

Roadside Repairs and Expedients

No matter how much you may love them, motorcycles are not nearly as technologically advanced as automobiles. Due to the motorcycle's relative unpopularity as compared to cars, the industry has been lacking the encouragement to improve and innovate. Moreover, the motorcycle's engine and electrical system are much more exposed to the elements than in automobiles, and bikes are generally pushed harder than cars. Due to these factors, it is no surprise that roadside breakdowns are a lot more common.

Most motorcycle shops will offer towing services designed specifically for motorcycles. Unfortunately, they are not open twenty-four hours a day. Of course you could call AAA (American Automobile Association) or another roadside assistance service that tows automobiles. If push comes to shove, your bike can be slung behind a tow truck, but it is infinitely better to trailer it into the shop when it can't get there on its own. Because most tow companies don't have motorcycle trailers, you should do whatever you can to try and get your bike there yourself.

Road expedients, or makeshift tricks, will keep your bike running long enough to get you to the garage. Remember: These are not valid repair methods. While each may offer the promise of getting you out of the rain, it will also increase the risk of serious failure at a later date.

When you find yourself at the side of the road, make sure you are in a safe place before you start laboring over your bike. If you are literally by the roadside, warn oncoming traffic of your presence with road flares and other warning devices like reflective triangles and flash lights. If you have a passenger who is not needed for the operation, have him or her stand guard and warn you if a mishap is about to occur. If you have a chase vehicle or if you can call someone with a car, block your work with a car or truck that has its hazards on.

The rest of this chapter will explore what you should be prepared for on the road, and provide some remedies that will help you get going again.

Chain: You can easily replace a chain if the new chain is fitted with a "maintenance link" (see previous chapter for detailed instructions).

Cooling system leaks: Leaks at the top portion of the radiator are often impossible to fix along the side of the road. Leaks in the radiator body or at the cooling fins can be fixed temporarily with over-the-counter radiator stop-leak products. When you pour such a fluid inside the radiator, it will seal the radiator as it leaks back out through the hole. This means you will have to ride a bit before you can judge whether the product worked. Leaks in radiator hoses can sometimes be temporarily repaired with duct tape. Both of these repairs are quick fixes, and should be used only to get you to a proper repair facility.

Brake and running lights: The quick remedy for a missing running light is much less costly than what will happen when a motorist doesn't notice you on the road. Hand signals may be legal in some states, but motorists generally have no idea what they mean. Never ride with burned-out lights—especially with burned-out brake lights. Always pack extra brake and running lights. Most lights require nothing more than a screwdriver to repair. However, some require very special screwdrivers, so make sure you have the right ones before heading out on the road.

Body parts: Occasionally a spill will result in damage to a body part that causes interference with the normal operations of the motorcycle. If such is the case, you can pull it out of the way and hold it in place with duct tape.

Headlights: It is impractical to carry a full-size spare headlight with you at all times. Fortunately, many motorcycles now use headlight inserts. These are smaller bulbs that you twist into what used to be the headlight itself on older motorcycles. Check to see what type of headlight you have ahead of time and, if possible, pack a replacement.

ESSENTIALS

Consider this problem as you search for motorcycle accessories. A popular custom-headlight arrangement is a bracket that allows the mounting of two large rectangular automotive headlights where there was once a smaller motorcycle headlight. However, these arrangements make it difficult to carry a replacement bulb.

Oil leaks: The only oil leak that may be corrected by a roadside remedy is one occurring in rubber tubing, like the ones that connect the engine to the oil cooler. If you tightly wrap the tubing with a few layers of duct tape, it should hold for a short time. Before long, however, pressure and heat will eat away at this quick fix.

Road flares: Ideally, roadside repairs are not actually conducted by the side of the road, but rather in a parking lot or some other off-road location. But sometimes you don't have that option, especially with blown tires. For those occasions, it is always a good idea to pack some road flares.

Wet plugs: No matter how good you have become at that choke setting, you will eventually flood your engine while trying to start it. In a pinch, you could always pull the plugs, clean, dry, and reinstall them, but when you consider the price of new plugs, you can see why it's probably best to just carry replacements. For a few bucks, you can turn an hour of cleaning and drying into a couple minutes of replacing.

Fixing a Flat Tire

Even brand-new tires are subject to road hazards, both seen and unseen, so if you drive over or through debris, make sure to check your tires afterward. It is infinitely better to find out about a tire that is going flat when you are sitting still than a tire that suddenly becomes flat while you are moving.

If a tire goes flat while you are on the road, you will probably have to call for towing service, because if a flat tire goes even a short distance under load, it will rip itself to pieces. However, if you spot the problem along the way or if your tire is lucky enough to have survived a moving flat, then you might be able to limp home or to the next repair facility—if you packed the right equipment.

ALERT

The following procedure is an emergency-only solution for a flat tire. Get a pressurized can of sealant and connect it to your valve stem. If it works, it will both inflate the tire and temporarily repair the leak. Make absolutely sure you follow the instructions on the can to the letter and take the can to the repair facility, to show them exactly what they are dealing with. If this approach fails at speed, you will regret ever having tried it.

Plugs: Plugs will only work with tires that do not have inner tubes. Fortunately, the majority of tires on the road fall into this category. You can purchase plug kits at most motorcycle and automobile shops—the kits should include everything you need to plug a tire and get back out onto the road, except, of course, for the air to refill your flat tire (see the next section).

Patches: Patches have no place in motorcycle maintenance. They are used on inner tube–type tires and require the removal of the wheel and tire to install. That sort of repair is beyond the scope of what the average biker is prepared to do by the side of the road. Once the tire is broken down that far, there is no reason not to replace the inner tube rather than patching it.

Refilling the Tire

There are a couple of options for replacing tire pressure by the side of the road. The best is an electronic or mechanical air pump. Unfortunately, these devices are often bulky and expensive. Another option is a CO_2 kit, which utilizes the same CO_2 cartridges as home seltzer-water dispensers and BB guns. Even if you can't find a motorcycle shop nearby, you can usually find the cartridges at hardware, sporting-goods, and even grocery stores. If you find yourself in a grocery store, be careful not to buy the ones for whipped cream, as they contain a nitrous oxide rather than carbon dioxide, and will not fit the inflator tool. The final, and probably best, option is air in a can. These look very much like Fix-A-Flat cans do, but they have no sealant.

ESSENTIALS

Repairing a tire by the side of the road is really a matter of knowing what type of tires you use and then packing accordingly. All tire repairs should be considered temporary fixes. When you consider the stakes, you should be able to see how proper tire repair is limited to tire replacement.

Harley-Davidson Engine

1925
Harley-
Davidson

1936
Harley-
Davidson

1937
Harley-
Davidson

1942
Harley-
Davidson

1949
Triumph

1972
Yamaha

1972
Triumph

1975
Norton
850

1989
BMW

1990
BMW

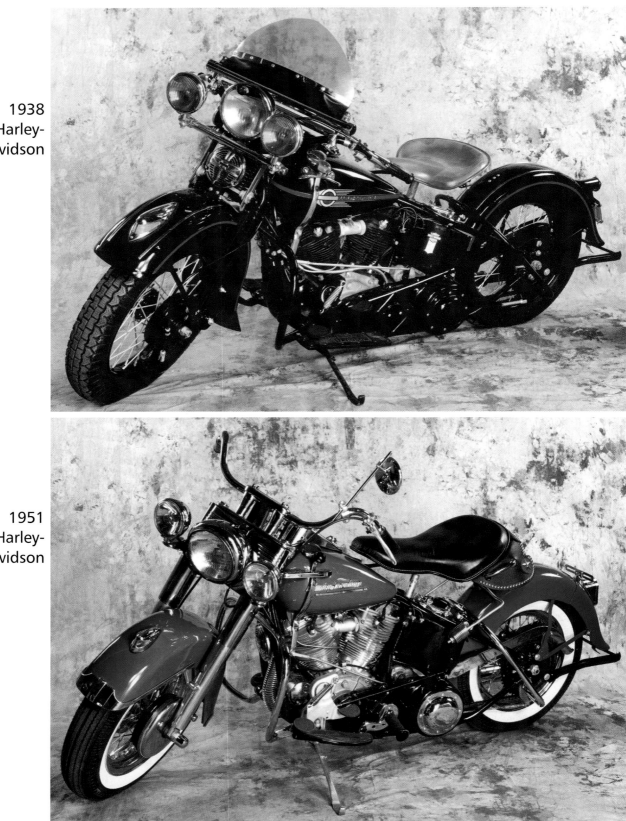

1938
Harley-
Davidson

1951
Harley-
Davidson

1955
Harley-
Davidson

1959
Harley-
Davidson

2001
Suzuki
GSX600B

2002
Suzuki
DLI

2002
Suzuki
SV650SB

Suzuki Motorcycle photographs courtesy of Suzuki.

CHAPTER 16

Kings and Queens of the Road— Riding in Groups

Riding a motorcycle need not be a solitary experience. On the contrary, this machine has the power to bridge the gap between people. Whether you ride with a passenger or as a group, you can definitely make biking a social experience. This chapter offers some tips on how to ride with a passenger, as well as the etiquette of riding in a group.

Riding with Passengers

Inviting a companion to travel with you can make your motorcycle rides much more pleasant, but it can also make riding much more dangerous. When you invite a passenger, you also invite a new set of concerns for safety. Even if your passenger moves exactly as you do around the turns, their additional weight will cause your motorcycle to respond differently. Your motorcycle will accelerate slower, brake longer, and turn wider. It is your responsibility as operator to remain in control of the motorcycle even with these changes in handling.

No Passenger Seat Means No Passenger

This rule is very simple, yet very important: If your bike doesn't have a passenger seat, it should never carry a passenger. If your motorcycle came equipped with a seat that has been removed, you will simply need to replace it. If it did not, however, you will have to check with the manufacturer to find out why, and what kinds of safety issues you should be concerned with. If your bike was not designed for a passenger at all, any modifications that you add to it will be at your own risk.

Although "pee pads" are a wildly popular addition to many street cruisers, simply bolting a cushion to the rear fender does not make a motorcycle safe for a passenger. If the rear fender is not designed to support the passenger's weight, it will bend and rub the rear tire. If it seems to support the weight while sitting still, there is no way of knowing what it will do when it hits that first big bump.

Passenger Foot Pegs

In addition to a passenger seat, your motorcycle should have passenger foot pegs. If you have removed the passenger pegs and want to reinstall them, reposition them in the same location. If you don't, then at least consider the change very carefully. The number one complaint passengers usually have about their experience on a motorcycle is the muffler burn that came from improperly positioned passenger pegs.

Passengers need to know where to put their feet and where not to. Explain that the foot pegs are the only place for their feet. Point out the exhaust and how hot it will get. If this isn't enough to keep their feet planted on the pegs, explain what will happen if their legs or feet should come in contact with road debris or other motorists.

Never let a passenger wrap their legs around your waist or rest their legs on your thighs. This raises the center of gravity, interferes with driver operations, and completely negates the passenger's ability to stay planted in even a mild turn.

It's a Matter of Weight

Any passenger means extra weight, and extra weight means different handling. If your passenger weighs the same as you, then the rider weight doubles. Even if your passenger is only half your weight, you are increasing the suspension load by 50 percent at rest. This means that the force exerted on all suspension parts will increase proportionately. Many manufacturers have taken this problem into consideration. Some have incorporated methods of easily changing the dynamics of how the motorcycle's suspension responds to differing rider weight. But just how much you will be able to adjust a motorcycle for the changing weight depends on the manufacturer.

At a very minimum, you should be able to adjust the preload. This is typically accomplished by twisting a knob that is either mounted on each rear shock absorber or, in some cases, there is a single knob that adjusts both. Other motorcycles are equipped with an "air ride" system by which you adjust either rear or both front and rear shocks by adjusting the air pressure in them. The exact method will be different depending on your model and can be found in the operator's manual.

Mounting and Dismounting

The passenger is always the last to get on and the first to get off. Do not let your passenger get on the motorcycle until after you have taken it off the kickstand or center stand. You might remember that the kickstand comes up before weight goes down, but your passenger might not. Further, the passenger seat generally rides higher than the operator's seat, so sometimes it's impossible for the passenger to keep the weight off the motorcycle while straddling it. Besides, when the operator mounts the motorcycle, his or her right leg swings through the area where the passenger sits. To make this easy to remember, just tell yourself that a passenger can never be on your bike if you are not on it.

Communicating with Your Passenger

There are intercom systems that make it easier for operator and passenger to communicate. If an intercom is not available, you and your passenger should come up with other methods of communication, in case speaking is not possible.

Here is a simple example. You are giving your friend a ride. As you approach a turn, you will hear him say something like "turn that way," but you won't see the arm flailing in the air to lead the way. Avoid the confusion ahead of time. A tap on the right shoulder means "turn right." A tap on the left shoulder means "turn left." A single tap on the right thigh means "rest stop." A double tap on the right thigh means "emergency stop." The exact format of these signals is unimportant. What's important is for the operator and passenger to know what they are ahead of time.

Static and Dynamic Passengers

Your operator's manual won't tell you what you can expect to find in your passenger's mind. Chances are, your passenger has never operated a motorcycle. Comparatively speaking, being the passenger in an automobile requires no thought. So just what is your passenger thinking? Is your passenger thinking? Before you let them get on your motorcycle, make sure they are on the right page. Have them participate in your preride checks and explain that when it comes to motorcycles, passengers have a unique responsibility to be either a dynamic or a static passenger. Here is what that means:

Dynamic passengers: Unless you ride a full touring model, it is best to have a dynamic passenger. This type of passenger will lean and respond to the road along with you. However, if it becomes clear that the passenger only leans now and then, it is better that they do not lean at all.

Dynamic passengers should know that the chicken bars (passenger handles) are there for looks only and that they should never grasp them, because doing so will interfere with their ability to follow your lead when it comes to leaning. Instead, they should wrap their arms around the operator at the waist. This way they can take cues from the way the operator leans.

Static passengers: If you are on a full touring model, it might be almost impossible for your passenger to lean with you if his or her position on the motorcycle is too far back to ride comfortably while maintaining the contact necessary to know what you are doing when you are doing it. In that situation, it is best that the passenger not lean at all. Such a passenger would be called a static passenger.

Never Mix the Two

The key to being able to lean safely with a passenger is knowing what kind of passenger you have. Make it clear to your passenger that you need to avoid the unexpected. The dynamic passenger cannot suddenly become static, and vice versa, without changing the way the motorcycle will perform. If that change occurs in the middle of a turn or a panicky situation, bad things can happen. If the passenger is going to be dynamic, the passenger will greatly improve your ability to handle the motorcycle in the most stressful situations. However, if they should suddenly fail in their ability to respond as you respond, they could be responsible for some of the worst accidents. You will have to spell this out for most passengers. If you don't think they understand, then don't let them on your motorcycle.

Riding in Groups

The Lone Wolf Biker image is one of the greatest misconceptions about bikers. Yes, most bikers pride themselves on being individuals, but they are also social creatures. If you spend any time around other bikers, you will discover that even a short ride can be enhanced if a few good friends join in. In a small-group setting, you can quickly learn about each other's habits, both on the road and off. You can discover your companions' weaknesses and strengths, and will soon learn how to protect them from their weaknesses and rely on their strengths.

The main drawback to riding in a small group is that there isn't usually anyone in charge. No one person has the privilege and responsibility to ride in the front to keep a safe speed and lead the way, and no one has been put in the back in case anything goes wrong. This can lead to competition between participants. Someone will get out front and want to see if those behind can keep up. If this occurs, let the lead bikers have their fun. If you do not pursue, they will quickly leave you behind and have no one to show off for. Soon, they will probably slow down and get with the program.

Riding with Clubs

Clubs are another story altogether. Most will have a certain set of rules made to uphold a safe riding environment and make sure that all members enjoy their scheduled rides. If you are not willing to ride within the confines of a particular riding club's rules, find a different club or go it alone.

Many club functions feature alcohol. This is fine as long as it is after you are done riding. It is very popular for a tour to end with a hog roast, barbecue, or other kinds of feasts and revelry. Check ahead of time to see if there is camping available after the activities. Many club functions will be conducted in conjunction with local taverns, as, for example, with Poker Runs.

A Poker Run is usually a charity event. Participants pay a fee, which goes to the run's designated charity. At the beginning of the run, riders leave one at a time, with a few minutes in between. Along the route, there are defined checkpoints where you pick up a playing card. These check points are often taverns. The last checkpoint is where the real festivities will generally begin.

ESSENTIALS

Because there isn't much of a hurry to these events, it is tempting to stop for a drink or two. Make those drinks nonalcoholic, because even if you think one beer won't hurt you, you will have several more checkpoints to stop at—the goal of the Poker Run is to get the best poker hand (hence the title).

Riding Formations

There are three main formations for riding in groups. Each has its place, as well as advantages and disadvantages.

Riding Single File

When riding in small groups or when the nature of the road dictates, you should always ride single file. This means all in the same lane, one person behind the other at a safe distance. If it weren't for concerns other than your group, this would be an ideal way to ride. Unfortunately, this riding formation will do nothing to help make your party stand out.

Riding Abreast

Riding in a standard abreast formation means that two bikers share a single lane, one on the left and one on the right. The benefit to this formation is that it causes the motorcycles to be seen much better, especially at night. Other motorists will often mistake you for automobiles and give you the distance you deserve.

Unfortunately, if other motorists think that you are an automobile, they will not be ready for you to act like a motorcycle. If you are riding abreast and split up for an off- or on-ramp, it may give the traffic behind you pause while they try to figure out how a car just split in half. If that pause comes when they should be putting on the brakes, bad things may happen.

Additionally, riding abreast does not give you the out that you have when the lane is all yours. You won't have nearly as much room to avoid debris, swerving motorists, and other road hazards. Beyond that, you can never be sure the other motorcyclist is proficient enough to hold position.

ALERT

It might seem very tempting to pull alongside another motorcycle to say hello, but it is generally not a good idea. When you join another motorcycle in the same lane, even at the stoplight, your move may be interpreted as an invasion of space.

Riding Staggered Abreast

The middle ground between riding single-file and riding abreast is to ride staggered abreast, which is why this formation is preferred among groups both large and small. One motorcycle rides in the left portion of a single lane, the next one back to the right but a length or two behind, and so on. In this formation, the group will appear larger than it actually is, and will be more visible to other motorists. The exact distance will change with speed. The idea is that motorcycles that are directly behind each other are at a safe minimum distance. Increase this distance for inexperienced riders as they may swerve from left to right or right to left unexpectedly.

Touring with Large Groups

The person who arranges the tour for a large group is known as the tour captain. It might seem like a fanciful title borrowed from the military, but it accurately describes the role. The tour captain is responsible for the strategy involved in the battle against discord. If you are the tour captain, your mission is to move all participants from point A to point B. Fighting you every way is discord, a natural force that the ancients personified as the goddess Discordia. She is the one who spills the oil and diesel fuel on the road, tosses loose nails at tires, and causes even the best preventative maintenance from missing a critical problem. Don't look at her as an enemy, because such an attitude will just make things worse. Think of her as the ever-increasing challenge to improve your abilities as captain.

The Chase Vehicle

Your first concern should be the chase vehicle. The chase-vehicle rider and tour captain should have CB radios. Cell phones will work in a pinch, but there are some areas where cell phones lose their service.

QUESTIONS?

What is a chase vehicle?
A chase vehicle is the vehicle that travels at the very rear of the tour and that would be capable of transporting an injured participant to the hospital. Ideally, the chase vehicle is a truck or trailer that can also transport bikes that break down along the way.

It's a good idea to place a banner on the chase vehicle (if there is room) that warns about the motorcycles in front of it. These banners can normally be made on vinyl by copy, sign, and print shops. The simpler the banner, the better: "Motorcycles Ahead—Be Careful" is a good example.

No matter what the chase vehicle is, make sure it carries the basics. Extra fuel, light medical supplies, fire extinguisher, and tools are mandatory. Food and water are also good ideas. Remember that the greater the distance and the more members the touring group has, the greater the need for a chase vehicle. Each additional motorcycle and mile means you have an additional chance at a mishap or breakdown. Very large tour groups are sometimes chased by medical personnel or paramedics with appropriate equipment.

In Case of Emergency

Know the participants and their bikes as best you can. Plan fuel stops in accordance with the motorcycle with the least range. Place your most experienced rider in the rear of the pack (this person is sometimes called the tour lieutenant).

If a motorcycle goes down or off to the side of the road, all the other bikers except the lieutenants should continue on, as long as they can do so safely. If it is safe to do so, the second lieutenant speeds up and goes around the tour to assume the captain's position in front. The captain then follows the second lieutenant to the first rest area or exit and the entire tour follows. The lieutenant tells the captain what has happened and the captain calls the chase vehicle. Deciding what happens next depends on the individual circumstances.

FACTS

The tour lieutenant's job is to keep an eye on what is going on from the rear and to race forward to tell the tour captain what is going on or to stop instantly to help a downed motorcycle. The tour lieutenant rides together with the second lieutenant, who should be an equally experienced biker.

If a motorcyclist is injured and cannot be transported by the chase vehicle due to possible spinal injuries, then the captain should call for an ambulance. If it is nothing more than quick maintenance problems, then the captain can choose to wait on the stragglers. If the repair problem is going to take a while, the captain might choose to pitch in for the night rather than press on without a chase vehicle.

CHAPTER 17

Meeting the Family

Motorcycle clubs can be some of the most rewarding organizations you can belong to. They offer fellowship and community, as well as vast quantities of knowledge that might otherwise take you much longer to acquire. The following chapter will introduce you to the clubs that may become your new extended family.

What's in a Club

Today's motorcycle clubs or MCs may be classified as either AMA-sanctioned or outlaw (non-AMA) clubs. There are many organizations that are neither AMA nor outlaw, but few that will use the term motorcycle club, because some folks resent that label.

When it comes to motorcycle organizations, the use of the word "club" isn't as open-ended as the more general use of the word. For the most part, factory-sponsored and public organizations are not considered motorcycle clubs—words like "association" and "group" are used to make this distinction, though, of course, there are exceptions to every rule.

If you want to form your own motorcycle club and fly your own independent colors, you have two options. You can join the AMA, which will sanction your club and give you the right to display their patch with your colors. This means you will play by the AMA rules, which are easy to acquire in print form from the AMA itself. If you don't join the AMA, it will be assumed that you are playing by the rules of the outlaw clubs. The problem with doing the latter is that those rules are discovered only after years of personal experience. Outlaw motorcycle clubs tend to be territorial, and for good reason, but they generally won't go out of their way to disturb AMA-sanctioned clubs.

Brand-Specific Organizations

Many bikers are fanatics when it comes to brand loyalty. Some will go so far as to say there is only one kind of motorcycle, or only one kind of biker. These are usually Harley-Davidson devotees, but their counterparts are found among followers of other motorcycle types and models as well. Although it might seem like these folks are a bit exclusive for your tastes, you will quickly find that brand-exclusive organizations offer a type of support that you just can't find in other organizations. At brand-exclusive organizations you will find people of a mind like yours when it comes to your biking preferences, since the same factors that caused you to purchase the type of motorcycle that you did may have been a factor in the purchase of their motorcycle. For that same reason, members of a brand-exclusive organization will be able to offer you much know-how and information when it comes to your motorcycle.

FACTS

Not all brands have a corresponding club, however—manufacturers are just now catching on to the many benefits they can receive by directly sponsoring an owners' group. For a complete list of motorcycle organizations, listed by state, refer to Appendix C.

BMW Motorcycle Owners of America (BMW MOA)

This organization boasts members in all fifty states as well as in Canada, South America, and Europe. Membership includes frills like a member's card, jacket patch, and motorcycle sticker. But there's a great deal more than frills to joining this organization. Perhaps the best benefit of membership is the *BMW MOA Anonymous* book. This is a coded listing of all members who have made their information public for both emergencies and social activities. Listings are arranged by area code, phone number, and degree of assistance offered. With over 12,000 members included, you can see how it can add a great peace of mind to long road trips. Membership also comes with access to the toll-free phone number necessary to reach the folks listed in the coded handbook, hence the term "anonymous." In addition to the *BMW MOA Anonymous* book, members also receive the monthly *BMW Owner's News*.

BMW MOA offers chartered clubs in each of the fifty states as well as in Canada, France, Germany, and Mexico. Moreover, if you can't find a chartered club in your area, this organization will offer you assistance in chartering and starting a club of your own.

Gold Wing Road Riders Association (GWRRA)

This is the world's largest club that is dedicated to a single motorcycle model rather than a brand—the Honda Gold Wing. Recently, membership has been opened to include the Valkyrie model as well. Established in 1977 and boasting over 75,000 members, GWRRA offers many benefits, and they differ from other brand-focused groups—their motto is: "Friends for Fun, Safety, and Knowledge." Some members claim that the GWRRA is the world's largest club of its kind, and the world's largest family.

BSA
Bantam

Photo courtesy of Seattle Support Group.

Chapters can be found in most areas; they provide social activities and organize touring outings—the Gold Wing/Valkyrie was designed to serve as a touring motorcycle. While most brand-exclusive organizations focus on the motorcycles themselves, GWRRA also offers safety classes and discounts at dealerships, hotels, travel agents, and campgrounds.

Members of GWRRA receive the *Gold Book*, a Gold Wing–friendly service directory that lists names and phone numbers of members who can provide everything from general help to tools, hotels, camping space, trip assistance, and a helping hand when your bike breaks down. It also lists participating dealerships and motorcycle-part vendors.

GWRRA also offers a Rider Education program, which has been recognized by the Motorcycle Safety Foundation, as well as ongoing workshops and programs to improve rider skill and safety. These safety programs are often based on the nature of this particular class of biking, and often include such subjects as safely towing a trailer, how to improve passenger performance, and the particular service issues that affect these motorcycles.

Good Times Owners Club—Kawasaki

If you ride a Kawasaki and races are your thing, this club is a plus. If you don't like either watching or participating in motor sports, you might have to wait a while for the club offerings to get up to par with those that other manufacturer-oriented clubs offer its touring-focused members. Kawasaki has only recently shown a serious interest in touring motorcycles and activities.

Membership includes extra hospitality and VIP treatment at all races, rallies, and shows that are sponsored or cosponsored by Kawasaki, their quarterly newsletter, an atlas, free subscription to *Good Times* magazine, and, of course, the logo on membership card, pin, and patch.

FACTS

On the bright side, this organization's offerings really shine on race day. Whenever Kawasaki officially participates in sponsoring a race, they offer great hospitality to their members, including free helmet check-in, free or discounted tickets, and free race schedule for Team Kawasaki.

Kawasaki's discount schedule for members seems a bit lacking as well. They offer 10 percent off all accessories to members, but that discount does not apply to motorcycle parts. They also offer 10 percent off all Kawasaki-licensed products at participating locations. One might get the idea they will give you a discount only on items that will further promote the sales of their motorcycles, like jackets, gloves, and helmets that carry the brand name.

Harley Owner's Group (HOG)

Harley-Davidson started HOG in 1983 to reinforce brand loyalty and to provide a family alternative to the outlaw clubs that are stereotypically associated with Harley-Davidsons. It was clear that the organization had a bright future when membership approached 33,000 before the end of its introductory year. By 1985, members realized they were too diverse for one organization. Local chapters started to form to support a wide range of activities. One chapter might be focused on customizing, another on racing, another on family-oriented activities, and still others focused on a mix of these and other activities.

Harley
Davidson

Photo courtesy of Seattle Support Group.

HOG encourages touring with the ABCs of Touring program. This is a great excuse to hit the road and head out of town. Collect pictures of yourself and your bike in front of official signs denoting the location. These signs are generally either government-posted, or are the name signs belonging to Harley-Davidson dealerships. Once you have collected enough pictures, members can submit them to HOG for potential prizes and recognition. Pins, patches, and medallions are also awarded based on mileage and participation in touring events.

Harley-Davidson Engine

Photo courtesy of Seattle Support Group.

Publications such as *Harley-Davidson's Enthusiast* magazine are free with full membership. *Enthusiast* is the world's oldest continually published motorcycle magazine. Membership also includes *Hog Tails*, the official publication of the Harley Owner's Group.

Events and discounts available to HOG members include the Fly and Ride program, which allows you to rent a bike in locations where you wouldn't normally ride, as well as airfare, car rental, event, and hotel discounts. At various large motorcycle events, HOG treats its members with hospitality. Moreover, members can receive discounts on shipping their motorcycles from one location to the next. This can be a great benefit when moving your household or when participating in touring events that take place so far away, either time or geography prevent riding to them. Even the most die-hard biker will find it tough to ride from the United States to a European-based event.

ALERT

Local chapters are found at almost every Harley-Davidson dealer, so finding one in your area is as simple as finding your local phonebook directory. Joining a chapter means instant access to a community that may be hard to find without HOG.

At an additional cost, members can join the HOG roadside assistance program, a kind of AAA for Harley owners. This program is very affordable and provides better service than AAA (where it is available), because the folks providing the assistance are familiar with assisting bikers.

HOG also encourages safe riding by providing partial rebates for the successful completion of rider courses offered by the Motorcycle Safety Foundation; it also offers a toll-free support line, a touring handbook, and a members-only section on the HOG Web site.

Honda Rider's Club of America (HRCA)

Membership in HRCA is free to anyone who purchases a new Honda motorcycle. HRCA currently boasts over 125,000 members, and claims to have the most benefits of any motorcycle club in the world.

Members receive *Honda Red Rider*, the official magazine of HRCA, six times a year. Because HRCA is directly associated with Honda, their publication always includes information about new models. It also lists events, membership news, and a great deal more that can enrich your life on a Honda.

Membership also includes a twenty-four-hour toll-free roadside assistance plan, which is probably the best of the ones offered by any brand-specific organization. Unlike any other roadside service you may encounter, service extends to any motor vehicle with a Honda in it, on it, or towing it (as long as the bike is there when the transport vehicle broke down). This service is especially beneficial for off-road bikers.

ESSENTIALS Dedicated to encouraging safe riding both on and off the road, HRCA will reimburse a portion of approved Motorcycle Safety Foundation rider courses, and offer incentives for both off-road motorcycle safety courses as well as courses in All-Terrain Vehicle (ATV) safety.

Probably the best advantage of being a member of HRCA is being informed about the many happenings in this diverse community of motorcycle enthusiasts. Because Honda produces motorcycles for just about any imaginable purpose, the diversity of events sponsored and cosponsored by HRCA is staggering. Members receive listings and access to rallies and races in just about every category. Some of these events are exclusive to its members—in such cases, your membership card is your secret password. Others are open to the public, but your membership will often entitle you to deep discounts on ticket prices.

Harley
Davidson
Sportster

Photo courtesy of Seattle Support Group.

Interest-Specific Organizations

Other motorcycle organizations have been created along the lines of common activities rather than common makes or models. The following is a brief list of the most widely known groups.

- **The American Motorcyclist Association (AMA):** While they don't represent 99 percent of all bikers, they do represent a great portion. Currently the AMA is estimated to have over a quarter of a million members. The AMA is your source of information on local racing events, as well as other motorcycle-related activities.

- **American Historic Racing Motorcycle Association (AHRMA):** The American Historic Racing Motorcycle Association is exactly what its name sounds like. It is a nonprofit association dedicated to racing historic motorcycles, and its members include both racers and spectators. The AHRMA also offer activities, for both novice and seasoned riders.
- **American Sport Touring Riders Association (ASTRA):** Members of this organization demonstrate just how wide the new sport touring category might stretch.
- **Blue Knights International Motorcycle Club:** This nonprofit fraternal organization of active and retired law enforcement officers has over 14,000 male and female members.
- **Motor Maids:** This motorcycle organization was started by World War II's female dispatch motorcyclists who needed to find a peacetime way to express their newfound love for motorcycles. Today, Motor Maids is the oldest motorcycle organization for women in North America.
- **Motorcycle Safety Foundation (MSF):** MSF is a U.S. national nonprofit organization sponsored by the U.S. manufacturers and distributors of BMW, Ducati, Harley-Davidson, Honda, Kawasaki, Piaggio/Vespa, Suzuki, Victory, and Yamaha motorcycles.

The best and safest way to learn how to ride is to take an MSF rider course. In many states, successful completion of the MSF rider course is all you need to get your motorcycle endorsement or license. If that's not encouragement enough, successful completion of this fun and easy course means you can save money on most motorcycle insurance policies.

- **Retreads Motorcycle Club International:** This club boasts a 20,000-person membership. What are the two requirements for joining? You must have a love of motorcycles, and you must be at least forty years of age.

Other Motorcycle Organizations

Some of the best connections you can make are with much smaller organizations. Clubs aren't meant to be one-size-fits-all. Sometimes the most obscure, off-the-wall association of three or five people is exactly what you need. Almost every town will have these smaller groups. Some are listed in Appendix C, but the best way to find them is just to get involved in the local scene.

SSENTIALS

Bikes are the best conversation starters. It's next to impossible to find something about a motorcycle that an owner won't want to talk about. From there, you will be well on the way to meeting the rest of the family.

If you have an interest in racing, a trip to the track is your ticket. If custom bikes are your thing, watch the newspaper for information about local shows. Dealerships and specialty shops are a good place to meet motorcycle people. Almost every dealership in the world can tell you about the local hangouts and organizations. In short, keep your eyes open. If you see a row of bikes that suit your style outside a local tavern or coffee shop, then maybe it's time for a beer or a cup of coffee.

CHAPTER 18
Over the River and Through the Woods

Because the biker gene can kick in early, many street bikers get their start off-road. There are no age restrictions for riding behind your parents' barn—except, of course, those imposed by your parents. This chapter is an overview of what you can expect from off-road biking, but remember: In off-road biking, there are no road maps to follow.

What Makes Off-Road Riding Special

If you are one of those bikers who originally learned in the dirt, count yourself as one of the better street riders. Off-road riding skills transfer to road riding readily, but the same is not always true the other way around. If you have not yet learned how to ride a motorcycle, consider learning off-road before heading onto the public streets. Off-roading has some real advantages, especially if you are just starting off.

The dirt is much more forgiving than public streets. A mishap in the dirt usually leaves you a bit scraped, but none the worse for wear. Of course, you can still receive serious and even mortal injuries on a dirt track, but it is much less likely. One of the main reasons for the decreased danger is obvious—no cars, trucks, vans, or buses. You and your motorcycle are more likely to go down, but the outcome of that spill will be much easier to recover from, both physically and financially.

FACTS

Off-road motorcycling is much safer than riding in traffic, because you eliminate the number-one cause of motorcycle accidents: the left-hand turning motorist.

Off-road riding presents its own challenges. The riding surfaces are difficult to negotiate: You will have to contend with loose dirt, sand, holes, hills, gravel, trees, and other obstacles that are missing on asphalt roads and highways. However, these obstacles will all hone your riding skills. Your ability to predict riding surfaces will increase, and your ability to control your throttle and brake will improve (because your traction is lower and your throttle is crisper than when you are on a hard surface with a street bike).

Paused for Posture

Improper rider position can be a real pain in the butt—literally. If you sit when you shouldn't be sitting, you will quickly hurt your rear end. When your wheels are in the mud, you must expect the unexpected and be able to move quickly. That means being ready at the legs and not planted on your seat.

Riding could also be a pain on your feet, especially if you have the feet of an urban yeti. When you ride forward, there is a tendency in most riders to rotate their feet on the pegs so their toes face down, below the pegs. This can lead to broken toes, especially when riding over large rocks or stumps. Try to keep your feet horizontal with the motorcycle and don't let your toes drop below the pegs.

ESSENTIALS

Dirt bikes are much lighter than street bikes, so much more of the balance depends on your weight and where it is at the time. This means that you will have to change your position on the motorcycle with changing conditions.

Climbing Hills

There is a difference between climbing a hill and "hill climbing." Climbing a hill is just a part of off-road riding. Hill climbing is a sport unto itself, in which the only goal and challenge is to get on top of a monster hill. In this case, the other side of the hill has been made safe for the odd chance that you will make it over. These hills are usually so steep that there is no way you can see over the top on your travels toward it, and no way to slow down on the way up—a miniscule decrease in speed will force you to slide backwards down the hill that you are trying to scale with your bike.

ALERT

Hill-climbing competitions are the hardest off-road events to master, and they are also the most dangerous. Even with years of practice, experts often receive serious injuries—better to leave this sport to the well-experienced riders until you join their ranks.

When it comes to off-road riding, you should never attempt a hill that you aren't completely sure you can take, unless you are as well staffed as those hill-climbing events. If you don't make it to the top, there is a good chance you will land on your back with your bike on top of your chest. Even if you are sure you can make it up and over, always know what is on the other side. If this means walking the track ahead of time, then so be it.

QUESTIONS?

What do you do when you try to climb a hill but fail?
If you try to climb a hill and fail, there's just one course of action: Try again, only next time pick a smaller hill.

Approach the hill with both feet planted on the pegs. Accelerate in low gear before reaching the hill to acquire momentum. Even if it is a small hill, shift a bit of your weight onto the pegs to decrease that first bump on your butt. The steeper the hill is, the more you will want to shift your weight forward. The extreme of this will be to stand full up on the pegs and lean as far forward as you can while still retaining control of the motorcycle. The largest concern is that the motorcycle will flip backwards and land on top of you. Every bit of weight you shift forward will fight this danger.

Norton
Motorcycle

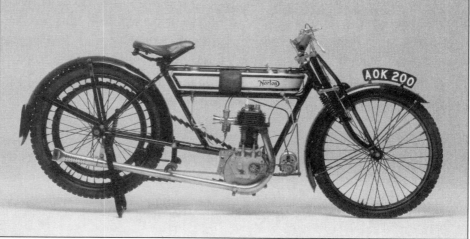

Photo courtesy of Seattle Support Group.

If you are new to off-roading and your bike starts to stall under the load, don't try to downshift. You will more likely wind upshifting too much weight onto the rear of the motorcycle and cause a back flip. Even if you do manage to downshift, you will probably pop the clutch and overaccelerate, which could also result in a back flip.

Instead, try to use the last of your forward momentum to get the bike turned around and headed back down the hill. If you come to a stop before you manage this, see if you can get a good footing on the outside (uphill) of your attempted turn. That way, even if your footing slips, your bike will slide out from under you in the opposite direction of your travel.

ALERT

If you do fall off your motorcycle, try to get as far away from it as possible. Your body hitting the ground isn't nearly as dangerous as your motorcycle hitting your body.

If you manage to get good footing, bring everything to a halt and regroup, then, with your clutch in and brake on, point your wheel toward the safest side, and gradually release your brake just enough to let you roll down and backwards while leaning into the hill. This will cause your bike to go sideways and you will probably fall down, but at least it will be in the right direction. If you manage not to fall, you will ride it backwards until you have enough room to turn your front wheel in the other direction to ride it the rest of the way down nose-first.

If you can't stay on top of it, try to hit the kill switch, then bend at the knee of the foot that is on the ground and use the other leg to kick off the foot peg. Your goal is to put as much distance between you and your motorcycle. When you hit the ground, let your one thought be to either stop planted in the dirt, or to slow your slide as much as possible. This will help you stay clear of the bike, which will probably go tumbling down the hill because all forward momentum stopped before you bailed. Remember, the leading cause of serious injury on off-road tracks is not when the rider hits the ground, but when the bike hits the rider.

Down the Hill

Going down a hill isn't nearly as challenging as going uphill. Gravity is more than willing to take over anytime you should let it. Riding down a hill while maintaining control of your motorcycle is another story entirely. Truth be known, on the mild hills that beginners should be starting on, they are much more likely to wipe out going down a hill than when they are climbing up.

ESSENTIALS

Your relationship with gravity will become a love/hate relationship. On your way up the hill, you will hate it. On the way down, you might learn to love it. Take advantage of that relationship and let it pull you down the hill rather than using the throttle.

Except in very extreme circumstances, you have a much better chance of riding it out if you negotiate the hill by pointing your bike straight down. Shift your weight as far back as you can without impairing your ability to control the motorcycle. Shift into low gear and let the engine drag. Sure, this will increase the wear on your engine, but it is an effective way to keep your speed down—off-road riding has never been gentle on motorcycle engines or other parts anyway. Avoid using the front brake as much as possible: Using it will cause the weight to shift forward, which is the last thing you want in this situation. Instead, rely on the rear brake, but be careful of losing traction when you do.

One way or the other, you will make it to the bottom of the hill. Like climbing a hill, if you know you are going to go down, kick off your bike and try to put as much distance as possible between it and yourself.

Slip-Sliding Away

Steering through high water and deep mud can be a messy challenge. To make matters worse, on the dirt track you generally find one with the other and you can never be sure what is under them unless you stop, get off your bike, and dance around in the puddle. If you are not familiar with the terrain, this is actually a good idea, especially when crossing what you have assumed to be a narrow stream. You are going to get wet anyway.

Your instinct might be to power up and let momentum transport you from one side to the next. This approach will probably work for that purpose, but there's no way of telling which way you will be facing on the other side, because you can't steer while you are hydroplaning. Instead, negotiate water slowly and with smooth control of both throttle and brake. Any time you change speed or direction, you welcome traction loss. With loss of traction comes loss of control. Point your eyes at the other side of the crossing and ease through the water at a constant speed.

Suzuki 750

Photo courtesy of Seattle Support Group.

Once you are on the other side, you will want to apply your brakes lightly as you ride to dry and clean them. If you went through particularly deep water, you might want to stop and check your oil. If there is any water in the crankcase, you will risk the engine by operating it further. This is true of both four-stroke and two-stroke engines, but tends to be more of a threat to four-stroke engines (because of the difference in design and location of crankcase breathers as opposed to those in two-stroke engines).

Riding in Mud

Riding through mud is only a bit different. The first thing to remember is that the person in front of you is probably going to be kicking clumps into the air with the rear wheel, so avoid riding directly behind another rider, even at what would normally be a safe distance. Other riders also mean ruts in the mud from those who have come before you. Tires seem to be attracted like magnets to ruts in the mud. Let them have it their way and look to where you are going, not where you are.

Mud can hide rocks, which will deflect your front tire and can cause you to lose control of your motorcycle. Always be ready for the unexpected when you can't see what's ahead.

If you find yourself bogging down, don't try to compensate with greater throttle—it will just dig you in deeper. If your rear wheel starts to slip, let off the throttle until it grabs hold again. If it does, move out of the mud with a very light throttle, being careful not to break traction. If all else fails, you may have to get off and push. It is not safe to try to operate the motorcycle while standing next to it, so expect the necessary energy to come from you and not the motorcycle. Be forewarned: This is going to be a difficult undertaking, especially if your feet cannot find solid ground from which to push.

2002 Moto
Guzzi VII
LeMans

Photo courtesy of Moto Guzzi North America, Inc.

Sinking in the Sand

Before you try to ride a motorcycle in sand, try running in it. You will quickly understand how every foot forward requires about six inches backwards. Now watch someone else run through the sand and notice how much is displaced with every step. That is why when you run in the sand, it feels like you are sinking with every step.

The key to riding in deep sand is not to tense up. Your motorcycle will slither between your legs like a snake. Instead of fighting the movement, move with it and maintain your balance.

When a motorcycle moves through deep sand (not sand on a hard surface), it feels more like sailing than biking. You cannot make sudden stops, and you're always worried about sinking. That sinking feeling is there because you are doing just that. Mastering sand means doing exactly what you don't want to do when tackling water. Just like running in sand, your rear tire will dig in with every revolution. To overcome this, you need to increase speed to a point where the tendency to dig in is compensated for by forward momentum.

With the rear wheel humming away, the next thing to worry about is the front wheel. You have to do everything you can to keep it from turning into a snowplow (going sideways). Shift your weight as far backwards as you can while maintaining control. This will lighten the front end and help it to go up and over—rather than into and through—the sand.

The closest thing to describing riding a motorcycle in sand is to say that it feels like you are riding a very large snake. You are never really going forward; it's more like a side-to-side motion with the occasional up and down movements.

At first, don't bother trying to steer, because almost any attempt to do so will just result in snowplowing. As you become more experienced, you will find that you can steer with the throttle and a bit of leaning. If you have ever practiced fishtailing in a parking lot during the first snow, you will understand exactly how it works. If not, try leaning left and goosing the throttle just a little bit, to see what happens. You will probably hit the ground a time or two, but after all it's just sand. If you really can't stand hitting the ground, then off-road just isn't your sport.

Loose Gravel and Dried Dirt

Riding on loose gravel and chunks of dried dirt is similar to riding in sand. Both are like riding a huge snake, but when you ride through gravel, the snake is always in the middle of a seizure. Your rear end will still want to dig in a bit, but your front wheel will be battered left and right by the onslaught of uneven surfaces.

You will still have that sinking feeling, but it won't be nearly as critical. You can maintain a slower speed, but try to be very steady about it. And there is one other significant difference: Rocks hurt more than sand.

What You Can't See Can Hurt You

When you ride off-road, be aware of everything and be ready for anything. Blind corners can hide downed trees. Water can hide deep crevices and craters. What might look like a little mud puddle could be the remnants of someone's attempt to mine for oil. If you stick to maintained courses, you could round a blind corner to find a bike down in the middle of the course. If you strike it out on your own, you will be amazed at the variety of hazards Mother Nature and Father Farmer can throw at you.

If you spend any time off-road, you will find out that you are going to run into things no matter how safe you think you are. If you hit something and bounce off to one side, fight the urge to use a leg to steady yourself. You will just wind up hyperextending the leg at the knee and ripping tendons. Instead, try to redistribute your weight to avoid the fall. If there's no way to avoid the fall, then think about your own protection rather than the protection of the motorcycle, and try to be as far away as possible from it when it comes down.

ESSENTIALS

To avoid the unexpected before it is too late, slow down when you don't know what's in front of you. Never ride faster than you can stop. This means that if you can only see ten feet in front of you, you should travel no faster than at a speed which would allow you to stop in nine feet.

If you are about to hit something small and there's no way out, you should try goosing the throttle and pulling back on the handlebars right before the front tire makes contact. When the front wheel is up and over, let off the throttle, and then goose it again as the rear wheel makes contact. This should not be attempted by novice riders. Moderately experienced riders should attempt this method only with objects lower than the lowest point of their motorcycle.

Tikes on Bikes: Children and the Off-Road Experience

Motorcycles are not safe. Neither is taking a bath. It doesn't matter how young or old you are, either activity can have disastrous results if not done responsibly. You will never make motorcycling safe for children, but you will never make anything safe for children. However, you can make motorcycling *safer*, and introduce your children to what might be the greatest love of their lives.

State laws about children riding on street vehicles tend to be rather straightforward these days. Motorcycles have no seat belts and there are no approved child seats for motorcycles, so even without motorcycle-specific laws children are pretty much excluded from the riding portion of the street scene. The laws for young adults vary from state to state.

The off-road experience is quite a different story. So far, the government has mostly allowed parents to decide what is right for their children, unless parents demonstrate a complete disregard for their children's safety. Parents should not rely on the manufacturer to know what is and is not right for their children. The factory cannot be depended upon to make these decisions; while the manufacturer may know its motorcycle, it does not know your children. It is hoped that you do.

FACTS

Generally speaking, a young adult will need a parent's permission in order to acquire a learner's permit (which allows for daytime riding only, requires wearing a helmet, and prohibits giving rides to passengers and riding on the highway). In most places, the age limit for getting a learner's permit is the age of sixteen.

Off-road motorcycling can be a rewarding family experience, but only when it is a part of the family and not just another activity the child participates in to keep him or her out of mom and dad's hair. If you just can't see yourself on two wheels and your child insists, then find an AMA-endorsed off-road class for children and young adults. But don't let your involvement end there. Kids should never ride without adult supervision, and they should never compete without a loving parent cheering their accomplishments and soothing their failures.

CHAPTER 19

Touring the World

Here is where you will finally learn the difference between bikers and motorcycle enthusiasts. Motorcycle enthusiasts like motorcycles. Bikers love motorcycles, and they love to travel on their motorcycles. For them, half the fun of a trip is getting there, and touring is just that—getting on the road.

Every Bike Is Not a Touring Model

All motorcycles can tour, but can your kidneys tour on just any motorcycle? Sure, you can add some hard bags and maybe even a tour pack to your bike, but if your motorcycle wasn't built with a serious attempt to dampen road and engine vibration, you are in for some serious shakes and quivers.

Good suspension on touring models is critical. If you are riding a classic motorcycle or even a wild custom-made machine, you should pay very close attention to what exactly is sprung and unsprung weight. If your rear tire is bolted directly to the frame, don't even think about going cross-country. Not only will your body be angry with you, it is entirely possible that the motorcycle's frame will complain as well. Rigid rear ends just don't make good touring motorcycles.

2002 Moto Guzzi Special

Photo courtesy of Moto Guzzi North America, Inc.

Touring Engines

Even cruisers have some serious shortcomings when it comes to touring. Although Harley-Davidson has long been associated with the open road, many of their motorcycles incorporate solid engine mounts that do absolutely nothing to isolate the operator and passenger from engine vibrations. When it comes to Harleys, avoid trying to tour on anything labeled Sportster or Softail: These tend to be the ones that really shake, rattle, and roll. In the case of other motorcycles, check to see if they have solid or rubber engine mounts. Solid engine mounts do not make good touring motorcycles. The best final drive for touring is by far the shaft. Simply put, it breaks less often. If you inspect it before a long trip, it is unlikely you will have any problems along the way. The shaft-drive's main disadvantage is that it detracts from handling, but this only becomes apparent under very hard acceleration, which is generally unnecessary for the purposes of touring. Unfortunately, shafts aren't always available for touring models. In this case, your next best bet is a belt final drive.

If you plan to attach a trailer to your touring bike, be sure your engine can handle the extra load. Factory specifications are the way to go when figuring what is a safe load for an engine to bear. If you've got more than a 1000cc engine, you are probably in good shape for hauling a trailer.

On Tour, Every Drop Counts

Most motorcycles do not have a fuel gauge, and those that do are never very accurate: When you fill up your gas tank, the arrow climbs down slowly, until it reaches the half-full mark, then speeds up between half-full and quarter-full, at which point it zips down to almost empty, and the engine sputters and dies. It's difficult to design a float system that can accurately judge the fuel in both of your fuel tanks. (Once the fuel is beyond the hump in the middle of most tanks that is necessary to facilitate the frame, one gas tank really becomes two gas tanks.) Road vibrations quickly take their toll, and what might have been a reasonably accurate gauge at the factory becomes a guesstimator a year later. Worse yet, the reading is sure to change with every bump.

Bikers are quick to tell you that you don't need a fuel gauge. When you run out of gas, you just turn the petcock to reserve and you've got plenty to make it to the next gas station. What they won't tell you is what happens when you forget to turn the petcock back to regular mode after you fill up. Well, you will use up all the gas in the main portion of the tank and all the gas in the reserve portion of your tank, and then you will reach down to turn the petcock to reserve, realize it is already in the reserve position, and your bike will do absolutely nothing, because there isn't one drop of gas left in the tank. Bikers call this "gas tank surprise," and it is one of the main reasons to never lend your motorcycle to anyone.

FACTS

Most motorcycles do not have fuel gauges. This means you will have to do a little math to figure out when it's time to fill up your bike. See Chapter 8 for details on how to calculate your gas needs.

Ignore the estimated range printed in your operator's manual. Manufacturers estimate range based on tank capacity and fuel economy under optimum conditions. Your tank capacity will change if it has a dent or has been modified in any way—if, for example, you have gel-coated it on the inside (a rust remedy). And when it comes to the manufacturer's estimates based on fuel economy, you have to remember that when you are dealing with a manual transmission, fuel economy is based primarily on how and when you shift. It's probably a safe bet that the factory test rider is shifting for the best possible fuel economy. Can you say the same about your own shifting habits?

What's Your Destination?

If you determine that your bike is good for touring, and know how much road it can reasonably be expected to handle, you can decide what your next touring destination will be. One of the great things about touring is that you don't have to go anywhere specific. Maybe you live in the Midwest and you just want to see the ocean. Did you know that New York is the second largest dairy state? Upstate is beautiful in the early fall. Late-fall roads are full of fallen leaves and get a bit slick. Get the idea? You don't notice trees and nature the same way when you ride inside an automobile. Of course there are also deer, so keep your eyes open and scan.

2002 Moto
Guzzi Special

Photo courtesy of Moto Guzzi North America, Inc.

Maybe you don't know where you want to go, you just know that you want to go. Do you want to go it alone? If so, just go for it. If you are not the loner type, consider going to a rally. These are great destinations for any tour because you can find a rally that meets any particular flavor of biking that you are interested in.

FACTS

If you are headed to a large rally, you will probably start meeting folks even before you arrive. It doesn't matter what route you take, because the rest of the crowd is probably coming from absolutely everywhere, especially if you are talking about the Bike Week at Daytona or Sturgis.

Bike Week at Daytona, Florida

The Bike Week at Daytona remains the mother of all motorcycle rallies and probably the mother of all parties. Originally started in 1941, it is not only the largest event of its kind in the world, but also one of the oldest. Right after the turn of the millennium, Bike Week celebrated its fifty-ninth incredible year. The only way to describe the number of people who had attended this event would be "more than you can imagine."

If it's racing you are into, you will find it here. The event was race-oriented long before it became a party, and in many ways it still is. You can find historic racing, classic racing, motocross, dirt track, drag racing, and, of course, the signature race of the event: the Daytona 200 Superbike race.

FACTS

Bike Week is not an exclusive Harley-Davidson party. Riders and manufacturers of just about every motorcycle ever made are in attendance each year: new and old, fast and slow, two-wheel and three-wheel, Asian and European—you will find all kinds of motorcycles here.

If you hear that the Daytona Bike Week is a TWO (Two Wheels Only) event, don't believe it. Even if you haven't purchased your first motorcycle, it's worth the trip because half of what makes the event so infamous is the nonmotorcycle entertainment. Besides, the place is so crowded that once you get there you might as well park and walk. You will find free beer, live bands, and wet T-shirt contests that inevitably turn into no T-shirt contests.

FACTS

Maybe Daytona Bike Week is not, strictly speaking, a family function, but it does not celebrate complete disregard for humanity either. The Real Ride for the Cure is a part of Bike Week that raises money for the American Diabetes Association, and the American Red Cross holds one of its largest blood drives there each year.

Bike Week is like the bikers' version of Mardi Gras. It's not the annual event for everyone, but it is something that everyone should experience at least once, especially when they are young enough to retain enough energy for the ride home.

Bike Week at Sturgis, South Dakota

There was a time when if you had to choose between Daytona and Sturgis, Daytona would win every time. Times change. The party in Daytona has gotten large and loud enough to concern some of the local law-enforcement agencies. The Mardi Gras–like conduct can result in either a night in jail or a steep fine. On the upside, there are only so many police officers and a horde of folk who are more inclined to look the other way at minor transgressions of law.

Sturgis has always been much more relaxed than Daytona. When bikers are more relaxed, law-enforcement officials become more relaxed as well, which makes for a much better event. When you leave Bike Week at Daytona, you will have enjoyed yourself immensely, but you'll be so exhausted, you'll be happy it's over. Leave Bike Week at Sturgis, and you will cry because you'll hate to leave.

ESSENTIALS

Like Daytona, you can find your fill of both racing and other activities aimed at both biker and partygoer at Sturgis—although mild compared to Daytona, Bike Week at Sturgis isn't always the best family-oriented vacation.

But the thing that really puts this rally apart from anything else you will ever experience is the feeling of unity. Maybe it's because the crowd is generally older. The extra years may have given the bikers at Sturgis the time necessary to realize that the important things in life are only symbolized in their bikes. Maybe it's the way citizens (nonbikers) smile at you as if they are genuinely happy that you are there—not because they want you to spend your money at their many shops.

Whatever it is, it is summed up with one look—Main Street. As far as the eye can see, motorcycles line the curbs on either side of Main Street. Two rows of bikes face each other down the center. A lane is left open between the center double row and each curb. Bikers move freely down each lane and seem to magically understand that each lane only goes in one direction. The first time you see it, you will stare in utter silence at the raw beauty of energy at rest, and you will understand in a moment that which takes years of biking to grasp.

SSENTIALS

A helpful tip: If you are restoring a classic motorcycle, bring some extra money to Sturgis. You will find just about every part you can imagine available for sale or trade.

Planning Your Trip

Now that you know where you want to go, you'll need maps to help you get there. A lot of clubs and organizations have come along to challenge AAA (American Automobile Association), but, for the most part, none have given it a very good run for its money. If you can afford a membership, it's a deal even if you use their services only to get free maps. Yes, free maps.

FACTS

AAA also offers something called a "trip tick," which points out just about every hotel and restaurant on your route, as well as a lot of the gas stations. And if that's not good enough for you, you might like to know that you will save a buck or two with hotel discounts for AAA members.

Touring Costs

So, how much is your trip going to cost? If half the fun is getting there, then you might as well figure half the expense of the trip will be spent getting there. How are those regularly scheduled preventative maintenance checks and services going? When was your last oil change? If any of the maintenance dates fall while you plan on being on the road, you'll probably want to attend to them before you leave. If your tour is particularly long, you might even be forced to stop for that oil change or service. Count on paying a bit more than you normally would at your favorite mechanic's shop.

Figuring fuel costs is relatively easy. You know your fuel mileage, you know how far you are going. Do the math. When you are done, be ready for sticker shock if you travel very far. Gas prices change wildly from state to state and region to region. Furthermore, you will always get sidetracked. Best to make all the calculations and then double the final result.

2002 Moto Guzzi

Photo courtesy of Moto Guzzi North America, Inc.

Where are you going to sleep? Professional truck drivers are not allowed to drive more than a specific number of hours without sleeping. Because they are expected to keep under the speed limit, that means they are allowed to travel only a specific number of miles as well. Bikers are not governed by such laws, and yet the very nature of a motorcycle requires more attention than driving a commercial truck. How long you can safely travel depends on the individual, with eight hours a day being a good estimate. Even if you do plan to do eight-hour runs, make sure to take breaks, especially if you feel that you are getting tired.

Staying at hotels requires additional expenses. Campsites are much cheaper than hotels, but you will need to pack more gear. Ultimately, finding an unofficial campsite is the cheapest way to go. Urban legend has it that camping under bridges is a good idea. While footbridges might be okay, underpasses are not a good idea. Not only is traffic below the underpass dangerous, traffic above is much noisier than you might expect.

Be aware of road pirates, especially on lonely country roads. Thieves are much more likely to be caught when operating in a busy parking lot and they know it. Your motorcycle can be split into a hundred pieces in the back of a full-sized van before it even gets out of state.

ALERT

Be aware that although the stereotype of the outlaw biker is often wrong, sometimes it is dead right. There are people out there who conduct criminal businesses while playing a biker, aping the stereotypes they probably saw in those old B-movies. You will be safe when surrounded by bikers, but being around posers is dangerous.

So, you know where you are, where you want to go, and about how long you want to travel each day. Use that trip tick from AAA to find a place to stay and call to verify prices and availability. Here is where a credit card comes in handy. (If you don't have one, get an ATM card that works like one.) If you are traveling during the tourist season, reserve your room and guarantee it with a credit card. If you are traveling off-season, it is better to "guesstimate" where you are going to stay and then have several options, should you want to travel faster or, on the contrary, spend an extra day on the road. Even in this case, you should know what to expect in advance, and always add some wiggle room to the figure.

Now that you know how much it will cost to get there, multiply the figure by two to get the total cost of the round trip. Hide the get-home money so that you don't lose it or spend it. You might want to hide the credit card in the same location.

What to Pack

Every time you go on a road trip, you will discover additional things that you never knew you needed. If you are preparing for your first touring trip, rely on common sense. Remember that tool bag that you are never supposed to touch? Touch it. Open it. Make sure everything is still there, including the first-aid supplies. Better to see now that something is broken or missing, rather than waiting until you actually need it. Make sure the bandages are still sealed and sterile in their nice little freezer Ziploc bags. Also, you might want to drop in a few automotive flares and a flashlight with fresh batteries.

Are you going to want to share your memories? If so, consider bringing a camera. Do you want to make your friends and family jealous even before you get back? Think about a digital camera. Many truck stops now feature pay-by-the-minute computers with wide bandwidth connections to the Internet. If you buy a digital camera with a floppy-disk drive, you can drop the disk out of the camera and into the rent-a-computer, and zip it off to your soon-to-be-jealous friends' e-mail boxes.

ESSENTIALS

Rain gear might not be on the top of the list to pack for cross-town trips, but if you are talking cross-country, that old banana suit might come in handy—the brighter the yellow, the better.

One of the rules of the road seems to be that the more you tour, the less clothing you will carry, *but* the longer a passenger tours with you, the more clothing he or she will want to bring. You'll have to come up with a happy compromise because you will also need to carry more nonclothing items. You can quickly run out of places to put packs, and anything more than a sleeping bag and bedroll is hard to hold down with a bungee net.

If you find yourself resorting to bungee cords and nets, make sure you pack evenly. Anything you strap to the outside of a motorcycle is going to cause increased wind resistance. This isn't much of a problem if it is even on both sides, but if you overload one side, the bike will pull and respond unpredictably to wind gusts and passing trucks. If you don't go the route of a touring pack, consider a luggage rack above the rear fender. If nothing else, it can provide a good solid place to secure the bungees.

What Are You Going to Eat?

The obvious question is: Are you going to pack your food, or are you going to buy as you go? Packing food with you is definitely more affordable, but all that food will take up more space. A reasonable alternative is to go grocery shopping as you need food, but you won't stick to a grocery budget, so you might as well plan to eat at small diners and truck stops.

ESSENTIALS

To add enjoyment to your trip, try making an effort to eat only at places you've never been to before. Some things never change. If you wait till you get home for that Happy Meal, the toy will still be included at no additional charge. But if you aren't interested in new places and experiences, you might as well stay home.

How will food affect your riding? Motorcycle travel is much more draining than automobile driving. You are also required to be more in control and aware of your surroundings. Mental wandering can cause lane wandering, so avoid instant uppers (sugar and candy) because they will provide an instant down the moment your body fights off the elevated sugar levels. Try to eat fuel foods in the morning; marathon foods like bread, pancakes, and waffles are far better than eggs and bacon, because they are high in carbohydrates and low in fat.

A cup of coffee and a can of soda won't kill you. But if it is all you drink, it just might. Caffeine dehydrates you, and you already know what's wrong with sugar. Even very mild dehydration can cause your mind to drift and your reaction time to slow.

CHAPTER 20

The Roundabouts of Road Racing

Motorcycle road racing is not new. Thirty seconds after the first motorcycle was built, someone asked how fast it could go. The next person asked if there was another one to race with. Basically, motorcycle racing comes in two kinds: racing around and around, and racing up and down.

All About Racing

Competition has always been a part of motorcycling, and manufacturers got right in on the action. Does anyone need a street-legal motorcycle that can do 200 miles an hour? Bikes like that aren't built out of necessity; they are built to race. And manufacturers joined a race of their own. Who will be the first manufacturer of a street-legal motorcycle that will do 150 mph? Okay, that race is finished. Now, who will be the first to make it 160, 170, 180, 190? And before you know it, you have a motorcycle that can ride at 200 mph, but no one can take advantage of that speed.

Competition is about survival. It is a primal instinct that has been driving humans to the very top of the food chain. It is the force that moves bikers to spend tons of money on chrome to make their street rides look just a bit better than the next. Racing is all these things and more. You don't have to be a racer to enjoy racing. It's all about entertainment. Think about a set of powerful motorcycles moving around an oval track with their riders maneuvering their bikes like an intricate game of chess. That's entertainment.

ESSENTIALS

No matter how fast your bike is, it won't really matter on race day, because if the factory will sell you a motorcycle that will go 200 mph, then it will sell your competition a motorcycle that can go 200 mph, and use that money to try and build a motorcycle that will do 210 mph.

A word on safety here: When you get right down to it, safe racers have nothing to prove and unsafe racers don't tend to last very long. The safe ones do it because they enjoy racing. Sure, winning feels good, but it comes only after many, many losses, none of which feel so great. If winning were the totality of the game, no one would play. Besides, if the trip weren't half the fun, you wouldn't need a motorcycle to get you there. Motorcycle-racing safety has improved with age. Today, this particular interest has one of the best safety standards of all forms of motor racing.

Back in the Day

Back in the first days of motorcycle racing, safety considerations weren't given much thought or attention. At first, races took place on public roads; very soon, it became clear that public roads weren't the ideal location. In the United States, race promoters quickly caught on, and began to construct tracks made specifically for hosting motorcycle races. In Europe, promoters weren't so quick to catch on and the Asian market hadn't become an influence just yet.

FACTS

Just like American bikers, motorcycle racers have had their own share of negative publicity. In the same way the U.S. public was misled by movies like *The Wild One*, the English public was misled about motorcycle racing safety by frequent reports of racing accidents. The English government responded against motorcycle racers by making it illegal to use a public road for racing.

In the United States, the owner of a classic cruiser is normally the one to be stereotyped as a hooligan, while motorcycle racers are seen almost as heroes. In Germany, the stereotypes are inverted—showing an interest in racing will significantly improve your chances of being viewed as a hooligan.

Grand Prix Racing

The Grand Prix is the most well-known and also the most expensive form of motorcycle racing. At its lowest end, you can expect to invest what you would in the highest-end street motorcycle. At its highest end, you will need multiple sponsors and a good business partner to juggle the numbers. Contrary to what a motorcycle dealer may tell you or the label they may place on a motorcycle, a Grand Prix motorcycle was built for nothing other than racing and was never designed to see traffic. When you see the word Grand Prix on a factory-made street bike, all the word means is that it looks a little bit like that particular manufacturer's Grand Prix racer bike.

The Isle of Man Tourist Trophy (TT)

Because English law prevented racing on public streets, race promoters decided to try and cut a deal with the much smaller government of the Isle of Man, where people were much more open to new ideas. The first motorcycle race was held on the island in 1907. To understand how progressive the people who lived on the Isle of Man were, consider the story of Cecil Williamson, who also set up shop there. Cecil was a witch, and he wanted to set up a community center for other witches. You can imagine how the good English folk felt about both these matters, but the people of the Isle of Man welcomed him to their island. Cecil set up in a 400-year-old farmhouse on the Isle of Man.

2002 Suzuki
GZ250

Photo courtesy of Suzuki.

Except during wartime, the TT races have been held on the Isle of Man since their humble beginnings. For the twenty-seven years prior to 1976, the raceway was part of the International Grand Prix Motorcycle World Championship. Unfortunately for those who suffer from bouts of nostalgia, but fortunately for racer and spectator safety, the Isle of Man course is no longer a sanctioned Grand Prix race. It lost that status in 1976 when it was decided by the *Federation Internationale de*

Motorcyclisme (Federation of International Motorcyclists, or FIM) that at least in the case of the Isle of Man TT, the English government was right about racing on public streets. This mountain circuit is not only one of the most famous, but one of the most dangerous as well.

Federation Internationale de Motorcyclisme (FIM)

So what is the FIM and how come it had the power to shut down the Isle of Man TT races? You might say that the FIM is to International Racing what the AMA is to American Motorcycling—the largest influence in its field. As the AMA functions in the better interest of the American motorcyclist, the FIM supports the international motorcycle racer and, to some degree, all motorcyclists in general. FIM has become the best-known sanctioning body for world-championship motorcycle racing, overseeing the international Grand Prix championship series, the international Superbike series, and many other smaller events.

QUESTIONS?

Why does FIM get to decide what is good for racers?
Because somebody has to. FIM moved the World Champion Grand Prix series from the Isle of Man because the track had seen an average of two deaths per year when calculated against its age.

When you are talking top-of-the-line Grand Prix, you are talking about the international Grand Prix championship series. It is a series of international races, which just about span the globe—except, that is, for a stop in the United States.

AMA Grand Prix Motorcycle Racing

While it doesn't have the prestige of the FIM's World Championship, the Yankees have the American Motorcyclist Association as a sanctioning body on which to depend. A lot of bikers resent the AMA for their seemingly intrusive attempts to sanction everything from clubs to helmets, but international races need an overseeing committee to organize and ensure the relative safety of races, and interstate competitions need the AMA.

Superbike Racing

"Superbike" is another term used incorrectly to sell motorcycles. If you see it on a factory-produced bike, it means that it is simply based on a Superbike. When you see the word "Superbike" in a manufacturer's catalog, all it means is that the motorcycle resembles the heavily modified motorcycle that this particular manufacturer uses in factory-sponsored races. As such, this word is nothing but a sales tool.

This bike is the middle of the road as far as expense. It was created for those who could not afford the exorbitant prices of Grand Prix racing. Seeing an opportunity to make money, the manufacturers caught on quickly and started creating street motorcycles that could be raced competitively right out of the show room. Of course, gearheads worked to make them even better, and the end result is that Superbike racing can be almost as expensive as Grand Prix racing.

In the United States, Superbike racing has become very popular because although the motorcycles are radically modified to perform almost to Grand Prix standards, they remain visually similar to the motorcycles that you might see in your neighboring bikers' garages.

This doesn't mean that the rest of the world doesn't love Superbike racing. As with the Grand Prix, FIM is in charge of international Superbike racing events, while the AMA sanctions events in the United States.

FIM World Superbike Series: Like their Grand Prix series, the FIM has built these races into some of the most prestigious events on the international arena. Unlike the Grand Prix, this series has been around only since 1988, and it is still possible to attend a FIM-sponsored World Superbike race in the United States.

AMA Superbike Racing: The FIM might be growing in this area of racing, but here the AMA set down the groundwork. Superbike racing was virtually established by the AMA and it's doubtful it will lose much of its control in the United States.

Supersport Racing

When it comes to Supersport racing, you can trust the manufacturers when they claim that their bikes are Supersport bikes, because "Supersport" refers to unmodified factory-production street-legal motorcycles. More than any other category of motorcycle racing, this form of racing is the sport for the people.

ESSENTIALS
The AMA prohibits the use of so-called "limited production" motorcycles in Supersport racing because a factory might make such a small number of bikes as to ensure the victory of their buyers. The AMA does make exceptions for safety modifications, but for the most part you ride what you bought.

Drag Racing

If you think that drag racing is a crude sport and requires no skill, because all you do is point a motorcycle forward and then ride it as fast as you can over a quarter-mile strip, then you have probably never been to a motorcycle drag race and definitely never participated in one.

FACTS
In one-eighth of a mile, the Harley top fuel record was set by Robert Stewart in September of 2001, at 178.95 mph in 4.159 seconds. The quarter-mile top fuel on a Harley was set by Steve Stordeur in June of 2001, at 212.90 mph in 6.389 seconds. As you can see, even Harleys can exceed 200 mph in less than 7 seconds.

"Top fuel" is a premium class, and it takes a premium cost to participate. Fortunately, there are entry levels into drag racing just as any other form of racing. In July of 2000, Doug Morrow set the Harley-Davidson Street Pro quarter-mile record at 146.88 mph in 9.583 seconds on a motorcycle that was only slightly modified from the way it was sold on the show room floor (a factory-stock motorcycle). What can you do in under ten seconds?

As with other forms of road racing, drag racing classes exist to encourage competition. Entry-level drag racing motorcycles are only mildly more than stock motorcycles.

Slow Racing

There is no sanctioning body for slow races; it does not offer international, national, or even state-level recognition; and if you want to find a sponsor, you had better keep your search very narrow and focus on local taverns and bowling alleys for the $1.98 that it will take to participate in one. But slow racing should be included in this chapter because it is technically a racing category. Furthermore, it really does require an enormous amount of skill, and because participation in slow racing will greatly improve your skills in other types of racing, as well as in city traffic.

When it comes to entry-level racing, it doesn't matter if you are talking road racing, dirt track, or slow racing. The important thing is that racing will improve your relationship with both your motorcycle and other motorcyclists. If you are interested, join in the fun!

The basic idea behind slow racing is to see who can take the most time to travel from point A to point B without putting a foot down to balance the motorcycle. Trikes and sidecars are, of course, prohibited—they would make a slow race impossibly time-consuming. When you toss in a turn or two, things get really challenging, because most riders have become so used to countersteering that when they are forced to steer due at very low speed, they end up turning in the wrong direction time and time again. Leaning does almost nothing for you when you ride at two miles an hour.

If You Want to Be a Motorcycle Road Racer

The truth is, motorcycle racing isn't nearly as dangerous as people tend to think. Not only do most races have sanctioning bodies to deal with safety concerns, the very nature of racing makes it a generally safe practice. When racing, everyone is going in the same direction, all vehicles are about the same size, cars don't make left-hand turns in front of you, and no one can say "I didn't see him" with a straight face. Even more importantly, the rules are spelled out beforehand, and everyone is on the same page.

FACTS

Most racetracks require racing licenses before they will let you participate in most of their races, but getting a racing license is much easier than you might have expected.

Most states have sanctioned raceways that host amateur nights. In the case of drag racing, some of these raceways have open entry or minimum requirements to participate.

Becoming a Motorcycle Racer

If you want to become a motorcycle road racer, there is some good news and some bad news. The bad news is that making a living without a serious investment of both time and money will be next to impossible. When it comes to racing, you will pick up your own tabs for a long time before the odd chance of a payoff. If it does come, don't be pompous about it, because it will take a great deal of luck in addition to experience. Professional racers require sponsors, and sponsors usually want something more than just a winner. They want winners who represent their product the way they want their product represented. If there isn't a match, then there isn't a sponsor. The good news is, you don't need a lot of money or a lot of experience to start. In fact, if you go spending a lot of money before you have the experience, it will probably make getting that experience just a bit more difficult. What you need in the beginning is the right competition—racers who are just a little bit more experienced than you. Even with the best equipment, you won't have the training and experience needed to be anything other than a danger to yourself and others. You will demonstrate that fact every time you get out on the track, and this will put more experienced racers off, though they might have been willing to give you a leg up and show you the ropes. So take it slow.

Riding is also a physical challenge, and will require you to be in excellent shape. You will use muscles that you didn't know you had to maneuver your motorcycle faster than the next. Your brain will need to get involved as well, to determine where in the pack you need to be and when. Besides, how much fun would it be to meet failure after failure when going up against better-experienced riders? Most people would rather lose a race they started with duct tape all over an old motorcycle than to have to put that duct tape on a brand-new bike right after the race.

Don't worry—when you begin, you won't be going up against experts. If you did, it would get boring watching you lose all the time. To make things more fair, the playing field is made level by splitting the main three categories—Grand Prix, Superbike, and Supersport—even further, into classes.

QUESTIONS?

So why get involved in motorcycle racing?
Well, if racing is in your blood, then you do it for the same reason you ride a motorcycle. You have no choice. It's the same reason people have to climb mountains and jump out of perfectly good airplanes. They have no other choice.

Generally, introductory classes demand smaller lightweight motorcycles and try to keep speeds well under 100 miles an hour. That might seem slow compared to what you see on the sports channel, but if you have never done 100 miles an hour on a motorcycle, all you have to do is get out on the highway, look down at the ground, and then multiply what you see by two. Chances are, the first time you are on the highway, you will think, "Oh my God, I am going to die." To know what it will be like the first time you are in a sanctioned road race, think about that first time on the highway, make it twice as bad, and then throw in some turns.

What Will It Cost to Feed Your Addiction?

Starting the addiction is relatively inexpensive. If you can spend between $2,000 and $3,000 on an introductory road racer, you're in! Figure more on the low side of that scale if you can do much of the work yourself.

It's best to make your first road racer a used bike. Stick with twins and thumpers under about 500cc. The Kawasaki Ninja 250R is great, except for all the plastic that you will probably break. Look for a deal on one that has been put down a time or two—that way you will save a bit of money. If not, then leave the fiberglass in your garage or put it up for sale. You will surely find someone else who has put one of those things down a time or two and would like to replace the nice-looking parts.

ALERT

Different racing organizations have different specifications for how a motorcycle has to be prepared for racing. What's that? Organizations? Of course. If you had to go it alone, wouldn't you have a much harder time getting started? To find local clubs, attend local races or call the AMA to find a sanctioned club in your area.

You will want to make contact with local racing clubs before you even think about purchasing or modifying a motorcycle. It is a good idea to attend a few entry-level races as well. Mingle with club members, and you might be able to find a really good deal on a motorcycle that has already been prepped with the race's particular racing criteria in mind. Remember, we are talking about an addiction, so there are plenty of entry-level bikes out there in the hands of racers that have entered higher classifications.

Even if you can't find a bike already prepped, don't worry. The criteria will vary from club to club, but they don't usually require more than an afternoon's worth of work. Generally speaking, most of the street equipment must be stripped out—turn signals, mirrors, license plate brackets, passenger foot pegs, side stands, and center stands must all go. Generally, headlights and taillights must be removed, though in some cases they may be taped. The idea here is that you don't want to leave anything that might rip into a person, motorcycle, or road, should the bike go down.

If your bike is liquid-cooled, you will have to run pure water. Antifreeze is out of the question because spills from the inevitable overheat are much less slick without it. (This step is described in detail in Chapter 22, which contains advice on preparing your bike for winter storage.) You will need number plates, but let that be decided by the race organization; depending on the race, plates may be color-coded and would require assigned numbers.

When you find a club that you want to race with, get their rulebook, visit a few races, and watch what goes on in the pits. Often, you should have no problems mingling with the racers and their bikes, but ask first. At Superbike and Grand Prix tracks, you will find that racers are less willing to give you a leg up, because real money is on the line. In those categories, you will find that a handful of racers always have the edge because their equipment is always new, hot, and paid for by sponsors.

Once you've seen what you can see, consider a course in motorcycle road racing. See Appendix C for a listing of schools and clubs. All schools charge a fee, but it is usually more than worth it, even if only for entertainment purposes. Clubs generally charge between $50 and $150 for a racing license after you have met club-specific criteria. Some clubs limit their criteria to successful completion of the courses offered by specific schools, others respect the licenses issued by other clubs. Once you have fulfilled the club's criteria and have your racing license, then it's off to the track. Getting started is that easy.

CHAPTER 21

Above and Beyond: Customizing Your Bike

For most people, simply purchasing a motorcycle is not enough to satisfy the addiction. Customizing is a widespread hobby among bikers, and includes everything from adding a few pieces of new chrome to creating an entirely new machine out of old motorcycle parts. Some fanatics work on one bike after another, until their garage is a virtual museum of motorcycles.

Why Fix It if It Isn't Broken?

There are many practical reasons to customize a motorcycle. Windshields, fairings, and saddlebags can turn a cruiser into a touring machine; crash bars and leg guards can make a motorcycle safer in spills; lights will make a bike more visible to other motorists. Rolling performance can be enhanced with after-market shock absorbers and improved suspension parts. Engine performance can be improved with better exhaust pipes, air filters, carburetors, and a host of other engine components.

But most commonly, motorcycles are modified for the sake of appearance. Bikers tend to be nonconformists, so it is only natural that they like their motorcycles to be individualized. Some like to add so much chrome that they no longer need headlights. Others invest in a custom paint job that costs more then the bike itself.

2002 Suzuki
Intruder
VS800

Photo courtesy of Suzuki.

Historic Backyard Customs

The original custom-motorcycle movement was alive and well before manufacturers began to imitate what bikers do in their backyards. It originally started in the United States, and later found its way to postwar Europe. Although the original European customizing techniques were vastly different from those in the United States, both were true custom motorcycles that no manufacturers had ever envisioned.

The Great American Bobber

When you think about choppers, you probably envision long rakes and small tires like those featured in the movie *Easy Rider*. Before, the 1960s, the term was used to indicate that the machine would outperform a factory-stock vehicle of the same make. Today, Harley-Davidson is one of the only manufacturers to use the term "chopper" in the older sense of the word.

Motorcycles were "chopped" down and built up into street monsters that were made with speed and handling in mind. Back in those days, backyard mechanics could improve greatly on what the factory was doing because they knew better. Old-school bikers had to know the ins and outs of every part of the engine because there wasn't really anyone else to do repair work for them. It was only natural that the folk who lived with the beasts knew how to make them run a whole lot better than the factory, which was having a tough enough time just keeping its doors open.

The Classic 1960s Chopper

With its high handlebars (also known as ape hangers), extended forks, tiny front tire, and tall sissy bar, the chopper just screams nostalgia. But it also screams warning. The steering dynamics of these creatures are so dangerous, only an expert builder can even come close to creating one that will perform with the worst of the stock motorcycles. Worse yet, many states have placed very strict regulations as to the angle and length of the fork. In short, it's best to leave the chopper-style customizing to custom motorcycles in the museum and the movies.

When it became clear that choppers were more about looks than about performance, the U.S. custom trend moved toward the low rider. These models lowered the riding position and stretched the length of the motorcycle at the frame. Controls and pegs moved forward for a more relaxed, leaning-back riding position.

Café Racers and the Birth of Crotch Rockets

The café racer was born in Europe and inspired by professional road racing motorcycles there. Whereas American customizing is chiefly concerned with appearance, the European bikers aimed at faster speeds. Explanations might include the superior European freeways that allowed for greater speeds, or the popularity of the racing bikes as opposed to touring bikes in the United States.

2002 Suzuki
GSX-600

Photo courtesy of Suzuki.

Whereas American bikers generally took off body panels to lighten the load, Europeans preferred to add a windshield and other covers, for the purpose of improving aerodynamics at high speeds. While Americans moved their foot pegs forward (highway pegs), café racers moved them to the back. While Americans moved their handlebar grips higher, the café racers moved their handlebars lower. In some cases, they removed the handlebars altogether, and mounted grips directly to the front fork (these grips became known as clip-ons).

Naked Racers

More café racers on the road meant more café racers in the junkyard. Body panels were expensive and broke easily in a spill. Motorcycles that were perfectly functional from a mechanical viewpoint were discarded after minor accidents.

Bikers know that a motorcycle is a terrible thing to waste, so what the insurance companies didn't think was worth saving became the next custom motorcycle. In this case, cleaver bikers created the "naked racer" look. With duct tape and a hammer in hand, all body panels and everything that isn't needed for either function, safety, or street-ability was removed. When finished, absolutely everything that can be painted is painted flat-black. With a few modifications, a pile of junk would become a naked racer.

ALERT Body parts do serve purposes other than fashionable appearance. For instance, the way a motorcycle cools its engine and feeds its intake is sometimes a function of body panels.

Does Art Imitate Life?

In this case, it's not hard to see what came first. Virtually every idea manufacturers have had was born in a gearhead's backyard. When it comes to motorcycles, the idea is always on the street before it is in production. The manufacturers know that bikers are resourceful, and watch them very carefully to know what the future market trends will be.

Today's factory-made street racer was yesterday's custom-made café racer. Today's factory bobber was yesterday's chopper. Even the naked racer has found its way into the assembly line. Though this style originated from the efforts to extend the life of a banged-up factory café racer by using duct tape and spray paint, it inspired the manufacturers to produce bikes like the Ducati Monster, Laverda Ghost, and the Triumph Speed Triple.

Customizing Your Ride

You might fall in love with a particular motorcycle on the show room floor, ride it home, and sit for hours in the realization that your dream is finally realized. But when you get out on the road you are going to find out that the factory is not as liberal as one might think when it comes to optional color schemes and accessories. When it comes to many motorcycles, you will get only a few color options. Even the mildest custom work can make the difference between blending in and standing out.

Custom-Light

Inexpensive and easily installed modifications can be made almost on a whim. There are plenty of appearance-altering features that cost very little and change nothing other than the motorcycle's look. Despite the relatively small price and ease of installation, these alterations can provide rewarding looks to an otherwise nondescript factory-made motorcycle.

Caliper covers: Caliper covers are usually thin pieces of chromed metal that clip onto the outside of disk-brake calipers. Many calipers get grimy and downright ugly after years of contact with brake fluid. Covers can add a pleasant look to an otherwise unsightly part.

Grip covers: You can buy grip covers in a variety of colors and styles. There are even models with hand-warmers and leather fringes, which scream "bead me and braid me."

Luggage racks: Luggage racks generally don't affect the performance of a motorcycle until they are loaded, but they do give you one more place to mount a bit of chrome.

Mirrors: You can customize the back side of replacement mirrors with colored housings, chrome, or a variety of logos and brand insignia.

Plug wires: You can find plug wires in just about every imaginable color from black to hot pink. You can also find glow-in-the-dark wires and even blinking spark-plug caps.

2002 Suzuki
ISV 650S

Photo courtesy of Suzuki.

Custom-Medium

When you are ready to make major decisions about customizing your motorcycle, you should consider the following two questions: What do you want? What are you willing to give up? The answer might seem as simple as money, but making sound decisions about customizing a motorcycle is more than just buying additional or replacement parts. With each addition and deletion, you modify the whole of your motorcycle in ways you may not have considered if you had made a quick decision.

Air filters: Factory air filters tend to be overly restrictive. This makes higher-flow after-market air filters very attractive. However, increased airflow means increased emissions. If you live in a state where you are required to have your motorcycle emissions checked on a regular basis, are you willing to change your air filter back and forth to comply when you have to comply, and then cheat when you want to cheat?

Carburetor and top end: If you spend any time reading about after-market carburetors and camshafts, you will believe that replacing a few parts can turn any motorcycle into a road monster. Performance improvements to your motorcycle's engine can dramatically improve your top end, but they can often destroy your ability to idle at low RPMs. With a high idle, you are more likely to pull through your brakes and cause a slide at low speeds. Even if this isn't a problem, you are likely to run into emissions laws if you are in a state that checks.

Chrome and custom paint: Chrome and custom-painted parts require extra cleaning time. Think of it this way: The amount of time you spend cleaning a motorcycle is directly related to the amount of money you spend on chrome and custom painting.

2002
Suzuki DLI

Photo courtesy of Suzuki.

Engine guards: These can protect both your legs and the engine during light spills, but they will also make your motorcycle a great deal wider. This can make it difficult to maneuver in tight places. Are you willing to give up maneuverability in tight places for engine and leg protection?

Exhaust pipes: Racing pipes can be just as attractive to the owner of a street racer as straight pipes can be to the owner of a cruiser.

They can increase engine performance and turn a few more heads. The problem is, you might turn the heads of a few people whose attention you do not desire. Noise and environmental regulations usually demand mufflers with intact baffles. Do you want to give up the comfort of knowing your exhaust can pass a roadside inspection?

Saddlebags and tour packs: The more packs you have, the more absolutely vital necessities you will be able to carry on your bike. However, additional storage space means additional weight, wind resistance, and the number of parts that can break in even a small mishap. Do you want to trade in street agility and efficient gas needs in return for extra storage on your cross-country tours?

Fairings and windshield: Anything that will keep the wind and weather off your body on a long trip is a blessing. But what about when you are just bopping around town? The windshield and (to a much greater extent) fairings add weight; moreover, it's safe to consider them easily breakable parts. Do you want to give up even slight off-road practicality for highway comfort?

E SSENTIALS   The cost of customizing your motorcycle will decrease with the amount of work you can do yourself. If you plan on doing a lot of custom work, plan on spending a lot of time in your garage.

Custom-Heavy

If neither light nor medium custom work will do, there is the custom-heavy approach. Sure, the costs will be heavy, too, but the changes in how the motorcycle looks or performs can be staggering as well. However, you can pretty much figure that any of these engine modifications will violate emission laws if performed on recent-production motorcycles.

Forced air induction systems: These systems are commonly called either "superchargers" or "turbochargers." Turbochargers are the most common. They use an exhaust-driven turbine to force air into the intake system. Superchargers work much the same way, but rely on either gears or belts to drive them directly from the engine.

Frame modifications: Frames are both modified or replaced for many reasons. Such modifications may be purely cosmetic, like chroming the entire thing, or they can be part of the overall effort to stretch the motorcycle, with the dual goal of better handling and better appearance. The real expense here is the complete disassembly and reassembly of your motorcycle.

Nitrous systems: Nitrous oxide is a gas that supports combustion. In and of itself, it offers virtually no performance enhancements. However, when it is injected into an engine along with extra fuel, it can drastically increase performance. Generally this is done with electric solenoids, which are only engaged when extra horsepower is needed. Although these are relatively easy to install, they are considered radical modifications—they will cause an increase in power that may be absolutely dangerous.

FACTS

When a motorcycle undergoes overboring and overstroking, the available horsepower of an engine can be increased dramatically. However, because the final product of an engine (power) is based on a great deal more than just displacement, it is important to have such a project designed by an expert who can determine necessary changes to the rest of the engine to accommodate increased engine size.

Overbore: The idea behind overboring an engine is that with a larger engine, more power will be available to turn the rear wheel. Overboring an engine is the process by which you increase an engine's internal size by decreasing the wall between the inside of the engine cylinder and the outside of the engine cylinder by "boring" the cylinder from the inside. With a larger cylinder bore, the engine can take in more fuel/air mixture and, theoretically, produce more power as a result. If the intended enlargement is relatively minor, you bore the cylinder blocks to a larger size and run larger pistons. If you want a more significant increase, it is necessary to replace the cylinder blocks with larger ones, allowing for a larger bore increase.

Stroking: Stroking an engine is the process that modifies the displacement of an engine by changing the crankshaft of the engine. This process often requires the change of the connecting rods as well, and may also necessitate the replacement of the pistons.

Buying a Motorcycle for a Customizing Project

If you don't want to give up anything except some time and money, you can keep your street bike and buy one especially for a custom project. If you ride a bike for any length of time, you are going to wind up with two or three anyway. You might as well make one of them your project bike. The benefits of customizing a project bike instead of your regular street motorcycle are many.

1. You can keep your knees in the breeze on your street ride in between turning a wrench on your project bike. This will give you time to find and install just the right parts.
2. If your project bike is never intended to hit the street, you can be as wild as you want on the paint and chrome.
3. Social opportunities will abound as you sift through swap meet after swap meet looking for that one part that no one has in their catalogs anymore.
4. If a motorcycle is not currently registered for road use, it is often exempt from mandatory insurance. If you are worried about theft or fire, chances are high that your homeowner's or renter's insurance will cover a project bike (but not a complete motorcycle).
5. Because you will be in no hurry to complete your project, you can spread out the expenses over a longer period of time.
6. Emission exemptions are usually made for classic motorcycles and sometimes for later models. If you don't want to adhere to the

regulations that affect modern motorcycles, check the laws in your area and then buy a motorcycle that is exempt due to its age.

When it's time to go out and buy a motorcycle that you plan to keep as a customizing project, be wary of fraud, and be sure you know exactly what you are getting. An easy oversight can be a costly mistake.

Professional Builders

Unless you have very deep pockets and a great deal of time on your hands, you are not going to be able to keep up with the professional builders. These folk make their bread and butter doing custom work for folk who can afford to pay for it, and use their wildest dreams to sell those services. The motorcycles that they show are like advertising for their services rather than motorcycles they are trying to sell. Usually, the motorcycles you see at bike shows are so far beyond what an average biker can hope to accomplish alone, their only real value is as an advertisement for a custom builder who also does less extreme work.

CHAPTER 22

In the End—
Winterizing
and Storage

If you don't have a project bike to visit with and work on during the winter, preparing your street bike for winter storage can be a painful but necessary experience. Motorcycles are impractical for winter use, and you can save money by storing them properly. This chapter will show you how.

The Benefits of Winter Storage

There are many very obvious reasons not to ride a motorcycle in the winter, as well as some not-so-obvious reasons to store it properly. Tires rot when they sit in the same position, gasoline goes flat, carburetors become caked with fuel additives as the fuel evaporates, and old oil becomes new grease. Beyond the mechanical considerations, there are also financial issues.

Most insurance companies will give you a discount for the months that your bike is in storage. If you are not putting it up for the winter, you should read your insurance policy carefully to make sure you are insured during the off-season.

ESSENTIALS   If you do not have a garage or the space to spare for motorcycle storage, you can usually find a dealership or repair shop that is willing to store your motorcycle for the off-season as part of a package deal with winterizing service.

Cleaning Your Bike

When it comes to cleaning motorcycles, there seem to be two schools of thought. First, there are people who insist on scrubbing down their bikes every time they drive down to the supermarket. Each time you clean a motorcycle, you run the risk of causing mild damage to the paint and chrome. Loose bits of grit might find their way into your rag and cause a scratch. The more water is applied to a motorcycle, the more likely it is to wash away lubricants that are found on brake calipers, inside cables, and in all sorts of other odd little places. This isn't usually a problem unless you are convinced that everyday scrubbings are in order.

Then there are the people who seem to think that road tar helps hold some of the smaller parts together. However, not only does built-up grime cause damage to cosmetics, it can make it downright impossible to identify more serious problems when they arise. When the entire lower end is covered in oil from a poorly adjusted self-oiling chain, you won't notice a real oil leak that might leave you stranded.

The ideal cleaning schedule is somewhere in between these two extremes. But no matter what your particular cleaning schedule will be, there is one cleaning that you should never miss: the cleaning that you do before putting your bike into storage. When gunk is left on paint, chrome, or even bare metal, oxidation and rusting will occur. When it is left there for three months without even the occasional rainstorm, a lot of oxidation and rusting will occur.

When you winterize your motorcycle, make sure to fill the gas tank to the top and add a fuel stabilizer. This will prevent rust from forming on the inside of the gas tank during storage, as rust is a form of oxidation. No oxygen means no oxidation.

When cleaning your bike for the winter, make sure to take the following steps:

1. Degrease the engine and lower end. You can find spray degreasers at any automotive or motorcycle-parts store. Apply it to the engine and lower-end parts (like the swing arm and wheels) *only*. Most degreasers are dangerous to body paints. Follow the instructions for the particular product for soak times, scrub with a soft brush, and then rinse completely. Don't move on to the rest of the wash until you are sure all the degreaser is washed off.

2. Wash the bike with mildly warm soapy water. It's a good idea to purchase soap intended for the task. Dish soap often contains chemicals that may speed up the paint-fading process. Use a soft sponge to wash. Toothbrushes are great for getting into small places. Dry with a chamois (available at any automotive or motorcycle-parts store).

3. Determine what is chrome and what looks like chrome. Polish all parts with the appropriate polish—make sure you don't use chrome polish on plastic parts that merely look like chrome. Also avoid using aluminum polish on chrome. If in doubt, do a magnet test. If a magnet sticks to a shiny surface, chances are it is chrome. If it does

not, but the surface looks metallic, then it is aluminum. If it isn't either chrome or aluminum, it is probably plastic. Using the wrong product can cause tiny scratches, which will dull the shine. Furthermore, using metal polishes on plastic parts can cause the surface to become soft and even melt.

4. Hard-wax the painted surfaces. Don't bother with soft wax or those wash-and-wax-in-one products. You can use Turtle Wax, or go the extra mile and purchase hard wax made specifically for motorcycles (though there is not much difference in the quality of the result). The one disadvantage of Turtle Wax: If you don't get it all off, it will leave a whitish-green film behind. Some motorcycle-specific wax dries clear. Once the wax has dried, buff it out until it shines.

You may be tempted to use "polishing" and "rubbing compounds" on your motorcycle. If used very sparsely, they can remove oxidation and smooth paint. But if you use them on a regular basis, they will soften, scratch, and damage paint. Best to steer clear from these products altogether, unless you are sure of how, when, and why they are used.

5. Coat all unpainted metal surfaces with WD-40 or other light oil to prevent corrosion. If you use this on your exhaust pipes, they might stink when you first start your bike in the spring, but it will keep the pipes from developing speckled rust spots from front to back.

Preparing the Engine

If you have a liquid-cooled motorcycle, remember that you should check your coolant level and mixture every week or so, and replace it every couple of years even if it seems to be perfect. The winterizing process is a good time to do just that. If you haven't reached the two-year mark since your last replacement, you should check the coolant level and the specific gravity to ensure that your coolant won't freeze during the winter, destroying an otherwise perfect engine in the process.

If it has been more than a couple of years since you last changed the coolant, do so in accordance with the operator's manual before moving on to the rest of the winterizing/storing process. This way, the engine will have time to run and circulate the new coolant before you put it up on a stand until spring.

Giving It the Lift

Kickstands just don't cut it when it comes to storage. Center stands are better, but they still leave the tires in contact with your garage floor, which may lead to rotting or flat spots. The best solution is to buy an after-market lift. In lieu of that, you might be able to get away with cinder blocks and two-by-fours. The goal is to get both tires off the ground while the motorcycle is planted solid and won't fall over when bumped or rocked during maintenance.

With either a little shopping or a little ingenuity, you should be able to find or construct a lift for just about any motorcycle. But if you can't manage it, then at a very minimum you should lay down a clean piece of cardboard and then roll your motorcycle onto it. Each week of storage, you should roll the bike a bit so that it does not rest on the same section of tire tread the entire winter.

Draining the Carburetor

If you do not drain the last bits of fuel from the carburetor, it will produce a shellac-like substance that will build up internally, which may cause the float to stick, the jets to plug, and the accelerator pump to fail. There are two ways to drain the carburetor.

The most-often used method is also the easiest one. Simply turn the petcock to the "off" position and then start the motorcycle. Let the motorcycle run until it runs out of fuel and you can be sure that most of the carburetor's float bowl is empty. This method will not work on vacuum-operated petcocks unless you pinch (not disconnect) the vacuum line. In this case, it's better to use the other method.

To use the second method, turn the petcock to the "off" position and then locate the float bowl drains on the carburetor. If you have more than one carburetor, do them one at a time. Open these drains, being careful to catch falling gasoline in a safe container—Styrofoam and some plastic cups will melt; you might try using an old military canteen cup or something equally durable.

When the fuel drains, examine it for signs of rust, flakes, or crud. If you see anything except clean fuel, turn the petcock to "prime," and see if you can flush out the junk from the float bowl. If you continue to see rust flakes or crud in the fuel that is coming out of the carburetors, maybe your gas tank is corroded on the inside from being stored without a full tank. Don't panic. You have several options and each will keep until spring.

1. Replace the gas tank. This is the most expensive route, but if you have a stock paint job you can probably purchase a new tank or find a used one at a fairly low price. If your paint is custom, you are going to have to settle for a mismatch or have the new tank custom-painted, which will cost a bit more.

2. Seal the corroded tank. This is less expensive, but doesn't always work well. The idea is similar to casting ceramics. A liquid is poured into the gas tank and allowed to sit for a bit. The fluid becomes thick at the edges (the inside walls of the tank), but remains pourable in the center. After a predetermined amount of time, the mixture is poured out of the tank and the portion that remains on the walls is left behind to harden and seal. If you choose this route, have a professional do it. The kits available to motorcycle owners just don't seem to do a good job.

3. Add an after-market fuel filter. Some people believe that every motorcycle should have a fuel filter, but the only motorcycles that definitely do have them when they arrive from the factory are the

fuel-injected ones. If you install a glass-body fuel filter between the petcock and carburetor(s), you will be able to see the junk that would normally flow into the carburetor. When it gets full, just replace the insert or clean it out. It shouldn't really be thought of as an alternative to fixing the fuel tank, but when you are on a budget, it will keep things running.

The Battery

It is a good idea to remove rings and other jewelry before working on any part of a motorcycle. It is a great idea to do so before working with the battery. Before removing the battery, clean it with a wire brush and a mixture of baking soda and warm water. Once you can place this solution on the battery without a strong fizzing response, it's safe to disconnect the terminals. Always remove the negative battery terminal first. You will probably have to disconnect a hold-down clamp or two.

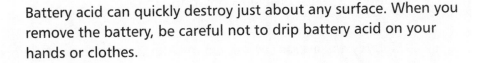

Battery acid can quickly destroy just about any surface. When you remove the battery, be careful not to drip battery acid on your hands or clothes.

Remove the battery and store it in a well-ventilated but warm place. It should be away from pets, children, and friends whose IQ sometimes sinks below 85 when they drink (or even when they don't drink). Do not store the battery on concrete. For some reason, even warm concrete seems to suck energy right out of a battery. Also, do not store it on anything that you plan on ever using, or that you wish to keep in good condition—even a slight vapor of battery acid will eat away at most surfaces.

Now for the real kicker. There is a fifty-fifty chance that you will wind up using last year's battery for nothing more than trade-in value in the spring. If you've got the money, buy a new one each season. You won't need to worry about battery storage, and you'll have the assurance that an old battery won't strand you somewhere at the worst time.

The Rest of the Story

There are a few other steps to take before your winterizing process is over and you can leave your motorcycle to hibernate for the winter. A short outline follows.

Oil: You will want to drain the oil and dispose of it properly. Follow the instructions listed in Chapter 14, but don't bother changing the oil filter because you will be doing that in the spring when you change the oil again. Why change the oil in the spring if you changed it in the fall? Well, you don't want your bike to sit with used oil in it during the winter, but you don't want to run it with the oil that sat in it over the winter either. So you will have to do it twice, when you winterize your bike, and when you bring it out of winter storage.

ESSENTIALS

Always use motorcycle-grade oil in the grade recommended by the manufacturer of your bike. Automotive oil might be cheaper, but it can cause problems down the road.

Motorcycle covers: Even if you are storing your motorcycle inside an unheated garage, better to let the bike stand uncovered. Even if the manufacturer of the cover claims it will breathe, it's better to let the dust accumulate and then just clean it off in the spring. Covers accumulate moisture, which causes rust and paint damage. Only use motorcycle covers if you are storing your bike outside—but if you are storing your bike outside, shame on you!

Soft bags: It's best to remove soft bags during storage. They will keep much better inside. If they must be kept outside, consider coating them with an approved preservative.

Hard bags: Spray the inside of hard bags with Lysol and then wipe dry. If you can find moisture guards or antimildew pads at your local hardware store, it is a good idea to toss a couple into each bag.

Leather seats: Ideally, remove seats and padded cushions of any kind and bring them inside for the winter. Extremely cold weather can crack and damage leather and other motorcycle-seat material. The process itself requires nothing more than dealing with a few screws. If you can't bring the seats and cushions inside, treat with the preserving agent that matches the material they are made from. If in doubt, see the operator's manual. Never use Armor All or similar products—they are likely to make seats too slick.

Although it is okay to visit with your motorcycle during the wintertime, you shouldn't attempt to sit on it or apply any pressure to leather, vinyl, plastic, or fiberglass parts. Extreme cold can make these parts brittle.

Air filter: Make sure the air filter is present and there is no way for air (or small critters) to get inside. Loose cowling is normally the culprit, so make sure everything leading from the air filter is sealed. Although it might sound strange, try wrapping the air filter with aluminum foil before storing if you suspect that there are mice in the storage area. You never know—one might decide to use your air filter as a nest (it's happened before).

Spark plugs: As an extra precaution against seizure, remove the spark plugs and coat the threads lightly with graphite. Then screw them back into their sockets. Like the battery, you will probably want to throw these away in the spring, but they work great for keeping junk out of the engine during the winter. You'd be amazed at the number of parasites that think spark-plug holes make great wintertime nests.

Chains: If your chain uses O-rings (which are internally lubricated), you should clean and lubricate them heavily with products approved for O-ring chains. These chains lubricate themselves only when they are in use, so when you store them they become dry. This wouldn't be a problem if the lubricant were not also the rust inhibitor. If you have an older motorcycle that does not use O-ring chains, you don't have to be so picky about cleaning and lubricating products, but it is still a good idea to check with the owner's manual.

O-ring chains are self-lubricating to a degree. Each link rides in an oil bath that is sealed by the O-ring. Using improper external lubrication and cleaning products can damage these O-rings and seriously compromise the life expectancy of the chain.

Shaft: Check the oil in the rear-wheel pinion assembly before storing.

Tools: Coat all of your metal emergency tools with WD-40 or other light oil. Don't bring them inside because you will just forget where you put them when it comes time to get back on the road.

Grips: Coat with approved protectant. Never use Armor All or other similar products (also refer back to the note on storing leather seats).

APPENDIX A

Catalog of Contemporary Motorcycles

This appendix is a comprehensive list of motorcycle models, organized by manufacturer. Note that the prices listed were valid at the time of publication, and will vary depending on the dealer. Use these prices as guidelines and points of comparison only.

Engine displacement may be listed in cubic centimeters (cc) or cubic inches (ci), depending on the manufacturer. To convert cubic centimeters into cubic inches, multiply by 0.061023. To convert cubic inches into cubic centimeters, multiply by 16.3872.

AMERICAN DIRT BIKE
www.americandirtbike.com

ADB doesn't offer production-line bikes. Each motorcycle is manufactured as a custom machine. These are street-legal "dual sports."

Avenger 605 Dual Sport ($8,995). Street/Dirt. Available in 350cc, 600cc, or 614cc to 635cc air-cooled single cylinder four-stroke engines with a five-speed transmission and a chain final drive. Although these are reportedly "dual sport" motorcycles, they beg for dirt.

Avenger 605 Motorcross ($7,995). Dirt. Available in 350cc, 600cc, or 614cc to 635cc air-cooled single-cylinder four-stroke engine with a five-speed transmission and a chain final drive. A trimmed-down version of the dual sport.

ATK
www.atkusa.com

This is a purely American Company that mainly produces single cylinder "thumper" style dirt bikes. A few of their four strokers are street-legal "Dual Sports," but that is definitely not their main aim.

350 Enduro Electric Start ($6,795). Street/Dirt. Available with a 350cc air-cooled four-stroke single-cylinder "thumper" engine with a six-speed wide-ratio transmission and a chain final drive.

500 Enduro Electric Start ($7,395). Street/Dirt. 500cc air-cooled four-stroke single-cylinder "thumper" engine and a five-speed wide-ratio transmission and a chain final drive.

605 Enduro Electric Start ($7,595). Street/Dirt. Same as the 500cc, but with a 605cc engine.

125 LQ Enduro ($4,995). Dirt. With a 124.9cc liquid-cooled two-stroke single-cylinder "thumper" engine with a six-speed wide-ratio transmission and a chain final drive.

250 LQ Enduro ($5,695). Dirt. Same as the 125 LQ, but with 249cc displacement.

260 LQ Enduro ($5,695). Dirt. Same as the 125 LQ, but with 251cc displacement.

500 DTW Dirt Track ($8,795). Dirt. Has a 494cc air-cooled four-stroke single-cylinder "thumper" engine with a five-speed transmission and a chain final drive.

600 DTW Dirt Track ($8,995). Dirt. Same as the 500 DTW, but with a 598cc engine.

500 Motard ($7,395). Dirt. 494cc air-cooled four-stroke single-cylinder "thumper" with a five-speed wide-ratio transmission and a chain final drive.

600 Motard ($7,595). Dirt. Same as the 500 Motard, but with a 598cc engine.

BIMOTA
www.bimota.it

If money is no concern but speed is, these bikes might be for you. Bimota is an Italian company that limits most of its production to street racers. These bikes aren't exactly commonplace in the United States, but they are well worth the extra money.

500 V-Due ($20,295). Street Racer. 499cc liquid-cooled four-stroke v-twin engine (90 degree) with a six-speed transmission and chain final drive.

Mantra ($17,030). Street Racer. 904cc air-cooled four-stroke v-twin engine (90 degree) with a six-speed transmission and a chain final drive.

SB6 ($20,295). Street Racer. 1074cc liquid-cooled four-stroke four-cylinder inline engine built around the Suzuki GSX-R and a five-speed transmission and a chain final drive.

SB8R ($23,595). Street Racer. 996cc liquid-cooled four-stroke v-twin engine (90 degree) with a six-speed transmission and a chain final drive.

SB8S ($26,595). Street Racer. 996cc liquid-cooled four-stroke v-twin engine (90 degree) with a six-speed transmission and a chain final drive. This is essentially the SB8R, but with a few extras that are probably not worth the extra $3,000.

YB11 ($20,295). Street Racer. 1002cc liquid-cooled four-stroke inline four-cylinder engine with a five-speed transmission and a chain final drive.

BMW
www.bmwmotorcycles.com

German engineering screams precision—in everything from watches to motorcycles. The Bavarian Motor Works is no exception. Categorizing BMWs is tricky; the line between street racer and touring bikes is often blurred.

S650GS ($8,100). Street Racer. 652cc liquid-cooled four-stroke single-cylinder "thumper" engine with a five-speed transmission and chain final drive.

R1150GS ($14,500). Street Racer. 1130cc air-cooled four-stroke opposed-twin engine with a six-speed transmission and an enclosed drive shaft final drive.

R1150RT ($16,290). Touring. 1130cc air-cooled four-stroke opposed-twin engine with a six-speed transmission and an enclosed drive shaft final drive.

K1200RS ($16,990). Street Racer. 1171cc liquid-cooled four-stroke inline four-cylinder engine with a six-speed transmission and an enclosed drive shaft final drive.

K1200LT ($16,990). Touring. 1171cc liquid-cooled four-stroke inline four-cylinder engine with a five-speed transmission and an enclosed drive shaft final drive.

R1100S ($13,900). Street Racer. 1085cc air-cooled four-stroke opposed-twin engine with a six-speed transmission and an enclosed drive shaft final drive.

R1100RS ($15,600). Street Racer. 1085cc air-cooled four-stroke opposed-twin engine with a five-speed transmission and an enclosed drive shaft final drive.

R1200C ($14,500). Cruiser. 1170cc air-cooled four-stroke opposed-twin engine with a five-speed transmission and an enclosed drive shaft final drive.

BUELL
www.buell.com

Erik Buell is a former Harley-Davidson employee who decided that Harley style and performance needed a boost, and left the motor company to form his own company that built bikes based on the HD Sportster engine. Buell's company was successful enough to get the attention of Harley-Davidson, which later purchased it. These machines are Harley-Davidsons on steroids, which makes them a little bit hard to categorize. Basically, you can think of all Buell motorcycles as street racers.

Cyclone M2 ($8,995). Street Racer. 1203cc air-cooled four-stroke v-twin (45 degree) with a five-speed transmission and a Kevlar belt final drive.

Lightning X1 ($10,995). Street Racer. 1203cc air-cooled four-stroke v-twin (45 degree) with a five-speed transmission and a Kevlar belt final drive.

X1W White Lightning ($11,395). Street Racer. 1203cc air-cooled four-stroke v-twin (45 degree) with a five-speed transmission and a Kevlar belt final drive.

Firebolt XB9R (price pending). Street Racer. 984cc air-cooled four-stroke v-twin (45 degree) with a five-speed transmission and a constant path, 11 mm GT profile belt final drive. This is the newest addition to the Buell line.

Thunderbolt S3T ($12,495). Touring. 1203cc air-cooled four-stroke v-twin (45 degree) with a five-speed transmission and a Kevlar belt final drive.

Blast ($4,395). Cruiser. 492cc air-cooled four-stroke single-cylinder thumper with a five-speed transmission and a Kevlar belt final drive.

DUCATI
www.ducati.com

In 1996, this Italian company was purchased by the Texas Pacific Group, making it another American-owned motorcycle manufacturer. At the turn of the millennium, Ducati offered the MH900e, the first motorcycle to be sold exclusively online.

998 (approx. $16,500). Street Racer. 998cc liquid-cooled four-stroke l-twin engine with a six-speed transmission and a chain final drive. 11.4 to 1 compression ratio. Variations include the 998S (almost identical to 998, but about 24 pounds lighter) and the 998R (almost identical to the 998, but with a 12.3 to 1 compression ratio and 32 pounds lighter).

748 (approx. $13,500). Street Racer. 748cc liquid-cooled four-stroke l-twin engine with a six-speed transmission, a chain final drive, and an 11.5 to one compression ratio. Variations include the 748S (almost identical to the 748 with trim, suspension, and paint variances) and the 748R (Almost identical to the 748 with trim and suspension variances as well as an 11.3 to one compression ratio). The 748 series closely resembles the 998 series with the greatest difference being the engine size.

900 SS (approx. $8,200 to $11,000 depending on final setup). Street Racer. 904cc air-cooled four-stroke l-twin engine with a six-speed transmission and a chain final drive. The 900 Sport is a variation with trim differences and each is available with the smaller 748cc engine as the 750 SS and 750 Sport.

ST4 (approx. $12,500). Touring. 916cc liquid-cooled four-stroke l-twin engine with a six-speed transmission and chain final drive. Variations include the ST4s with 996cc engine and the ST2 with the 944cc engine. This motorcycle screams for a new category, Sport Touring.

Monster 900 i.e. ($9,995). Naked Street Racer. 904cc air-cooled four-stroke l-twin engine with a six-speed transmission and a chain final drive.

Monster 700 i.e. ($7,695). Naked Street Racer. 748cc air-cooled four-stroke l-twin engine with a six-speed transmission and a chain final drive. Variations include the 620 i.e. with a 618cc engine and a five-speed transmission and the Monster 400 with a 398cc engine.

Note: Additional variations to the Monster lineup of Ducati motorcycles include the liquid-cooled Monster S4 and the S4 Fogarty, both with 916cc engines, six-speed transmissions, and chain final drive.

HARLEY-DAVIDSON
www.harleydavidson.com

Harley-Davidson has beaten all odds time and time again. There is very little reason to list specific prices for Harley-Davidson motorcycles because if it's a buy-now situation, you will have to take what you can get and pay what the dealer wants. Listed here are price estimates gathered from dealer surveys.

It is important to know that Harley engines are mounted in two different ways. Sportsters and Softail models basically have the engine bolted right to the frame. Because the design of the engine causes a lot of vibration, these make very poor touring motorcycles—they can just about shake the kidneys right out of your body. To get around this, Harley touring motorcycles feature the Dyna chassis, which isolates the rider from the vibrations. The vibrations are still there, but you just don't feel them. So when someone tells you that every motorcycle is a touring bike, you can be pretty sure they never had the chance to ride Harleys. To determine which are which, just look for the words

Dyna, Glide, or Road in the title. Even if a bike doesn't come as a touring model, you can build it up. If, on the other hand, the words Softail or Sportswear are in the title, it is probably best used as a cruiser and a cruiser alone, because it is going to shake, rattle, and roll, no matter what you do to it. It's all part of the charm that is Harley-Davidson.

Dyna Convertible (approx. $14,500). Cruiser. 80ci air/oil-cooled four-stroke v-twin (45 degree) engine with a five-speed transmission and belt final drive.

Dyna Low Rider (approx. $14,000). Cruiser. 80ci air/oil-cooled four-stroke v-twin (45 degree) engine with a five-speed transmission and belt final drive.

Dyna Super Glide (approx. $11,000). Cruiser. 80ci air/oil-cooled four-stroke v-twin (45 degree) engine with a five-speed transmission and belt final drive.

Dyna Wide Glide (approx. $15,000). Cruiser. 80ci air/oil-cooled four-stroke v-twin (45 degree) engine with a five-speed transmission and belt final drive.

Electra Glide Classic (approx. $16,000). Touring. 80ci air/oil-cooled four-stroke v-twin (45 degree) engine with a five-speed transmission and belt final drive.

Electra Glide Ultra Classic (approx. $18,000). Touring. 80ci air/oil-cooled four-stroke v-twin (45 degree) engine with a five-speed transmission and belt final drive.

Electra Glide Standard (approx. $16,000). Touring. 80ci air/oil-cooled four-stroke v-twin (45 degree) engine with a five-speed transmission and belt final drive.

Fat Boy (approx. $15,000 if you can find one). Cruiser. 80ci air/oil-cooled four-stroke v-twin (45 degree) engine with a five-speed transmission and belt final drive. Ever since Arnold Schwarzenegger rode this bike in the popular movie *Terminator: Judgment Day*, it has been difficult to find on the show room floor and near impossible to find used. It's just as hard as finding a good lever-action 12-gauge shotgun.

Heritage Softail Classic (approx. $15,500). Cruiser. 80ci air/oil-cooled four-stroke v-twin (45 degree) engine with a five-speed transmission and belt final drive.

Heritage Springer (approx. $17,500). Cruiser. 80ci air/oil-cooled four-stroke v-twin (45 degree) engine with a five-speed transmission and belt final drive.

Road Glide (approx. $17,000). Touring. 80ci air/oil-cooled four-stroke v-twin (45 degree) engine with a five-speed transmission and belt final drive.

Road King (approx. $15,000). Touring. 80ci air/oil-cooled four-stroke v-twin (45 degree) engine with a five-speed transmission and belt final drive.

Road King Classic (approx. $16,000). Touring. 80ci air/oil-cooled four-stroke v-twin (45 degree) engine with a five-speed transmission and belt final drive.

Softail Custom (approx. $14,500). Cruiser. 80ci air/oil-cooled four-stroke v-twin (45 degree) engine with a five-speed transmission and belt final drive.

Springer Softail (approx. $15,000). Cruiser. 80ci air/oil-cooled four-stroke v-twin (45 degree) engine with a five-speed transmission and belt final drive.

Sportster 883 (approx. $5,500). Cruiser. 883cc air/oil-cooled four-stroke v-twin (45 degree) engine with a five-speed transmission and belt final drive.

Sportster 883 Hugger (approx. $6,000). Cruiser. 883cc air/oil-cooled four-stroke v-twin (45 degree) engine with a five-speed transmission and belt final drive.

Note: The difference between the Sportster 883 and the Sportster 883 Hugger is a little chrome and a lot of rider-location repositioning. The operator's seat on the Hugger is much lower than on the regular 883. If you have your heart set on an 883, try riding both, or at least take a seat on both of them: The Hugger is downright painful for someone of bigger-than-average size.

Sportster 1200 (approx. $7,750). Cruiser. 1200cc air/oil-cooled four-stroke v-twin (45 degree) engine with a five-speed transmission and belt final drive. If you are debating between this standard Sportster 1200 and the sportier Sportster Sport 1200, spend the extra money. This is a good entry level cruiser, but you will be so much happier with the more expensive model.

Sportster Sport (approx. $8,500). Cruiser. 1200cc air/oil-cooled four-stroke v-twin (45 degree) engine with a five-speed transmission and belt final drive. This motorcycle is quick enough in the turns that it borderlines on being called a street racer.

Sportster Custom (approx. $9,000). Cruiser. 1200cc air/oil-cooled four-stroke v-twin (45 degree) engine with a five-speed transmission and belt final drive. This is a Sportster with a mild chopper style that takes away from its ability to corner quickly. What this motorcycle loses in turning performance it gains in classic style.

HONDA

www.hondamotorcycles.com

Harley-Davidson may lead in the big-cruiser category, but Honda leads the entire market in every other category.

Gold Wing GL1800/GL1800A ($17,699–$17,999). Touring. 1832cc liquid-cooled four-stroke horizontally opposed six-cylinder engine with a five-speed transmission, including overdrive and an electric reverse. Shaft final drive.

Gold Wing with ABS ($18,699–$18,999). Touring. Same as above, but with antilock brakes.

CBR1100XX ($10,999). Street Racer. 1137cc liquid-cooled four-stroke inline four-cylinder with a six-speed transmission and a chain final drive.

RVT1000R ($10,999). Street Racer. 999cc liquid-cooled four-stroke v-twin (90 degree) engine with a six-speed transmission and chain final drive.

Super Hawk ($8,999). Street Racer. 996cc liquid-cooled four-stroke v-twin (90 degree) engine with a six-speed transmission and chain final drive.

CBR600F4I ($8,199). Street Racer. 599cc liquid-cooled four-stroke inline four-cylinder engine with a six-speed transmission and chain final drive.

CBR954RR ($10,599). Street Racer. 954cc liquid-cooled four-stroke inline four-cylinder engine with a six-speed transmission and chain final drive.

CB900F ($7,999). Street Racer. 919cc liquid-cooled four-stroke inline four-cylinder engine with a six-speed transmission and chain final drive.

Interceptor VFR800FI ($9,999–$10,999). Street Racer. 781cc liquid-cooled four-stroke v4 (90 degree) engine with a six-speed transmission and chain final drive.

VTX1800 ($12,499–$13,499). Cruiser. 1795cc liquid-cooled four-stroke v-twin (52 degree) engine with a five-speed transmission and shaft final drive.

Valkyrie GL1500CD ($13,099–$13,299). Cruiser. 1520cc liquid-cooled vertically opposed six-cylinder engine with a five-speed transmission and shaft final drive.

Shadow Spirit VT1100C ($7,999). Cruiser. 1099cc liquid-cooled four-stroke v-twin (45 degree) engine with a five-speed transmission and shaft final drive.

Shadow Ace VT750CD ($5,999–$6,399). Cruiser. 745cc liquid-cooled four-stroke v-twin (52 degree) engine with a five-speed transmission and chain final drive.

Shadow VLX Deluxe VT600CD ($5,299). Cruiser. 583cc liquid-cooled four-stroke v-twin (52 degree) with four-speed transmission and chain final drive.

Shadow VLX VT600C ($4,999). Cruiser. 583cc liquid-cooled four-stroke v-twin (52 degree) with four-speed transmission and chain final drive.

Rebel CMX250C ($2,999). Cruiser. 234cc air-cooled four-stroke parallel twin-cylinder engine with a five-speed transmission and chain final drive.

Nighthawk CB250 ($3,399). Cruiser. 234cc air-cooled four-stroke parallel twin-cylinder engine with a five-speed transmission and chain final drive.

Nighthawk CB750 ($5,799). Cruiser. 747cc air-cooled four-stroke inline four-cylinder engine with a five-speed transmission and chain final drive.

CRF450R ($6,299). Dirt. 449cc liquid-cooled four-stroke single-cylinder engine with a five-speed transmission and chain final drive.

CR250R ($5,899). Dirt. 249cc liquid-cooled two-stroke single-cylinder engine with a five-speed transmission and chain final drive.

CR125R ($4,999). Dirt. 125cc liquid-cooled two-stroke single-cylinder engine with a five-speed transmission and chain final drive.

CR80R Expert ($2,999). Dirt. 83cc liquid-cooled two-stroke single-cylinder engine with a six-speed transmission and chain final drive.

CR80R ($2,899). Dirt. 83cc liquid-cooled two-stroke single-cylinder engine with a six-speed transmission and chain final drive.

XR650R ($5,999). Dirt. 649cc liquid-cooled four-stroke single-cylinder engine with a five-speed transmission and chain final drive.

XR650L ($5,499). Dirt. 644cc air-cooled four-stroke single-cylinder engine with a five-speed transmission and chain final drive.

XR400R ($5,299). Dirt. 397cc air-cooled four-stroke single-cylinder engine with a five-speed transmission and chain final drive.

XR250R ($4,699). Dirt. 249cc air-cooled four-stroke single-cylinder engine with a six-speed transmission and chain final drive.

XR200R ($3,299). Dirt. 195cc air-cooled four-stroke single-cylinder engine with six-speed transmission and chain final drive.

XR100R ($2,099). Dirt. 99cc air-cooled four-stroke single-cylinder engine with a five-speed transmission and chin final drive.

XR80R ($1,799). Dirt. 80cc air-cooled four-stroke single-cylinder engine with a five-speed transmission and chain final drive.

XR70R ($1,399). Dirt. 72cc air-cooled four-stroke single-cylinder engine with a three-speed transmission (automatic clutch) and a chain final drive.

XR50R ($1,099). Dirt. 49cc air-cooled four-stroke single-cylinder engine with a three-speed transmission (electric clutch) and chain final drive.

KAWASAKI

www.kawasaki.com

Kawasaki is best known for speed and performance. Recently, this manufacturer has begun to expand beyond production of bikes that race from one stoplight to the next, and are quickly building up their client base in the cruiser and touring categories.

Ninja ZX12R ($10,999). Street Racer. 1198cc liquid-cooled four-stroke inline four-cylinder engine with a six-speed transmission and belt final drive.

Ninja ZX9R ($9,499). Same as the Ninja ZX12R, except with an 899cc engine.

Ninja ZX7R ($8,799). Same as the Ninja ZX12R, except with a 748cc engine.

Ninja ZX6R ($7,699). Same as the Ninja ZX12R, except with a 599cc engine.

Ninja ZX6 ($6,999). Similar to the Ninja ZX6R, except with a lower compression ratio engine.

Ninja 500R ($5,099). 498cc liquid-cooled four-stoke parallel twin-cylinder engine.

Ninja 250 R ($2,999). Same as the Ninja 500R, except with a 248cc engine.

ZZ-R1200 ($10,499). Street Racer. 1164cc liquid-cooled four-stroke inline four-cylinder engine with a six-speed transmission and belt final drive.

ZRX1200R ($7,899). Naked Street Racer. 1164cc liquid-cooled four-stroke inline four-cylinder engine with a six-speed transmission and belt final drive.

ZR-7S ($5,999). Naked Street Racer. 738cc air-cooled four-stroke inline four-cylinder engine with five-speed transmission and belt final drive.

Super Sherpa ($3,999). Street/Dirt. 249cc air-cooled four-stroke single-cylinder engine with a six-speed transmission and chain final drive.

KLR250 ($4,149). Street/Dirt. 249cc liquid-cooled four-stroke single-cylinder engine with a six-speed transmission and chain final drive.

KLR650 ($4,999). Street/Dirt. 651cc liquid-cooled four-stroke single-cylinder engine with a five-speed transmission and chain final drive.

KLX110 ($1,699). Dirt. 111cc air-cooled four-stroke single-cylinder engine with a three-speed transmission and chain final drive.

KLX300R ($4,699). Dirt. 292cc liquid-cooled four-stroke single-cylinder engine with a six-speed transmission and chain final drive.

KDX220R ($4,399). Dirt. 216cc liquid-cooled two-stroke single-cylinder engine with a six-speed transmission and chain final drive.

KDX200 ($3,999.). Dirt. 198cc liquid-cooled two-stoke single-cylinder engine with a six-speed transmission and chain final drive.

KX500 ($5,199). Dirt. 499cc liquid-cooled two-stroke single-cylinder engine with a five-speed transmission and chain final drive.

KX250 ($5,799). Dirt. 249cc liquid-cooled two-stroke single-cylinder engine with a five-speed transmission and chain final drive.

KX125 ($4,949). Dirt. 124cc liquid-cooled two-stroke single-cylinder engine with a six-speed transmission and chain final drive.

KX100 ($3,449). Dirt. 99cc liquid-cooled two-stroke single-cylinder engine with a six-speed transmission and chain final drive.

KX85 ($3,199). Dirt. 84cc liquid-cooled two-stroke single-cylinder engine with a six-speed transmission and chain final drive.

KX65 ($2,849). Dirt. 64.7cc liquid-cooled two-stroke single-cylinder engine with a six-speed transmission and chain final drive.

KX60 ($2,299). Dirt. 60cc liquid-cooled two-stroke single-cylinder engine with a six-speed transmission and chain final drive.

Vulcan 1500 ($9,999–12,999). Cruiser. 1,470cc liquid-cooled four-stroke v-twin engine with a five-speed transmission and shaft final drive. Style and price variances include the Drifter, Classic, Mean Streak, and Nomad.

Vulcan 800 ($6,799–7,499). Cruiser. 805cc liquid-cooled four-stroke v-twin engine with a five-speed transmission and chain final drive. Style and price variances include the Classic and the Drifter.

Vulcan 750 ($6,099). Cruiser. 749cc liquid-cooled four-stroke v-twin engine with a five-speed transmission and shaft final drive. Available factory options can push this cruiser almost to the touring class.

Vulcan 500 LTD ($4,699). Cruiser. 498cc liquid-cooled four-stroke parallel-twin engine with a six-speed transmission and chain final drive.

Eliminator 125 ($2,499). Cruiser. 124cc air-cooled four-stroke single-cylinder engine with a five-speed transmission and chain final drive.

Retro W650 ($6,599). Cruiser. 676cc air-cooled four-stroke parallel-twin engine with a five-speed transmission and chain final drive. This motorcycle has the look of the original Japanese motorcycles. It is definitely a cruiser, but is anything but a Harley clone.

Police 1000 (No standard listing price). Cruiser. 998cc air-cooled four-stroke inline four-cylinder with a five-speed transmission and chain final drive. Buying one of these new is problematic as the factory does not generally ship them to dealerships and there is no standard list price to be found. However, you might be able to find one at an auction for a good price.

Voyager XII ($12,299). Touring. 1196cc liquid-cooled four-stroke inline four-cylinder with a five-speed transmission and shaft final drive. This is a good alternative to the much higher priced Honda Gold Wing.

Voyager 1500 Nomad ($12,999). Touring. 1470cc liquid-cooled four-stroke v-twin engine with a five-speed transmission and shaft final drive. This is a good alternative to the much higher priced Harley-Davidson touring models.

Concourse ($8,199). Touring. 997cc liquid-cooled four-stroke inline four-cylinder engine with a six-speed transmission and shaft final drive. This bike is really a blend between a cruiser and a street racer into a hybrid touring motorcycle.

KTM
www.ktmusa.com

KTM was founded as a motorcycle manufacturer in Mattigofen, Austria, in 1953. When considering KTM motorcycles, take extra care to note that the same letters in the model are used to denote both two-stroke and four-stroke engines as the offered engine gets larger. As an example, there is the KTM 380 SX with a two-stroke engine as well as the KTM 400 SX with a four-stroke engine. Although the engines are only a little different in displacement, the difference between two- and four-stroke engines is profound.

KTM 125 SX ($4,998). Dirt. 124.8cc liquid-cooled two-stroke single-cylinder engine with a six-speed transmission and chain final drive.

KTM 250 SX ($5,948). Dirt. 249cc liquid-cooled two-stroke single-cylinder engine with a five-speed transmission and chain final drive.

KTM 380 SX ($6,148). Dirt. 368cc liquid-cooled two-stroke single-cylinder engine with a five-speed transmission and chain final drive.

KTM 400 SX ($6,498). Dirt. 398cc liquid-cooled four-stroke single-cylinder engine with a six-speed transmission and chain final drive.

KTM 520 SX ($6,748). Dirt. 510.4cc liquid-cooled four-stroke single-cylinder engine with a four-speed transmission and chain final drive.

KTM 200 MXC ($5,648). Dirt. 193cc liquid-cooled two-stroke single-cylinder engine with a five-speed transmission and chain final drive.

KTM 300 MXC ($6,198). Dirt. 297cc liquid-cooled two-stroke single-cylinder engine with a five-speed transmission and chain final drive.

KTM 400 MXC ($6,998). Dirt. 398cc liquid-cooled four-stroke single-cylinder engine with a six-speed transmission and chain final drive.

KTM 520 MXC ($7,248). Dirt. 510.4cc liquid-cooled four-stroke single-cylinder engine with a six-speed transmission and chain final drive.

KTM 200 EXC ($5,798). Dirt. 193cc liquid-cooled two-stroke single-cylinder engine with a six-speed transmission and chain final drive.

KTM 250 EXC ($6,148). Dirt. 249cc liquid-cooled two-stroke single-cylinder engine with a five-speed transmission and chain final drive.

KTM 300 EXC ($6,298). Dirt. 297cc liquid-cooled two-stroke single-cylinder engine with a five-speed transmission and chain final drive.

KTM 380 EXC ($6,398). Dirt. 368cc liquid-cooled two-stroke single-cylinder engine with a five-speed transmission and chain final drive.

KTM 400 EXC ($7,098). Dirt. 398cc liquid-cooled four-stroke single-cylinder engine with a six-speed transmission and chain final drive.

KTM 520 EXC ($7,348). Dirt. 510.4cc liquid-cooled four-stroke single-cylinder engine with a six-speed transmission and chain final drive.

KTM 640 LC4 Duke II (TBA). Street Racer. 625cc liquid-cooled four-stroke single-cylinder engine with a five-speed transmission and chain final drive.

KTM LC8 (TBA). Street Racer. 942cc liquid-cooled four-stroke v-twin (75 degree) engine with a six-speed transmission and chain final drive.

LAVERDA

www.laverda.it

These bikes have been almost impossible to get in the United States since the Reagan administration increased motorcycle importation tax. Basically, everything they produce is the same motorcycle. The Formula has a full fairing, the Ghost has no fairing, and the motorcycles between have partial fairing.

Formula ($10,795–$12,995). Street Racer. 747cc liquid-cooled four-stroke parallel twin-cylinder engine with a six-speed transmission and chain final drive. Variations include the 750 S and the 750 S Carenata.

Ghost ($6,995–$8,995). Street Racer. 748cc liquid-cooled four-stroke parallel twin-cylinder engine with a six-speed transmission and chain final drive. Variations include the 750 Ghost Strike, the 650 Ghost Strike (668cc engine), and the 650 Ghost.

MOTO GUZZI

www.motoguzzi-us.com

This company can be thought of as the Italian Harley-Davidson. It is Italy's oldest motorcycle manufacturer and its European brand loyalty is similar to Harley's brand loyalty in the States.

California EV ($14,990). Touring. 1064cc air-cooled four-stroke v-twin (90 degree) with a five-speed transmission and shaft final drive.

California Stone Metal ($9,290). Cruiser. 1064cc air-cooled four-stroke v-twin (90 degree) with a five-speed transmission and shaft final drive. This is the cruiser version of the California EV.

V11 Sport Scura ($13,990). Street Racer. 1064cc air-cooled four-stroke v-twin (90 degree) with a six-speed transmission and shaft final drive.

V11 Le Mans Tenni ($13,990). Street Racer. 1064cc air-cooled four-stroke v-twin (90 degree) with a six-speed transmission and shaft final drive. This model is a little bit heavier than the V11 Sport Scura and has a slightly larger fairing.

MZ

www.motorradna.com

This is a German motorcycle company that few heard about before the fall of the wall and the reunification of East and West Germany. Now they are making noise with their Yamaha-powered thumpers.

Skorpion ($4,995–$6,495). Street Racer. 660cc liquid-cooled four-stroke single-cylinder with a five-speed transmission and chain final drive. Models include the Traveler and the Tour.

Black Panther ($6,195). Street/Dirt, more on the Street side. 660cc air-cooled four-stroke single-cylinder with a five-speed transmission and chain final drive.

Street Moto ($6,195). Street/Dirt, more on the Street side. 660cc air-cooled four-stroke single-cylinder with a five-speed transmission and chain final drive.

125 SX ($3,595). Street/Dirt, more on the Dirt side. 124cc air-cooled four-stroke single-cylinder engine with a five-speed transmission and chain final drive. Minor variations can be found in the 125 SM, RT 125, and the 125 FunX.

1000S (TBA). Street Racer. 996cc liquid-cooled four-stroke parallel-twin engine with a chain final drive. Price and details are pending, but if this one is as solid as their other motorcycles, it will be a real challenger to the street-racer category.

SUZUKI

www.suzuki.com

This once-small company has come a very long way since it first started offering motorcycles to the U.S. market in 1963. With the turn of the century, their product line is going strong and their offerings have never been better.

GSX ($7,999–$10,399). Street Racer. 988cc liquid-cooled four-stroke four-cylinder engine with a six-speed transmission and chain final drive. Variations are in engine sizes between 599cc and 988cc.

GS550 ($4,399). Street Racer. 487cc air-cooled four-stroke two-cylinder engine with a six-speed transmission and chain final drive.

TL1000R ($9,599). Street Racer. 996cc liquid-cooled four-stroke v-twin (90 degree) engine with a six-speed transmission and chain final drive.

DL1000 ($8,899). Street Racer. 996cc liquid-cooled four-stroke v-twin (90 degree) engine with a six-speed transmission and chain final drive. This motorcycle is very similar to the TL1000R, but with a milder compression ratio and price.

HAYABUSA 1300 ($10,849). Street Racer. 1299cc liquid-cooled four-stroke four-cylinder engine with a six-speed transmission and chain final drive.

Katana ($6,299–$7,299). Street Racer. 750cc air/oil-cooled four-stroke four-cylinder engine with a six-speed transmission. Price difference is found in the engine selection. Available in 750cc and 599cc.

Bandit 1200 ($6,999–$7,399). Street Racer. 1157cc air/oil-cooled four-stroke four-cylinder engine with a five-speed transmission and chain final drive. Models include Bandit 1200 and 1200S.

Bandit 600S ($5,849). Street Racer. 599cc air/oil-cooled four-stroke four-cylinder engine with a six-speed transmission and chain final drive.

SV650 ($5,799–$6,199.). Street Racer. 645cc liquid-cooled four-stroke v-twin (90 degree) with a six-speed transmission and chain final drive. Model variations include the SV650 and SV650S.

Intruder LC VL1500 ($9,999). Cruiser. 1462cc air/oil-cooled four-stroke v-twin (45 degree) engine with a five-speed transmission and shaft final drive.

Intruder 1400 ($8,349). Cruiser. 1360cc air/oil-cooled four-stroke v-twin (45 degree) engine with a five-speed transmission and final shaft drive.

Intruder Volusia ($6,599). Cruiser. 805cc liquid-cooled four-stroke v-twin (45 degree) engine with a five-speed transmission and final shaft drive.

Intruder 800 ($6,399). Cruiser. 805cc liquid-cooled four-stroke v-twin (45 degree) engine with a five-speed transmission and shaft final drive.

Marauder ($5,999). Cruiser. 805cc liquid-cooled four-stroke v-twin (45 degree) engine with a five-speed transmission and chain final drive.

Savage ($4,299). Cruiser. 652cc air-cooled four-stroke single-cylinder engine with a five-speed transmission and belt final drive.

GZ250 ($2,999). Cruiser. 249cc air-cooled four-stroke single-cylinder engine with a five-speed transmission and chain final drive.

DR650SE ($4,999). Street/Dirt. 644cc air/oil-cooled four-stroke single-cylinder engine with a five-speed transmission and chain final drive.

DR250SE ($3,899). Street/Dirt. 199cc air/oil-cooled four-stroke single-cylinder engine with a five-speed transmission and chain final drive.

DR-Z400 ($5,349). Street/Dirt. 398cc liquid-cooled four-stroke single-cylinder engine with a five-speed transmission and chain final drive. Model variances include the DR-Z400S and DR-Z400E.

DR-Z250 ($4,699). Street/Dirt. 249cc air/oil-cooled four-stroke single-cylinder engine with a six-speed transmission and chain final drive.

DR-Z125/L (TBA). Street/Dirt. 124cc air-cooled four-stroke single-cylinder engine with a five-speed transmission and chain final drive.

RM250 ($5,899). Dirt. 249cc liquid-cooled two-stroke single-cylinder engine with a five-speed transmission and chain final drive.

RM125 ($4,999). Dirt. 124.8cc liquid-cooled two-stroke single-cylinder engine with a six-speed transmission and chain final drive.

RM85 ($3,099). Dirt. 84.7cc liquid-cooled two-stroke single-cylinder engine with a six-speed transmission and chain final drive.

TRIUMPH

www.triumph.co.uk

Triumph produced its first motorcycle in Coventry, England in 1902, and the company has been going strong ever since.

TT600 ($8,299). Street Racer. 599cc liquid-cooled four-stroke inline four-cylinder engine with a six-speed transmission and a chain final drive.

Daytona 955I ($10,999). Street Racer. 955cc liquid-cooled four-stroke inline three-cylinder engine with a six-speed transmission and a chain final drive.

Sprint ST ($10,799). Touring. 955cc liquid-cooled four-stroke inline three-cylinder engine with a six-speed transmission and chain final drive. This motorcycle comes from the factory with full fairing and hard bags.

Sprint RS ($9,499). Street Racer. 955cc liquid-cooled four-stroke inline three-cylinder engine with a six-speed transmission and a chain final drive. Similar to the Sprint ST, but with only a partial fairing and none of the extra trim.

Speed Triple ($10,499). Street Racer. 955cc liquid-cooled four-stroke inline three-cylinder engine with a six-speed transmission and a chain final drive. The Speed Twin is the naked version of the Daytona with no fairing.

Tiger ($10,799). Street Racer. 955cc liquid-cooled four-stroke inline three-cylinder engine with a six-speed transmission and chain final drive. With its large fuel tank and optional hard bags, this street racer is a quick convert to the touring class.

Trophy 900 ($10,999). Touring. 885cc liquid-cooled four-stroke inline three-cylinder engine with a six-speed transmission and chain final drive. One variation, the Trophy 1200 is essentially the same motorcycle, but with an 1180cc inline four-cylinder engine.

Bonneville ($6,999). Cruiser. 790cc air-cooled four-stroke parallel-twin engine with a five-speed transmission and chain final drive. This is the classic style that became popular during the Japanese invasion.

Legend TT ($7,799). Cruiser. 885cc liquid-cooled four-stroke inline three-cylinder engine with a five-speed transmission and chain final drive. Looks like a cross between classic Japanese invasion and Harley clone.

Thunderbird ($8,999). Cruiser. 885cc liquid-cooled four-stroke inline three-cylinder engine with a six-speed transmission and chain final drive. Similar to the Legend TT, but with an extra gear.

Adventurer ($8,999). Cruiser. 885cc liquid-cooled four-stroke inline three-cylinder engine with a five-speed transmission and chain final drive. Similar to the Legend TT.

URAL

www.ural.com

Ural is probably one of the most enjoyable motorcycle manufacturers to talk about. They started their business during World War II by smuggling BMW motorcycles from Germany into Russia. From there, it was all backwards engineering until they had their own models. All current-production Urals feature sidecars. These are street/dirt motorcycles, but they should be thought of as the Jeeps of the motorcycle world. Definitely built for in-the-dirt adventure, but not the way other dirt bikes are.

Patrol ($10,390). Street/Dirt. 649cc air-cooled four-stroke opposed-twin "boxer" engine with a four-speed transmission and a shaft final drive. This is the only U.S. street-legal motorcycle with an engageable sidecar drive shaft. This "two wheel drive" system offers major benefits when used as a dirt bike. There are plans to introduce the newer 750cc engine to this model, but a date has not been set.

Tourist ($8,495). Street/Dirt. 750cc oil/air-cooled four-stroke opposed-twin "boxer" engine with a four-speed transmission and shaft final drive.

VICTORY

www.victory-usa.com

In the early 1990s, the executives of Polaris Industries tossed around the idea of becoming the first American manufacturer of a new line of motorcycles since the Great Depression. On June 26, 1997, they released the motorcycle that would mark that accomplishment, the Victory V92C. At the time this list was compiled, Victory had not released the 2002 prices and the 2001 models have changed so much that listing them would be pointless. Expect to see prices between $14,000 and $15,000, depending on model and trim.

V92C (TBA). Cruiser. 1507cc air/oil-cooled four-stroke v-twin (50 degree) engine with a five-speed transmission and belt final drive.

V92C Deluxe (TBA). Cruiser. 1507cc air/oil-cooled four-stroke v-twin (50 degree) engine with a five-speed transmission and belt final drive. This is basically the V92C with extra trim and a full windshield.

V92TC (TBA). Cruiser. 1507cc air/oil-cooled four-stroke v-twin (50 degree) engine with a five-speed transmission and belt final drive. The main difference between the V92C and V92TC line is that the V92TC routes its exhaust to both sides of the motorcycle, while the V92C runs both pipes down the same side.

V92TC Deluxe (TBA). Cruiser. 1507cc air/oil-cooled four-stroke v-twin (50 degree) engine with a five-speed transmission and belt final drive. The Deluxe model means more trim.

YAMAHA

www.yamaha-motor.com

Yamaha holds a very interesting place in the motorcycle industry. Yamaha sales rest firmly on the accurate reputation for building some of the most dependable motorcycles available and the tremendous value they offer.

Road Star ($10,999–$11,199). Touring. 98ci air-cooled four-stroke v-twin (48 degree) engine with a five-speed transmission and belt final drive. This is the base model of the Road Star line.

Road Star Ventura ($16,399–$16,899). Touring. 79ci liquid-cooled four-stroke v4 (70 degree) engine with a five-speed transmission and shaft final drive.

Road Star Warrior ($11,999). Cruiser. 102ci air-cooled four-stroke v-twin (48 degree) engine with a five-speed transmission and a belt final drive.

Road Star Silverado ($12,399–$12,599). Cruiser. 98ci air-cooled four-stroke v-twin (48 degree) engine with a five-speed transmission and a belt final drive.

Road Star Midnight Star ($11,799). Cruiser. 98ci air-cooled four-stroke v-twin (48 degree) engine with a five-speed transmission and a belt final drive. Very similar to the Silverado, only trimmed down a bit.

V Star Silverado ($6,899). Cruiser. 40ci air-cooled four-stroke v-twin engine with a five-speed transmission and shaft final drive.

V Star 1100 Silverado ($9,299). Cruiser. 65ci air-cooled four-stroke v-twin (75 degree) engine with a five-speed transmission and belt final drive.

V Star Classic ($8,199–$8,399). Cruiser. 65ci air-cooled four-stroke v-twin (75 degree) engine with a five-speed transmission and shaft final drive.

V Star Custom ($7,899). Cruiser. 65ci air-cooled four-stroke v-twin (75 degree) engine with a five-speed transmission and shaft final drive.

V Max ($10,899). Cruiser. 1200cc liquid-cooled four-stroke v4 (70 degree) engine with a five-speed transmission and shaft final drive. This motorcycle is a cross between a Cruiser and a Street Racer.

Virago 250 ($3,399). Cruiser. 249cc air-cooled four-stroke twin (60 degree) engine with a five-speed transmission and a chain final drive.

YZF-R1($10,299). Street Racer. 998cc liquid-cooled four-stroke inline four-cylinder engine with a six-speed transmission and chain final drive.

YZF-R6 ($7,999). Street Racer. 599cc liquid-cooled four-stroke inline four-cylinder engine with a six-speed transmission and chain final drive.

YZF-600R ($6,999). Street Racer. 599cc liquid-cooled four-stroke inline four-cylinder engine with a six-speed transmission and chain final drive.

FX1 ($8,499). Street Racer. 998cc liquid-cooled four-stroke inline four-cylinder engine with a six-speed transmission and chain final drive.

XT225 ($3,999). Street/Dirt. 223cc air-cooled four-stroke single-cylinder engine with a six-speed transmission and chain final drive.

TW200 ($3,599). Street/Dirt. 196cc air-cooled four-stroke single-cylinder engine with a five-speed transmission and chain final drive.

YZ426F ($5,999). Dirt. 426cc liquid-cooled four-stroke single-cylinder engine with a five-speed transmission and chain final drive.

YZ250 ($5,899). Dirt. 249cc liquid-cooled two-stroke single-cylinder engine with a five-speed transmission and chain final drive.

YZ250F ($5,499). Dirt. 249cc liquid-cooled four-stroke single-cylinder engine with a five-speed transmission and chain final drive.

YZ125 ($4,999). Dirt. 124cc liquid-cooled two-stroke single-cylinder engine with a five-speed transmission and chain final drive.

YZ85 ($3,249). Dirt. 85cc liquid-cooled two-stroke single-cylinder engine with a six-speed transmission and chain final drive.

WR426F ($6,199). Dirt. 426cc liquid-cooled four-stroke single-cylinder engine with a five-speed transmission and chain final drive.

WR250F ($5,699). Dirt. 249cc liquid-cooled four-stroke single-cylinder engine with a five-speed transmission and chain final drive.

TT-R250 ($4,699). Dirt. 249cc air-cooled four-stroke single-cylinder engine with a six-speed transmission and chain final drive.

TT-R225 ($2,999). Dirt. 223cc air-cooled four-stroke single-cylinder engine with a six-speed transmission and chain final drive.

TT-R125 ($2,399–$2,599). Dirt. 124cc air-cooled four-stroke single-cylinder engine with a five-speed transmission and chain final drive. Variations include the TT-R125L.

TT-R90 ($1,699). Dirt. 89cc air-cooled four-stroke single-cylinder engine with a three-speed transmission, automatic clutch, and chain final drive.

PW-80 ($1,349). Dirt. 79cc air-cooled two-stroke single-cylinder engine with a three-speed transmission, automatic clutch, and chain final drive.

PW- 50 ($1,149). Dirt. 49cc air-cooled two-stroke single-cylinder engine with a single speed automatic transmission and chain final drive.

Appendix B

Glossary of Terms

The following glossary contains three categories of words: technical terminology (marked TT), biker slang or babble (marked BB), as well as other words you might need to know (left unmarked).

13 (BB): Indicates the mother club of a motorcycle club that has branched out or hived off into other areas. May also refer to a local club's leader who was originally a member of the mother club.

ABS: See **antilock brakes system.**

After-market (TT): Any merchant selling motorcycle equipment, parts, or accessories that are not **Original Equipment Manufacture** (OEM) products.

Airheads (BB): Air-cooled cylinder heads. In particular, the BMW boxer twins.

AMA: American Motorcyclist Association.

Antilock brakes system (ABS) (TT): A system by which the motorcycle can identify a skidding wheel and respond by releasing hydraulic pressure on brake pads just long enough to stop the skid. Antilock brake systems are often expensive, but they do keep your steering functional in a panic stop.

Ape hangers (BB): Disproportionately high handle bars commonly seen during the chopper days of custom motorcycles. They are dangerous and should be avoided.

BAB (BB): Born Again Biker—someone who had to sell a bike to pay the bills, but bought another as soon as finances allowed.

Baggage (BB): A term referring to a passenger who does not lean with the operator (a static passenger).

Barrels (BB): Used to refer to the throat of the carburetor or the cylinder body.

Basket case (BB): An entire motorcycle, completely disassembled.

Bathtub (BB): Sidecar.

Belt final drive (TT): A system by which the power to drive a motorcycle is transferred from the transmission to the rear wheel by a belt rather than a chain or shaft.

Bicycle lane (BB): The space between the two yellow lines. Also used by some synonymously with **lane splitting**. Both are very bad ideas.

Big end (BB): The top speed of a motorcycle. This term is sometimes used to make it clear that one is not talking about the **top end**, which can denote either top speed or the top half of an engine.

Big slab (BB): Any interstate or large multilane freeway that extends for great distances.

Big twin (BB): A specific reference to the larger of the Harley-Davidson v-twin engines. Even if a v-twin engine is larger than what the largest Harley has to offer, it is not typically called a "big twin."

Biker-friendly (BB): Usually a reference to a business that encourages bikers as patrons. Sometimes refers to employers, friends, and others open to the lifestyle.

Binders (BB): Brakes.

Blinkers (BB): Turn signals.

Blown (BB): Reference to either an engine that has failed or to one that has been either supercharged or, in some cases, turbocharged.

Bobber (BB): A reference to the post–World War II custom craze where most of the body work was removed from motorcycles.

Bobtail (BB): A reference synonymous with **bobber**, but more often used to refer to Harley-Davidsons.

Bone yard (BB): Salvage yard; source for used parts.

Bore (TT): The size of an engine's **cylinder**. When multiplied with the stroke (also called the **cycle**), the solution yields the cylinder's displacement.

Bottom end (TT): The portion of the engine where the crank rides. On almost all motorcycles (with the exception of Harley-Davidson), bottom end also refers to the transmission.

Boxer (TT): An engine with two opposing **cylinders**.

Brain bucket (BB): Helmet.

Bubble gum machines (BB): Police car or motorcycle. If a rider in front of you or in oncoming traffic pats his or her head or helmet, it usually means there is one ahead.

Burn out (BB): In racing, this term means to lock the front brake and throttle up in order to cause the rear tire to spin. This will cause a burning smell as friction heats up the rear tire. Drag racers burn out prior to the start of the race, to soften the rubber and get a better grip on the racetrack when the green light comes on. This phrase also refers to what happens when you accelerate too quickly when a stoplight turns green.

Café racer (BB): A reference to the English custom craze of the 1950s and 1960s. Supposedly, those motorcyclists would drink coffee and then race from one café to the next, hence the term "café racer." A café chop is a stock motorcycle to be converted into a café racer.

Cage (BB): Automobile.

Cagers (BB): Automobile operators.

Cam (BB): Short for **camshaft**.

Camshaft (TT): A revolving rod in the engine with lobes on it for controlling the opening and closing of the valves.

Cans (BB): Mufflers.

Canyon carving (BB): Riding twisty roads very quickly, especially when those roads move in and out of canyons and other cutaway areas of mountains.

Captain (BB): Leader of a particular tour; a particular rank of members in motorcycle clubs.

Carb (BB): Short for **carburetor**.

Carburetor (TT): A device that uses the differing pressures to mix fuel and air prior to its induction into an engine.

Center stand (TT): A stand that holds the motorcycle in an upright position as opposed to a side stand, which causes the motorcycle to lean to the side.

Center stand tang (TT): A part of the center stand onto which you place your foot when lifting the motorcycle onto the stand.

Chain final drive (TT): A system by which the power to drive a motor-cycle is transferred from the transmission to the rear wheel by a chain, rather than a belt or shaft.

Chase vehicle (TT): In organized long-range touring, this is a vehicle that follows behind the motorcycles, in case one breaks down. Usually a chase vehicle is a truck, capable of transporting a broken motorcycle.

Chassis (TT): Usually a reference to the frame and suspension on a motorcycle; however, some high-tech models use the engine case itself as part of the chassis.

Cherry top (BB): Another slang term for police car.

Chopper (BB): Originally used much the same way **bobber** was used, it came to describe motorcycles with an extended fork, high han-dlebars (**ape hangers**), and no rear suspension (hard tails).

Citizen (BB): Nonbiker. This term is used mostly in the Harley-Davidson community, but it is gaining popularity elsewhere as more people explore biking and recognize the backlash that some citizens express.

Clip-ons (BB): Handlebars that are attached directly to the front fork instead of at the top of the fork as is the case with most motorcy-cles. This is done to lower the riding position.

Clutch (TT): The mechanism by which the engine is disconnected from the transmission to facilitate gear change.

Coaster (TT): A plate used to block the holes when a **reed valve** is removed.

Colors (BB): Motorcycle club patches, usually worn on denim vests over leather jackets. This is usually a reference to outlaw **MCs** and not **AMA**-approved club patches. The difference is easily identified: AMA clubs have an AMA patch on their colors somewhere. Outlaws do not.

Combustion chamber (TT): The portion of the **cylinder** head where combustion takes place. This is also where the spark plugs reside and on four-stroke engines, where both the intake and exhaust valves are mounted.

Commuter (BB): Refers either to a motorcycle used often to travel to and from work or to a biker who uses a motorcycle as the primary transportation to and from work.

Connecting rod (TT): Not to be confused with a push rod, the con-necting rod is what connects the **cylinder** to the crankshaft.

Constant-radius turn (TT): A steady turn throughout, as opposed to sharper at the beginning or the end. See also **decreasing-radius corner** and **increasing-radius corner**.

Contact patch (TT): That portion of the tire's tread that is in contact with the road.

Corn snakes (BB): Dried corn stalks that blow across country roads in the fall.

Counterbalance (TT): A weight inside a motorcycle engine that helps dampen some of the vibration. On an automobile, this device rides

outside the engine case and is called the harmonic balancer. On a motorcycle this would be far too dangerous as the device spins with engine speed.

Countersteering (TT): The method of steering a motorcycle at all but the lowest speeds by turning right to go left.

Cowling (TT): Body work that covers the engine, transmission, and/or midportion of the motorcycle.

Crash bar (BB): Highway bar, engine bar, or leg guard that is actually built to provide protection and not just good looks or a place to put your feet.

Cross-over pipe (TT): In a multicylinder engine, this is the portion of the exhaust system that connects two or more of the exhaust pipes to provide greater exhaust flow.

Crotch rocket (BB): A slang term for "street racer."

Crown (TT): In engine terminology, this is the top of the piston. In road terminology, this is the high point of the road surface. Roads are often crowned to allow water to run off more freely.

Cycle (TT): The up-and-down motion of the **cylinder**. Used inter-changeably with the word **stroke**. When multiplied with the **bore**, the solution yields the cylinder displacement.

Cylinder (TT): The hole in the engine where the piston travels. Also see **cylinder block**.

Cylinder block (TT): The housing in which the **cylinder** is found, which is sandwiched between the lower end and the cylinder head.

Cylinder head (TT): The top of the engine that houses the spark plugs and (in four-stroke engines) both the intake and exhaust valves.

Death grip (BB): Holding on to a motorcycle so tightly that you risk your own safety. A beginner's common mistake.

Decreasing-radius corner (TT): A turn that is not constant and becomes more sharp as you transverse it. To use this term properly every time, just pretend the term radius means "ease," so a decreasing ease corner means it becomes less easy as you go. Less easy means sharper. Also see **constant-radius turn** and **increasing-radius corner**.

Detonation (TT): Preignition.

Dirt bike (TT): A motorcycle designed specifically for off-road use and never intended to be street legal. With the introduction of street/dirt or dual-sport bikes, the term **pure-dirt** has gained in popularity.

Dirty side (BB): A reference to the bottom of a motorcycle. "Keep the dirty side down" means "ride safely."

Disk (BB): Refers to that portion of the disk brake system that rotates with the wheels. The technical term is **rotor**.

Dog (BB): A motorcycle that spends a great deal of time in the back of a pickup truck.

Dresser (BB): A motorcycle that has been outfitted for long-distance touring with hard bags and tour packs as well as **fairing** and/or windshield.

Dual sport (TT): A cross between a street-legal motorcycle and a dirt bike. Generally, these are street motorcycles with a limited amount of off-road capabilities and are not suited for serious off-road competition.

Eating asphalt (BB): An accident where you hit the asphalt, usually face first.

Electronic fuel injection (EFI) (TT): The most common fuel injection system, by which fuel is forcefully introduced to the engine with electronically controlled injectors rather than a **carburetor**.

Evolution (TT): In the 1980s, Harley-Davidson introduced a redesigned version of its popular v-twin engine, called the Evolution.

Fairing (TT): A body part that protects rider and motorcycle from wind, weather, and the occasional bit of flying debris.

False neutral (TT): When you are neither in a gear nor in neutral, but the motorcycle behaves as if it is in neutral until it realizes (unpredictably) that it is not.

Fast-riding award (BB): Speeding ticket.

Flat cylinders (TT): Used to describe the cylinders found in the flat-four and flat-six engine that is unique to the Honda Gold Wing.

Flower pot (BB): A poorly constructed motorcycle helmet.

Fluid exchange (BB): Stopping for gasoline and restroom use.

Foot paddling (BB): A reference to walking a motorcycle at low speed.

Forks (TT): Found between handlebars and front wheel, most often these are telescoping tubes with built-in shock absorbers. Sometimes also used to describe the swing arm that mounts the rear wheel.

Front door (BB): Borrowed from trucker slang, this term refers to the lead motorcycle in a large group.

Fuel injection (TT): A system by which fuel is forcefully introduced into the engine without a **carburetor**.

Fuel management system (TT): The method by which the engine receives fuel. Refers to both **fuel injection** and **carburetors**.

Garbage wagon (BB): A term used mostly in the Harley-Davidson community to refer to large imported touring motorcycles. Most often used to denote the Honda Gold Wing.

Gasodometer (BB): A reference to the trip odometer when you remember to reset it at the gas station and you know what the range of a tank of gas is.

Gearhead (BB): A biker who works on his or her own motorcycle.

Gear set (TT): The transmission gears as a whole, especially when discussing the gear ratio of the transmission gears and how many gears the transmission offers.

Giggle gas (BB): Nitrous oxide, sometimes used in a system incorporated into a motorcycle to increase the speed and volume of combustion.

Hair dryer (BB): Turbocharger or a turbocharged motorcycle.

Hammer down (BB): Open the accelerator (another phrase borrowed from truckers).

Harley wrench (BB): An ordinary hammer or a pair of vice grips.

Head (BB): Slang term for **cylinder head**.

High-siding (TT): Rolling a motorcycle away from the direction of a turn.

HOG: The Harley Owner's Group.

Hog (BB): Any Harley-Davidson motorcycle

Horsepower (TT): A measurement of raw power, either of the engine or of the motorcycle itself.

Hydroplane (TT): Traveling atop water. This reduces and in some cases eliminates your ability to steer effectively.

I (BB): The interstate.

Increasing-radius corner (TT): A turn that is not constant and becomes less sharp as you transverse it. To use this term properly every time, just pretend the term radius means "ease." So an increasing ease corner means it becomes more easy as you go. More easy equals less sharp. See also **constant-radius turn** and **decreasing-radius corner**.

Inline X (TT): Refers to the configuration of X engine cylinders as being lined up in a row.

JAC (Just Add Cash) (BB): This is a person who becomes an instant biker by purchasing bike, gear, and everything a biker needs short of heart and soul in one trip.

Jugs (BB): The **cylinder blocks** or **barrels**.

Knucklebuster (BB): The name given to an adjustable wrench after many mishaps when the wrench slipped.

Knucklehead (BB): The lovely name given to Harley-Davidson's first overhead-valve engine in 1936. Also used to refer to old-school bikers.

L-twin (TT): A type of v-twin engine where the difference between cylinder angles is 90 degrees.

Lane splitting (TT): Riding between the lanes of other motorists. Some states actually allow this legally. Every sane and experienced rider will advise against it.

Laying it down (BB): Originally, an emergency procedure involving deliberately putting a motorcycle down in a way that causes the least amount of damage. Currently, this phrase refers to any crash in which the bike lands on something other than its tires.

Lieutenant (BB): The last motorcycle rider in a tour, who is, preferably, the most experienced.

Lifer (BB): One who has always been and always will be a biker.

Lugging (BB): Riding a motorcycle in a gear that is too high for the conditions.

Main jet (BB): Interstate highway. This term was probably borrowed from aviation as it is also a reference to the jet stream.

Main jet (TT): The primary jet in the **carburetor** that is responsible for regulating the air/fuel mixture.

Manual transmission (TT): The type of transmission that is found on virtually every modern motorcycle. There are very few exceptions; most of them have been out of production for several years.

MC (BB): Motorcycle Club; this abbreviation usually refers to an **outlaw** motorcycle club.

MSF: Motorcycle Safety Foundation.

Naked (BB): A motorcycle that has no fairing or other covers.

Naked racer (BB): A street racer that has been stripped as a result of an accident, or the manufacturer's recent attempt to duplicate that style. Also known as a street fighter.

OEM: See **Original Equipment Manufacturer**.

Oilheads (BB): Air and oil–cooled cylinder heads. In particular, refers to the BMW **boxer** twins that came after the airheads.

Oil lane (BB): The middle of a lane that tends to collect leaking motor oil from cars and trucks.

Oil pump gear (OPG) (TT): Most often used to refer to the nylon variety that reportedly fails frequently in Kawasaki Vulcans.

One-percenter (BB): After the **AMA** blamed the problems that occurred at Hollister, California, in 1947 on the 1 percent of bikers who are members of outlaw motorcycle clubs, one-percenters held on to that title; they wanted to make it perfectly clear that they were not interested in the American Motorcyclist Association's alleged attempt to control all bikers.

Open class (TT): Usually a racing reference to the type of racing that welcomes any motorcycle that is street legal with an engine displacement over 800 cubic centimeters. Also used to describe other classes of racing in which the specifications for participants are relatively wide-ranging.

Original equipment manufacturer (OEM) (TT): Refers to equipment, parts, or accessories that were produced or sold by the same company that made the motorcycle.

Orphans (BB): Models that are out of production and not supported by the original manufacturer. Usually these are rare motorcycles; be aware that their parts are not readily available. If this term refers to a biker, it means that he or she was a member of an outlaw club that is now defunct and is thus eligible to be recruited by other clubs. It is considered very bad taste to leave one outlaw club and join another, unless you have been orphaned.

OTB (BB): Flying over the bars in a sudden stop.

Outlaw (BB): Generally speaking, any motorcycle club that is not represented by the **AMA**. This term does not denote criminal intent.

Outlaw biker (BB): A reference to a member of an American motorcycle club (**MC**) that is not endorsed by the American Motorcyclist Association.

Overbored (TT): A cylinder whose **bore** has been increased beyond the original factory specifications. Overboring increases the dis-

placement and in most cases increases the amount of available horsepower, but it also drastically changes the power range and can sometimes decrease overall motorcycle performance.

Overhead cam (TT): A system in which the **camshaft** rides above the valves and directly operates the valves, thus decreasing the number of parts necessary to operate the engine. Whenever you have less parts, you have less parts to break, and you tend to increase performance by decreasing friction.

Pads (BB): Tires or seats.

Pads (TT): The brake part that comes into contact with the **rotor** or **disk** to cause the vehicle to stop.

Pan head (BB): A loving term given to Harley-Davidson's second overhead-valve engine, which was introduced in 1948.

Parallel twin (TT): A two-cylinder engine with pistons that are arranged side by side and move on a vertical plane.

Pavement surfing (BB): Sliding down the pavement after exiting a motorcycle at high speed.

Pegging (BB): Pegging involves the rider of a running motorcycle placing his foot on the passenger peg of a disabled motorcycle in order to push it along. This is not a safe practice.

Pipes (BB): Exhaust pipes.

Piston (TT): Mechanism that rides inside the **cylinder** and takes the brunt of the ignition force and **preignition** knocks.

Pledge (BB): One who is attempting to gain membership in a motorcycle club but has not yet met the requirements.

Plugs (BB): Spark plugs.

Preignition (TT): A condition where the air/fuel mixture ignites prior to desired position. Most often caused by using fuel that is of a lower grade than what the manufacturer recommends, but may also be caused by hot spots on damaged **pistons** or when an excess of carbon builds inside the combustion chamber or on the pistons due to improper fuel/air ratios or bad/incorrect fuel.

Primary drive (TT): A method by which the engine's crankshaft connects to the transmission; usually a heavy chain would be employed as a primary drive.

Pocket rocket (BB): A slang reference to street racers, especially the smaller versions of larger **crotch rockets**.

Probate (BB): A probationary member of a motorcycle club.

Production models (TT): Motorcycles built for sale to the general public.

Push rods (TT): An engine part that transfers the motion of a **camshaft** to the valve system via **rocker arms.** Push rods are not used in overhead-cam systems because the camshaft in those systems is in direct contact with the valves.

Putt (BB): Used as either a noun to refer to a motorcycle or as a verb to refer to riding it.

Power band (TT): The **RPM** range in which an engine produces the majority of its power.

Power shower (BB): Riding the highway at high speeds in the rain.

Pure-dirt (BB): A word that has come about as a result of the misuse of the term **dirt bike** to mean **dual sport**.

Radial tires (TT): A reference to the method in which the cords of a tire are arranged during its manufacturing process. This process generally produces a more durable tire.

Rain grooves (TT): A series of grooves cut into the road surface to channel water away from danger areas.

Reed valves (TT): The type of intake **valve** used in a two-stroke engine.

Repair link (TT): A chain link found in some final-drive chains that can be removed to facilitate chain repair. A repair link is an aftermarket roadside solution to broken chains and can help you limp home.

Road agent (BB): Yet another term for police officer.

Road gators (BB): Chunks of tire left behind by large trucks.

Road rash (BB): Friction injury acquired by **pavement surfing**.

Rocker arms (TT): A device in the **cylinder head** that pivots the motion of the push rod and to open and close the **valves**.

Rolling basket (BB): A motorcycle that is assembled enough to roll, but not to run.

Rolling chassis (TT): A motorcycle minus engine and transmission.

Rotor (TT): The portion of a disk-brake system that turns with the wheel. In an ignition distributor, the portion of the distributor that rotates with the engine.

RPM (TT): A measurement of engine (not motorcycle) speed as revolutions per minute.

Rubber mounts (TT): Engine mounts that use rubber and rubberlike materials to isolate the engine vibrations from the frame.

Rubbers (BB): Tires.

Run (BB): Riding for a specific charitable goal. As in "Toys for Tots Run," where toys are delivered to children, or "Poker Runs," where revenue gathered from participation fees go to specific charities.

Scooter (BB): Motorcycle.

Shaft final drive (TT): A system by which the power to drive a motorcycle is transferred from the transmission to the rear wheel by a drive shaft rather than a **chain** or **belt**.

Shaft jacking (TT): The main disadvantage to shaft final-drive systems. When you accelerate, the shaft twists and because that twisting is opposed to vehicle travel, the motorcycle tends to want to move in the opposite direction of the twist.

Shovelhead (BB): A reference to Harley-Davidson's third overhead-valve engine introduced in 1966.

Sidecar (TT): A small compartment with a third wheel that attaches to the side of a motorcycle to allow you to ride with an extra passenger or for extra storage space. In some very rare cases, this third wheel is powered by the motorcycle's engine. In another very rare case,

the third wheel provides an electric reverse. Usually, the third wheel is completely unpowered.

SIPDE (BB): A term coined by the Motorcycle Safety Foundation (**MSF**) that describes the method of assessing traffic conditions: scan, identify, predict, decide, and execute.

Sissy bar (BB): The backrest behind the passenger seat. This term is most often used to describe particularly high backrests. Sometimes this term is also used to describe the handles that a passenger can hold on to.

Skid lid (BB): Helmet.

Skin (BB): The painted surface of body parts on a motorcycle.

Skins (BB): Riding leathers.

Sled (BB): Motorcycle.

Slug (BB): Piston.

Sneakers (BB): Tires.

Solid mount (TT): The method by which an engine is mounted to the frame, with no attempt to use the engine mount to dampen vibrations.

Speed shifting (BB): Shifting without using the clutch. This is almost impossible on most motorcycles and downright dangerous on almost all.

Splitting the case (BB): Taking apart the lower end of a motorcycle engine.

Springer (TT): A motorcycle that uses large springs on the front forks to dampen road shock. This term used to be part of the biker jargon before Harley-Davidson started using it to describe factory-production motorcycles with that option.

Squid (BB): One of the nicer terms used to describe someone who rides a motorcycle on the street the way one rides a motorcycle at the racetrack. Also used to describe an underexperienced motorcycle operator who is taking entirely too many chances. *Stupidly quick*, *underdressed*, and *imminently dead* pretty much mean the same thing.

Stay vertical (BB): Do not crash, keep the dirty side down, ride safely.

Straight pipes (BB): Exhaust pipes with no baffles.

Street fighter (BB): See **naked racer**.

Stretch (TT): The length of the front fork's down tubes.

Stroke (TT): The up-and-down motion of the **cylinder**. Used interchangeably with the word **cycle**. When multiplied with the **bore**, the solution yields the **cylinder displacement**.

Stroker (BB): See **two-stroke engine**.

Suicide shifter (BB): A hand-operated shift arm.

Suspension (TT): All parts of the motorcycle that connect sprung to unsprung weight, including springs, shocks, and forks. Some also include the tires, because they help suspend the motorcycle from the road.

Sweeper (BB): The last rider in a group.

Tar snake (BB): Uneven cracks in the road that have been sealed with tar.

T-bone (BB): The type of accident where a motorcycle runs into the side of a car.

T CLOCK (BB): A term used to remind you of preride checks: tires, controls, lights, oil, chain, and kickstand (remember to retract it).

Team (BB): A group of riders within a group of riders on a tour, run, or other organized long ride.

Thumper (BB): Most correctly used to describe large-displacement single-cylinder four-stroke engines because of the sound they produce. Sometimes the line between large and small is hard to find, and other times the word is even used to describe two-stroke engines, though they don't have the same sound.

Ton (BB): One hundred miles an hour.

Top end (BB): The highest speed a motorcycle can reach without tearing itself apart.

Top end (TT): The upper part of the engine consisting of the intake system, cylinders, and pistons. Everything above the **bottom end**.

Torque (TT): In a motorcycle, this is the amount of twisting force provided by either the engine or the rear wheel. When comparing torque between motorcycles, it is important to make sure you are comparing the same measurement (engine or wheel). Ultimately it is the available torque at the rear wheel that makes the difference. Torque is what causes **shaft jacking** in motorcycles that have a shaft final drive.

Touring bike (BB): A motorcycle suited to and equipped for long rides.

Traction (TT): The amount of grip a tire has on the road.

Travel (TT): The amount of distance the sprung and unsprung weight of a motorcycle can move relative to each other.

Trike (TT): A three-wheeled motorcycle that does not have a sidecar.

Twisting the wick (BB): Accelerating.

TWO (BB): Two Wheels Only. You may encounter this phrase on invitations to rallies and parties. If you see this term, forget about coming with your sidecar.

Two up (BB): Riding with a passenger.

Two-stroke engine (TT): An internal-combustion engine whose power stroke is found on every downward movement of the piston. These engines are not generally found on street motorcycles because they are not environmentally friendly.

Unitized transmission (TT): A design in which the transmission is built into the same compartment as the engine's lower end. Virtually all modern motorcycles use a unitized transmission. Harley-Davidson is the most-recognized exception.

V4 (TT): An engine that has four cylinders, which point at the crankshaft in a V shape.

Valve (TT): Device that internally restricts flow either in direction or in timing. In the case of the engine valves, this ensures that both air/fuel mixture and exhaust move through the engine at the right time and in the right direction. In the case of petcock valves, the valves restrict fuel flow when the motorcycle is not running. There are many other valves found throughout the engine.

Valve guides (TT): In the case of engine valves, these are metal tubes in the **cylinder head** that house the valves to provide better seal and to assist in the ease of cylinder-head repair.

Valve job (BB): Reseating and sometimes replacing the valves in the cylinder head.

Valve train (TT): All parts used to open and close intake and exhaust valves.

V-twin (TT): An engine that has two cylinders, which point at the crankshaft in a V shape.

WOT (BB): Wide Open Throttle.

Wrench (BB): When used to describe a person, this term refers to a mechanic.

Wrenching (BB): Fixing or maintaining a motorcycle or other motor vehicle.

Clubs, Associations, and Resources

Many of these organizations are endorsed by or are affiliated with larger sanctioning bodies, but some remain independent. All motorcycle clubs listed here are sanctioned by the AMA. Note that many of these organizations are operated out of private homes, so please call during respectable hours or send a polite e-mail. The listings are arranged by state.

Alabama
Predators Motorcycle Association
Montgomery, AL
Phone: (334) 264-4506
E-mail: *derl@worldnet.att.net*

Perry Mountain Motorcycle Club
Selma, AL
Phone: (334) 872-4286
E-mail: *hhollingsh@aol*

Birmingham Trails
Birmingham, AL
Phone: (205) 251-6296

North Alabama Trail Riders
Harvest, AL
Phone: (256) 837-0084
E-mail: *wintrak@hiwaay.net*
Web site: *www.natra.dirtrider.net*

Clanton Track and Trail
Clanton, AL
Phone: (205) 280-0601

The Rockford Men's Club
Wetumpka, AL
Phone: (334) 953-3598
E-mail: *phillipmcmillan@max2.maywell.af.mil*

Retread Motorcycle Club (Mid South)
Millbrook, AL
Phone: (334) 288-1080
E-mail: *dave36054@aol.com*
Web site: *www.retreads.org*

Arizona
Wheels of Man Motorcycle Club
Phoenix, AZ
Phone: (602) 849-6550
E-mail: *donshuck@cs.com*
Web site: *www.wheelsofmanmc.com*

Huns Motorcycle Club
Tucson, AZ
Phone: (520) 887-4777
E-mail: *daveseck@earthlink.net*

Sun Riders Motorcycle Club
Tucson, AZ
Phone: (520) 324-3941
E-mail: *ptchs298@cs.com*

Central Arizona Trials
Phoenix, AZ
Phone: (602) 840-3640

Arizona Trail Riders
Cave Creek, AZ
Phone: (602) 766-1750
E-mail: *don.o.hood@aexp.com*
Web site: *www.arizonatrailriders.org*

Phoenix International Touring Society
Mesa, AZ
Phone: (480) 314-7334
E-mail: *azbeemers@yahoo.com*
Web site: *www.azbeemers.com*

Central Arizona Road Riders
Prescott, AZ
Phone: (520) 776-9024

Abate of Arizona
Phoenix, AZ
Phone: (602) 678-4012
Web site: *www.abateofaz.com*

Lost Dutchman Motorcycle Club
Mesa, AZ
Phone: (480) 820-9719
E-mail: *pat.carr@intel.com*
Web site: *www.lostdutchmanmc.com*

Jerome Bike Jamboree
Jerome, AZ
Phone: (520) 634-0037
E-mail: *buddyc1@msn.com*

Arizona Motorcycle Association
Phoenix, AZ
Phone: (602) 795-5995
E-mail: *mark@hugeindustries.com*
Web site: *www.hugeindustries.com*

California
Lodi Motorcycle Club
Lodi, CA
Phone: (209) 368-5154
E-mail: *lodicycleclub@aol.com*

San Francisco Motorcycle Club
San Francisco, CA
Phone: (415) 821-1208
E-mail: *erniejay@hotmail.com*
Web site: *sf-mc.org*

Four Aces Motorcycle Club
Ridgecrest, CA
Phone: (760) 375-1009
E-mail: *richie@adnetsol.com*

Stockton Motorcycle Club
Stockton, CA
Phone: (209) 466-6781
E-mail: *disney4steff@prodigy.net*

Salinas Ramblers Motorcycle Club
Salinas, CA
Phone: (831) 784-5220
E-mail: *driveline@mbayweb.com*
Web site: *www.salinasramblersmc.org*

Capital City Motorcycle Club
Sacramento, CA
Phone: (916) 442-8242
Web site: *www.capitalcitymc.com*

San Jose Dons Motorcycle Club
San Jose, CA
Phone: (408) 226-7004
E-mail: *san-jose-dons-@yahoo.com*

Richmond Ramblers Motorcycle Club
Pinole, CA
Phone: (510) 223-2453

Hill Toppers Motorcycle Club
Garden Grove, CA
Phone: (714) 994-1170
E-mail: *wirecutco@aol.com*
Web site: *www.hilltoppersmc.com*

Polka Dots Motorcycle Club
Fair Oaks, CA
Phone: (916) 366-6523
E-mail: *bbuffingto@evalcompcorr.ca.gov*

Cal Poly Penguins Motorcycle Club
San Luis Obispo, CA
Phone: (805) 782-9675
E-mail: *bradley@calpoly.edu*
Web site: *www.penguinsmc.org*

Port Stockton Motorcycle Club
Linden, CA
Phone: (209) 887-3283
E-mail: *motorcycledave@webtv.net*

Southern California Dirt
Weldon, CA
Phone: (760) 378-4285
E-mail: *dirtdiggers@eee.org*

Valley Climbers Motorcycle Club
Suisun City, CA
Phone: (707) 429-1154
E-mail: *sfreitas@speinyco.com*

Far West Motorcycle Club
Eureka, CA
Phone: (707) 725-2775
E-mail: *dlwjb@northcoast.com*
Web site: *www.farwestmotorcycleclub.com*

Viewfinders Motorcycle Club
Riverside, CA
Phone: (909) 276-8200
E-mail: *prmc1@mindspring.com*

Redwood Riders Motorcycle Club
Santa Rosa, CA
Phone: (707) 568-7745
Web site: *members.tripod.com/
    redwood_riders*

Freedom Seekers Motorcycle Club
Sacramento, CA
Phone: (916) 922-2924
E-mail: *seekerjohn1@aol.com*
Web site: *www.freedomseekersmc.com*

Hearts of Thunder Women's
    Motorcycle Club
Martinez, CA
Phone: (925) 787-1977
E-mail: *hotmc@earthlink.net*

Northern Valley Local 31 ABA
Chico, CA
Phone: (530) 345-3318
E-mail: *dnunley@compuserve.com*

Abate of California
Ventura, CA
Phone: (850) 641-2334
E-mail: *info@abate.org*
Web site: *www.abate.org*

Warriors of Brotherhood Motorcycle Club
Auberry, CA
Phone: (559) 855-4367
E-mail: *ragzandsuzie@netptc.net*

Los Borrachos Motorcycle Club
Ventura, CA
Phone: (805) 525-5420
E-mail: *ricepaddy@thegrid.net*

Desert Motorcycle Club
Pomona, CA
Phone: (626) 854-7368
E-mail: *dezmcrace@aol,com*

Huntington Beach Motorcycle Club
Lakewood, CA
Phone: (714) 628-2384
E-mail: *dbarnett@de.ittind.com*

Sonoma Country Sports Cycle
Cotati, CA
Phone: (707) 778-8316
E-mail: *pcd1@prodigy.net*

Dirt Diggers North Motorcycle Club
Orangevale, CA
Phone: (800) 426-4869
E-mail: *info@hangtownmx.com*

Chaparrals Motorcycle Club
Placentia, CA
Phone: (714) 528-3007
E-mail: *badams814@aol.com*

Desert Vipers Motorcycle Club
Anaheim, CA
Phone: (714) 779-5313
E-mail: *russell.boyd@ae.ge.com*

Badgers Motorcycle Club
Pine Mountain, CA
Phone: (661) 242-2712
E-mail: *dpostma@qnet.com*
Web site: *www.badgersmc.org*

Merced Dirt Riders
Modesto, CA
Phone: (209) 634-4810
E-mail: *merced_dirt_riders@yahoo.com*
Web site: *http://home.off-road.com/~larry-
    roak/home.html*

Sierra Old Timers Motorcycle Club
Crockett, CA
Phone: (510) 787-2596
E-mail: *sierraotmc@lanset.com*

Sacto P.I.T.S.
Woodland, CA
Phone: (530) 753-2519
E-mail: *laurag@the-printer.net*

Training Wheels Motorcycle Club
Santa Ana, CA
Phone: (714) 554-0116
E-mail: *acrashaw@earthlink.net*

California Enduro Riders
Fremont, CA
Phone: (510) 445-0883
E-mail: *bmcarey18@juno.com*

Valley Observed Trails
Garden Grove, CA
Phone: (714) 530-8587
Web site: *www.motorcycle-adventure.com*

Tankslappers Motorcycle Club
El Cajon, CA
Phone: (619) 595-7189
E-mail: *julieraces@home.com*

Los Altos Dirt Bikers
San Jose, CA
Phone: (408) 297-7640
E-mail: *malucas@pacbell.net*

Time Keepers Motorcycle Club
Los Gatos, CA
Phone: (408) 584-1737
E-mail: *timekmc@timekeepersmc.com*

High Sierra Motorcycle Club
Truckee, CA
Phone: (530) 582-9912
E-mail: *bdart@oakweb.com*

South Coast BMW Riders
Laguna Niguel, CA
Phone: (949) 495-8886
E-mail: *suekjimb@home.com*
Web site: *www.scbmwrc.com*

Racers Under the Son
Whittier, CA
Phone: (562) 943-0297
Web site: *www.ruts.org*

Elsinore Valley Touring
Villa Park, CA
Phone: (949) 476-5203
E-mail: *mandmgoodman@earthlink.com*

Redneck Roosters
Concord, CA
Phone: (925) 674-1381
E-mail: *hairscrambler@volcano.net*

Nevada County Woods Rider
Chicago Park, CA
Phone: (530) 273-4813
Web site: *www.woodsriders.org*

Leading Links Motorcycle Club
Los Angeles, CA
Phone: (818) 246-4915
E-mail: *burns111@ik.netcom.com*
Web site: *www.sidecarcross.com*

Motorcycle Riders Association
Riverside, CA
Phone: (909) 678-9410
E-mail: *briantb@aol.com*

Shamrock Road Riders
Upland, CA
Phone: (626) 812-1228
E-mail: *charlie.conyer@aerojet.com*

American Trails Association
Diamond Bar, CA
Phone: (909) 860-1857
E-mail: *bmark909@aol.com*

Antelope Valley Touring Society
Lancaster, CA
Phone: (661) 943-2213
E-mail: *hoffelt@qnet.com*

Fun Team Racing
Fullerton, CA
Phone: (714) 879-5529
E-mail: *funteamreg@aol.com*

Ghost Riders Motorcycle Club
San Jose, CA
Phone: (408) 265-2122
E-mail: *rickwheeler@earthlink.net*

Southern California Motorcycling
Santa Ana, CA
Phone: (714) 775-8246
Web site: *www.sc-ma.com*

Orange County Dualies
Fullerton, CA
Phone: (760) 948-4012
E-mail: *dualies@yahoo.com*
Web site: *www.dualies.com*

Red Hot Riders
San Diego, CA
Phone: (619) 460-0669
E-mail: *jbranch@home.com*
Web site: *www.redhotriders.com*

San Diego Off-Road Coalition
El Cajon, CA
Phone: (619) 595-7189
E-mail: *jallen@foxjohns.com*
Web site: *www.sdorc.org*

BMW Clubs of Southern California
Pomona, CA
Phone: (909) 629-2132
E-mail: *brownbmw@earthlink.com*

Santa Cruz Vampires Motorcycle Club
Aptos, CA
Phone: (408) 930-7048
E-mail: *vampires@tower.org*
Web site: *www.santacruzvampires.com*

Vulcan Riders Association
Ceres, CA
Phone: (209) 531-1181
E-mail: *zortoe@aol.com*

Colorado
Harry's Roamers Motorcycle Club
Denver, CO
Phone: (303) 759-2299
E-mail: *junkdoc@uswest.net*

San Juan Trail Riders
Durango, CO
Phone: (970) 884-0737
E-mail: *dale@sanjuantrailriders.org*

Front Range Trail Riders
Englewood, CO
Phone: (303) 796-8732
E-mail: *dmidthun@earthlink.net*

Motorcycle Road Racing Association
Northglenn, CO
Phone: (303) 530-5678
Web site: *www.mra-racing.org*

Pitkin Hotel and Road Tea
Colorado Springs, CO
Phone: (719) 475-2437
E-mail: *ama@apexsportsinc.com*

Rocky Mountain Motocross Association
Brush, CO
Phone: (970) 842-3299
E-mail: *suzysweney@aol.com*
Web site: *www.rmxa.com*

Colorado 500
Basalt, CO
Phone: (970) 927-4010
E-mail: *wallyd@rof.net*
Web site: *www.colorado500.org*

Connecticut
Bridgeport Motorcycle Association
Shelton, CT
Phone: (203) 925-8921
E-mail: *pwbdev@hotmail.com*

New London Motorcycle Club
Quaker Hill, CT
Phone: (860) 848-3341
Web site: *http://members.aol.com/nlmcclub/
home.html*

New England Hill Climbers
Hartford, CT
Phone: (860) 289-9428
E-mail: *neha2711@aol.com*

New England Trail Riders
Collinsville, CT
Phone: (860) 693-9111
E-mail: *netraman@yahoo.com*
Web site: *www.netra.org*

River Valley BMW Association
Naugatuck, CT
Phone: (203) 720-7409
E-mail: *crvsecretary@juno.com*
Web site: *http://members.aol.com/crvbmwr/
crvbmwr.html*

New England Motocross Association
West Suffield, CT
Phone: (860) 668-5129
Web site: *www.nemamx.com*

British Iron Association of Connecticut
Amston, CT
Phone: (860) 565-0186
Web site: *www.britironct.org*

Connecticut Ramblers Motorcycle Club
Ellington, CT
Phone: (860) 875-2189
E-mail: *motoxrs@crols.com*
Web site: *http://members.dencity.com/ctram/*

Pathfinder Motorcycle Club
Danbury, CT
Phone: (800) 999-2003
E-mail: *m.stone@ix.netcom.com*

Berkshire Trailriders Association
Suffield, CT
Phone: (860) 627-7986
Web site: *www.mudslinger.org*

Delaware
Southern Chester County Motocross
Wilmington, DE
Phone: (302) 654-8848
E-mail: *graniti@aol.com*

Delaware Enduro Riders
St. Georges, DE
Phone: (302) 834-4568

Diamonds Motorcycle Club
Claymont, DE
Phone: (302) 383-2403
E-mail: *rwchappell@compuserve.com*

Florida
Daytona 200
Daytona Beach, FL
Phone: (904) 252-2132

Orange County Cruisers
Minneola, FL
Phone: (352) 394-7657
E-mail: *iam@web-rider.net./occi*
Web site: *www.web-rider.net/occi*

Florida Trail Riders
Debary, FL
Phone: (407) 668-9700
E-mail: *dbarydan@earthlink.net*

Daytona Dirt Riders Association
South Daytona, FL
Phone: (904) 761-6123

Central Florida Trail Riders
Sorrento, FL
Phone: (407) 598-4118
E-mail: *hodgert@worldnet.att.net*

River City Dirt Rider Association
Jacksonville, FL
Phone: (904) 247-1062
E-mail: *guadagno@rcdr.org*
Web site: *www.rcdr.org*

Georgia
American Sport-Touring Riders Association
    (ASTRA)
PO Box 672051
Marietta, GA
Phone: (770) 222-0380
Web site: *http://adamsimages.com/mc/*
    astra.html

Atlanta Motorcycle Club
Doraville, GA
Phone: (404) 728-7243
E-mail: *goman42@gateway.net*

Georgia Sportbike Association
Conyers, GA
Phone: (404) 861-2020
E-mail: *rocky@georgiasportbike.com*
Web site: *www.georgiasportbike.com*

Cherokee Cycle Club
Gainesville, GA
Phone: (770) 967-3381
E-mail: *llcufr@mindspring.com*

Georgia Recreational Trails
Alpharetta, GA
Phone: (404) 215-4102
Web site: *http://garta.home.mindspring.com*

Greater Gwinnett Motorcycle Club
Loganville, GA
Phone: (770) 978-7362
E-mail: *pjhartl1@aol.com*
Web site: *www.ggmotorcycleclub.com*

Milemakers Motorcycle Club
Jasper, GA
Phone: (706) 692-6909
E-mail: *milemaker136613@mindspring.com*

Idaho
Desert Rats of Idaho
Meridian, ID
Phone: (208) 888-9881
E-mail: *pmwhite@micron.net*

Boise Ridge Riders
Boise, ID
Phone: (208) 384-5141

Idaho Coalition for Motorcycle Safety
Boise, ID
Phone: (208) 345-6231

Black Derby Racing
Nampa, ID
Phone: (208) 466-6630
E-mail: *dtk@boi.hp.com*

South West Idaho Wings
Nampa, ID
Phone: (208) 467-0316
E-mail: *rnschmier@aol.com*

Illinois
Rock River Riders Motorcycle Club
Sterling, IL
Phone: (815) 625-4414
E-mail: *pezjust@essex1.com*

Variety Riders Motorcycle Club
Ottawa, IL
Phone: (815) 434-3669
Web site: *www.howdyneighbor.com/*
    varietyriders

Pekin Motorcycle Club
East Peoria, IL
Phone: (309) 696-8672
E-mail: *nsales4848@aol.com*

Canton Motorcycle Club
Glasford, IL
Phone: (309) 389-3832
E-mail: *wfodbiker@aol.com*

Forest City Riders Motorcycle Club
Poplar Grove, IL
Phone: (815) 765-2511
E-mail: *forestcityriders@msn.com*

Belleville Enduro Team
Swansea, IL
Phone: (618) 277-2213
Web site: *www.betdirt.com*

Cahokia Creek Dirt Riders
Springfield, IL
Phone: (217) 529-4636
E-mail: *fireniron3746@aol.com*

Springfield Milers BMW Motorcycle Club
Springfield, IL
Phone: (217) 498-8368
E-mail: *motomike@fgi.net*

Honda Sport Touring Association
Hillsboro, IL
Phone: (217) 534-7698
E-mail: *fredz@cillnet.com*
Web site: *www.ridehsta.com*

Northern IL Sidecarists
St. Charles, IL
Phone: (630) 584-0548
E-mail: *okie137@hotmail.com*

Chicago Norton Owner's Club
Claredon Hills, IL
Phone: (630) 887-8041
E-mail: *flamingocycles@juno.com*

Little Egypt Off-Road Motorcycle Club
Harrisburg, IL
Phone: (618) 252-2062
E-mail: *tsmlm@shawneelink.net*

Team D.R.N.
Island Lake, IL
Phone: (847) 487-6543
E-mail: *bvanorden@ameritech.net*

Indiana
Mid West Motorcycle Club
Indianapolis, IN
Phone: (317) 888-4401
E-mail: *mwmc_info@yahoo.com*

Wabash Cannonball Motorcycle Club
Wabash, IN
Phone: (219) 563-5744

Riders Motorcycle Club
Goshen, IN
Phone: (219) 642-4701
E-mail: *webmaster@ridersmc.org*
Web site: *www.ridersmc.org*

Tri-State Motorcycle Club
Garrett, IN
Phone: (219) 637-8050

Indiana, Illinois, and Kentucky Enduro Riders
Evansville, IN
Phone: (812) 491-1293
E-mail: *quadzilla63@hotmail.com*

Midnight Riders Motorcycle Club
Kokomo, IN
Phone: (765) 452-7654

Chesterton Motorcycle Club
Chesterton, IN
Phone: (219) 926-6715
E-mail: *drew1955@gte.net*

Gourmet Riders Motorcycle Club
Goshen, IN
Phone: (219) 533-6139
E-mail: *drgonzobsmc@aol.com*

Black Sheep Motorcycle Club
Goshen, IN
Phone: (219) 533-6139
E-mail: *blutobsmc@aol.com*

Friends on Wheels Motorcycle Club
Indianapolis, IN
Phone: (317) 366-3325
E-mail: *jcarr@brylane.com*

Iowa
Tri City Motorcycle Club
Bettendorf, IA
Phone: (319) 332-4775
E-mail: *mart57@home.com*

Soo City Cycle Club
Sioux City, IA
Phone: (712) 276-8428
E-mail: *knobyknees@aol.com*

Hawkeye Motorcycle Club
Dubuque, IA
Phone: (608) 763-2821
E-mail: *percival@pcii.net*

Rambling Wheels Motorcycle Club
Cedar Falls, IA
Phone: (319) 266-4654
E-mail: *morgans2@home.com*

HWY 175 Raceway
Arthur, IA
Phone: (712) 367-2331
E-mail: *rcrs175@netins.net*

Midwest Hillclimbers Association
Anamosa, IA
Phone: (319) 335-4366
E-mail: *mschultz@uiowa.uhl.edu*

Bent Lever Dirt Bike Club
Des Moines, IA
Phone: (515) 771-6358
E-mail: *putzlandolt@hotmail.com*

Cedar Valley Trail Riders
Center Point, IA
Phone: (319) 849-2109
Web site: *www.cvtr.org*

Des Moines Enduro Riders
Granger, IA
Phone: (515) 251-6739
E-mail: *acmurphy3@dwx.com*

Iowa Enduro Riders Association
Fremont, IA
Phone: (641) 933-4872
Web site: *www.iera22.com*

New Hartford Racing Inc.
Cedar Falls, IA
Phone: (319) 274-6684
E-mail: *morgans2@home.com*

Central Iowa Enduro Rider
Iowa Falls, IA
Phone: (641) 648-4205
E-mail: *jevans@cnsinternet.com*

Kansas
Tilted Horizon
Olathe, KS
E-mail: *webmaster@tiltedhorizon.com*
Web site: *www.tiltedhorizon.com*

Cessna Motorcycle Club
Wichita, KS
Phone: (316) 524-4941
E-mail: *gbirdranch@juno.com*

Kentucky
Louisville Motorcycle Club
Louisville, KY
Phone: (502) 363-6486

Owensboro Motorcycle Club
Owensboro, KY
Phone: (270) 685-8434

Hoosier Hilltoppers Motorcycle Club
Louisville, KY
Phone: (502) 241-2010
E-mail: *gleaf791@aol.com*

Pendleton County Motorcycle Recreation Park
Demossville, KY
Phone: (606) 472-3442

Apex Valley Raceway
Hopkinsville, KY
Phone: (270) 886-8564

Bluegrass Beemers
Lexington, KY
Phone: (859) 223-5459
E-mail: *kr4mo@yahoo.com*

Louisiana
Independent Bikers of America
Quitman, LA
Phone: (318) 259-3330

Louisiana Trail Riders Association
Baton Rouge, LA
Phone: (225) 621-1672
E-mail: *ltra2000@aol.com*

Breezy Hill Enduro Club
Pollock, LA
Phone: (504) 385-6090
E-mail: *acadcool@iamerica.net.com*

Maryland
Baltimore Ramblers Motorcycle Club
Reisterstown, MD
Phone: (410) 833-5795

Independent Riders Society
Pasadena, MD
Phone: (410) 437-9695
E-mail: *gollum@abs.net*

Blue Ridge Road Riders
Fredrick, MD
Phone: (301) 990-0234
Web site: *www.brrr.homestead.com*

Western Maryland Motorcycle Association
Union Bridge, MD
Phone: (410) 775-7209
E-mail: *trailcentre@frederickmd.com*

4 Seasons Road Riders
Mount Airy, MD
Phone: (410) 760-0072

Nation's Capital Norton Owners
Clear Spring, MD
Phone: (301) 791-5175
Web site: *www.ncno.org*

Enfield Bullet Owners Club
Smithsburg, MD
Phone: (301) 824-6582

Old Line Motorcycle Club
Silver Spring, MD
Phone: (301) 593-6411
Web site: *www.tritoncomputer.com/oldline*

Free State Motorcycle Club
Baltimore, MD
Phone: (410) 574-2374
E-mail: *normkiaunis@aol.com*

Shore Riders
Easton, MD
Phone: (410) 763-8155
E-mail: *gloie@hotmail.com*

Lynx Motorcycle Club
Bel Air, MD
Phone: (410) 879-6738
E-mail: *cclayton@surfbest.net*

Massachusetts
Tumbleweed Motorcycle Club
Brockton, MA
Phone: (508) 584-7162
E-mail: *strykers2@aol.com*

Quaboag Riders Motorcycle Club
Monson, MA
Phone: (413) 267-4414
Web site: *www.quaboagridersmc.com*

Springfield Motorcycle Club
Holliston, MA
Phone: (508) 429-1239

Cape Cod Motorcycle Club
Mashpee, MA
Phone: (508) 447-1935

Pilgrim Sands Trail Riders
Hanson, MA
Phone: (781) 294-8355
Web site: *www.pstr.org*

Tri-State Trail Riders Motorcycle Club
Newburyport, MA
Phone: (978) 462-3436

Knights of Life Motorcycle Club
Braintree, MA
Phone: (781) 848-3674
E-mail: *mph569@aol.com*

Michigan
Lansing Motorcycle Club
Lansing, MI
Phone: (517) 322-2237
E-mail: *katiewoo4@cs.com*

Knights of the Road Motorcycle Club
Inkster, MI
Phone: (734) 729-0727

Port Huron Motorcycle Club
Port Huron, MI
Phone: (810) 982-6798
Web site: *www.phmc-usa.org*

Bulldog Riders Motorcycle Club
Millington, MI
Phone: (517) 871-3899
E-mail: *torcojoe@mailcity.com*

Huron Valley Night Hawks
Ypsilanti, MI
Phone: (734) 480-9085
Web site: *www.hvnh.org*

Tri-City Competition Club
Auburn, MI
Phone: (517) 662-2599

Soaring Chicken Motorcycle Club
Canton, MI
Phone: (734) 397-8890
E-mail: *griff2sarge@netscape.net*

North Country Riders Motorcycle Club
Gaylord, MI
Phone: (517) 732-1570
E-mail: *davepagel@hotmail.com*

Red Bud Competition Club
Buchanan, MI
Phone: (616) 695-6405
E-mail: *mxoffice@redbudmx.com*
Web site: *www.redbudmx.com*

Michigan Gold Wing Association
Royal Oak, MI
Phone: (248) 542-7498
E-mail: *mgwa@compuserve.com*

Tri-City Travelers Motorcycle Club
Essexville, MI
Phone: (517) 893-7307
E-mail: *gobertei@isd.bay.k12lmi.us*

Para Dice Motorcycle Club
Grand Rapids, MI
Phone: (616) 754-3060
E-mail: *m.s.rose@worldnet.att.net*

Moscow Touring Club
Albion, MI
Phone: (517) 629-8942
E-mail: *ikglass7@hotmail.com*

Michigan/Ontario Trails
Fenton, MI
Phone: (810) 750-5258
E-mail: *bobcap@ameritech.net*

Wolverine Riders
Allen Park, MI
Phone: (313) 388-2592

Metro Triumph Riders
Ortonville, MI
Phone: (248) 489-4300
E-mail: *lolvlflyr@hotmail.com*

BMW Touring Club of Detroit
Brighton, MI Phone: (248) 324-8506
E-mail: *dallgood@ismi.net*
Web site: *www.bmwtcd.org*

Michigan Independent Riders Association
Holly, MI
Phone: (248) 634-7514
E-mail: *gdenise@tir.com*

Cycle Conservation Club
Rives Junction, MI
Phone: (517) 569-9999
E-mail: *cccbill@dmci.net*
Web site: *www.cycleconservationclub.org*

Buzzard Motorcycle Club
Harrison, MI
Phone: (517) 539-9417
E-mail: *jlipovsky@hotmail*

East Side Competition Riders
Fenton, MI
Phone: (810) 750-5258
E-mail: *bobcap@ameritech.net*

Great Lakes Trails Club
Holly, MI
Phone: (810) 230-7965
E-mail: *baherne@tri.com*

Minnesota
Flying Dutchmen Cycle Club
New Ulm, MN
Phone: (507) 354-2306
E-mail: *leskaren@newulmtel.net*

Golden Eagles Cycle Club
Owatonna, MN
Phone: (507) 451-7451
E-mail: *u2f2338@us.ibm.com*

Norsemen Motorcycle Club
Cambridge, MN
Phone: (763) 689-2760
E-mail: *nmc@norseman.org*
Web site: *www.norsemenmc.org*

Hi-Winders Motorcycle Club
Rochester, MN
Phone: (507) 753-2779
E-mail: *scmxpark@mr.net*

Range Riders Motorcycle Club
Cohasset, MN
Phone: (218) 326-9312
E-mail: *jgale@exchange1.mnpower.com*

River Valley Enduro Rider
Cold Spring, MN
Phone: (320) 363-7968
E-mail: *newelopitz@aol.com*

Travelers Motorcycle Club
Shakopee, MN
Phone: (612) 445-4379

Upper Midwest Trails Association
Faribault, MN
Phone: (507) 334-3284
E-mail: *spud@deskmedia.com*

Dirt Track Riders Association
Brooklyn Park, MN
Phone: (763) 560-7818
E-mail: *marnd1717@aol.com*

North Central Dirt Track
Cedar, MN
Phone: (612) 434-7487

Twin Cities Trail Riders
Jordan, MN
Phone: (612) 369-5107
E-mail: *ingo@tctrailriders.org*
Web site: *www.tctrailriders.org*

Mississippi
Mississippi HI-Point Enduro
Ellisville, MS
Phone: (601) 477-2119
E-mail: *roscoe@netdoor.com*

Masterlinks Enduro Team
Wiggins, MS
Phone: (601) 928-3783

Ridge Runners Enduro Team
Meridian, MS
Phone: (601) 483-3067
E-mail: *rlp4300@aol.com*

Missouri
BMW Gateway Riders Club
Saint Louis, MO
Phone: (314) 577-1322
E-mail: *jim.shaw@white-rodgers.com*

Missouri Mudders
Wentzville, MO
Phone: (314) 770-6302
E-mail: *michael.silger@avnet.com*

Motocross Parents MXP
Jonesburg, MO
Phone: (636) 488-3174
E-mail: *ditch83@jonesburg.net*

Midwest Trail Riders Association
Maryland Hts, MO
Phone: (314) 434-5095
E-mail: *ridemtra@hotmail.com*

Missouri Dirt Riders
Defiance, MO
Phone: (314) 504-7287
E-mail: *kinklr@cat2.com*

Shadow Riders Club
St. Ann, MO
Phone: (314) 506-0042
E-mail: *pphillips@carpetone.com*

Midwest Café Racing Association
Saint Louis, MO
Phone: (314) 481-8078
E-mail: *dadamridr36@juno.com*
Web site: *www.apci.net/~racenone*

Montana
Billings Motorcycle Club
Billings, MT
Phone: (406) 657-5251
E-mail: *chuckdbonnett@aol.com*

Montana BMW Riders
East Helena, MT
Phone: (406) 227-3367
Web site: *www.treasurestate.com/
mtbmwriders*

Nebraska
Cavalier Motorcycle Club
Murray, NE
Phone: (402) 235-3134

Rollin Plains Motorcycle Club
Omaha, NE
Phone: (402) 561-9504

BMW Riders Association of Nebraska
Lincoln, NE
Phone: (402) 483-6447
E-mail: *huels@nouix.net*

C C Riders Motorcycle Club
Omaha, NE
Phone: (402) 733-9283
E-mail: *ktmblack@home.com*

Nebraska BMW Nightriders
Milford, NE
Phone: (402) 761-3124
E-mail: *jr61907@alltel.net*

Midwest Trails Association
Omaha, NE
Phone: (402) 556-3333

TBQ Sport Club
Grand Island, NE
Phone: (308) 381-2143
E-mail: *dnitzel@kdsi.net*
Web site: *www.nohva.com*

Nevada
Western States Racing Association
Reno, NV
Phone: (775) 972-4907

Venture Touring Society
Pahrump, NV
Phone: (775) 751-3003
E-mail: *vtsmta@vtsmta.com*

Dust Devils Motorcycle Club
Reno, NV
Phone: (775) 325-1194
E-mail: *ltrip@earthlink.net*
Web site: *www.dustdevilsmc.com*

New Hampshire
Manchester Motorcycle Club
Litchfield, NH
Phone: (603) 424-9465

White Mountain Riders Motorcycle Club
Gorham, NH
Phone: (603) 752-3142

Lakeside Sharks Motorcycle Club
Laconia, NH
Phone: (603) 366-2000

Merrimack Valley Trail Riders
Bedford, NH
Phone: (603) 624-4004
E-mail: *no-new-eng@cff.org*

U.S. Classic Racing Association
Richmond, NH
Phone: (603) 239-6778
E-mail: *rscoy@k12.0it.umass.edu*
Web site: *www.race-uscra.com*

New Jersey
New Jersey Motorcycle Club
Bergenfield, NJ
Phone: (201) 385-1166

Meteor Motorcycle Club
Glendora, NJ
Phone: (609) 939-1192
E-mail: *meteormc1930@aol.com*

Dawn Patrol Motorcycle Club
Middlesex, NJ
Phone: (732) 356-5838
E-mail: *michaeleck@att.net*

Monmouth Shore Points Motorcycle Club
W. Long Branch, NJ
Phone: (732) 870-6805
E-mail: *cdbrock@home.com*

Central Jersey Competition
Edison, NJ
Phone: (732) 985-9016
Web site: *www.cjcr.com*

Blue Star Motorcycle Club
Linden, NJ
Phone: (908) 862-7471
E-mail: *rbkenney@read.com*

Redliners Motorcycle Club
Newark, NJ
Phone: (973) 760-9333
E-mail: *redliners@aol.com*
Web site: *www.redlinersmc.com*

Sober Disciples Motorcycle Club
Trenton, NJ
E-mail: *rollennj@webtv.net*

Iron Knights Motorcycle Club
Hoboken, NJ
Phone: (973) 748-1884
E-mail: *ironknightsmc@ironknightsmc.com*
Web site: *www.ironknightsmc.com*

Mavericks Motorcycle Club
Budd Lake, NJ
Phone: (973) 347-9407
E-mail: *thundrroz@aol*

Raritan Road Runners
Helmette, NJ
Phone: (732) 521-5029
E-mail: *webmaster@raritanroadrunners.org*
Web site: *www.raritanroadrunners.org*

Ridge Riders Motorcycle Club
Montclair, NJ
Phone: (973) 267-3922
E-mail: *chris.tlack@vs.uniti.com*

Competition Dirt Riders
Vineland, NJ
Phone: (856) 691-5371
E-mail: *endurodave@aol.com*

Bayshore Wheelers Motorcycle Club
Keyport, NJ
Phone: (908) 236-5503
E-mail: *bayshore@bayshorewheelers.org*
Web site: *www.bayshorewheelers.org*

Road Apples Motorcycle Club
Tom River, NJ
Phone: (732) 349-6544
E-mail: *bopp@weichertrealtors.net*
Web site: *www.geocities.com/apples08753*

Old Bridge Winter Riders
Old Bridge, NJ
Phone: (732) 679-5587
E-mail: *joeroob@yahoo.com*

Last Chance Motorcycle Club
Clifton, NJ
Phone: (973) 497-7630
E-mail: *ngardenst@aol.com*

Spokes-Women Motorcycle Club
E. Brunswick, NJ
Phone: (609) 777-3572
E-mail: *bcvc@aol.com*
Web site: *www.spokes-women.org*

Classic Iron Motorcycle Club
Chester, NJ
Phone: (908) 879-5052
E-mail: *hdxls82@cs.com*

New Mexico
Sandia Motorcycle Roadracers
Albuquerque, NM
Phone: (505) 292-8672
E-mail: *jromero466@aol.com*
Web site: *www.smra-racing.org*

Mesilla Valley Road Riders
Las Cruces, NM
Phone: (505) 526-6778
E-mail: *mvrr@zianet.com*
Web site: *www.zianet.com/mvrr*

Rio Grande Riders
Rio Rancho, NM
Web site: *www.riogranderiders.com*

New York
South Shore Motorcycle Club
East Meadow, NY
Phone: (516) 538-2801
E-mail: *heytom5@inane.com*

Ramapo Motorcycle Club
Nanuet, NY
Phone: (914) 623-4636
E-mail: *rmc@ramapomc.org*

Wayne County Motorcycle Club
Newark, NY
Phone: (315) 331-4764
E-mail: *wayne_county_mc@yahoo.com*
Web site: *www.geocities.com/wayne_
county_mc*

Springville Travelers Motorcycle Club
Eden, NY
Phone: (716) 992-4365
E-mail: *cmsimmons@wrat.com*

Conesus Lake Riders
Wayland, NY
Phone: (716) 669-2342
E-mail: *tigerfrank@aol.com*

Roamers Motorcycle Club
Watervliet, NY
Phone: (518) 270-5235
E-mail: *romersmc@aol.com*
Web site: *www.amadist3.com/rmc*

Cross Island Motorcycle Club
East Meadow, NY
Phone: (516) 483-1834
E-mail: *ci@crossislandmc.com*
Web site: *www.crossislandmc.com*

Dusk II Dawn Motorcycle Club
Bronx, NY
Phone: (718) 893-7424
E-mail: *davethemechanic@yahoo.com*

Hogs and Rice
Pomona, NY
Phone: (212) 353-4329
E-mail: *pault@cooper.edu*
Web site: *www.cooper.edu/~pault/test4.html*

Reality Racing Inc. Motorcycle Club
Deer Park, NY
Phone: (631) 587-1157
E-mail: *ruron69@aol.com*

Pony Express Motorcycle Club
Woodhaven, NY
Phone: (718) 296-9700
E-mail: *ponyexpress01nyc@aol.com*
Web site: *www.ponyexpressmc.com*

Iron Riders Motorcycle Club
Highland, NY
Phone: (845) 691-2651
Web site: *www.ironridersmc.com*

Southern Tier Hillclimber
Hornell, NY
Phone: (607) 324-7924
E-mail: *mcaneney@infoblvd.net*

Island Tribe Motorcycle Club
Holbrook, NY
Phone: (631) 471-5523
E-mail: *islandtribe@aol.com*

Storm Riders Motorcycle Club
Salt Point, NY
Phone: (845) 266-3182
E-mail: *secretary@stormridersmc.com*
Web site: *www.stormridersmc.com*

Ithaca Dirt Riders
Richford, NY
Phone: (607) 255-6648
E-mail: *vjd1@cornell.edu*

Thunder Ridge Motorcycle Park
New Berlin, NY
Phone: (607) 847-6815
E-mail: *tridgejim@usa.net*
Web site: *www.tridgejim.com*

Lost Wheels Motorcycle Club
Glenham, NY
Phone: (845) 297-6205
E-mail: *fellefax@aol.com*
Web site: *www.lostwheels.com*

Southern Tier Enduro Rider
Corning, NY
Phone: (607) 962-2961
E-mail: *sterglc@aol.com*

Kattskill Mountain Riders
Kingston, NY
Phone: (845) 331-9720
E-mail: *ym2902@netscape.net*

Adirondack Riders Motorcycle Club
Glen Falls, NY
Phone: (518) 792-1713
E-mail: *prplady@capital.net*

Syracuse Area Trail Riders
Baldwinsville, NY
Phone: (315) 456-2625
E-mail: *honda@dreamscape.com*
Web site: *www.satra.org*

Freedom Rider's Motorcycle Club
Cairo, NY
Phone: (518) 945-1758
E-mail: *frmc@amadist3.net*

Sirens New York City Motorcycle Club
Lindenhurst, NY
Phone: (212) 544-2870
E-mail: *zconk@earthlink.net*

Sport Touring Motorcycle Club
New York, NY
Phone: (973) 764-9642
E-mail: *jwilt@worldnet.att.net*
Web site: *www.sporttouringmc.com*

Celtic Motorcycle Club
Babylon, NY
Phone: (631) 422-8031
Web site: *www.celticmcc.com*

I Don't Know Motorcycle Club
Central Islip, NY
Phone: (631) 348-0722
E-mail: *idkmc1@aol.com*
Web site: *www.angelfire.com/ny3/idkmc*

Alliance Motorcycle Club
New York, NY
Phone: (212) 613-1490
E-mail: *arthur_corette@hias.org*

Nassau County Fire Riders
Port Washington, NY
Phone: (516) 944-3945
E-mail: *ralph.hummel@nassauwings.org*
Web site: *www.nassauwings.org*

New York Trail Riders
Fredonia, NY
Phone: (716) 366-6146
E-mail: *nytroatv@netsync.net*

CC Riders Motorcycle Club
Silver Springs, NY
Phone: (716) 493-2777
E-mail: *candccycle@wycol.com*

Western New York Off-Road Association
Brockport, NY
Phone: (716) 637-7142
E-mail: *raymond.goulet@kodak.com*

New York Cruisers
Scarsdale, NY
Phone: (718) 822-8878
Web site: *www.newyorkcruisers.com*

Scooter's Club
Willseyville, NY
Phone: (607) 657-4178
E-mail: *crich@ithaca.edu*

Ridin' Free Motorcycle Club
Wappingers Falls, NY
Phone: (845) 298-9228
E-mail: *tatoodavid61@cs.com*

Chai Riders Motorcycle Club
New York, NY
Phone: (212) 689-0063
E-mail: *info@chairiders.org*
Web site: *www.chairiders.org*

Liberty Riders
Brooklyn, NY
Phone: (718) 963-8762
E-mail: *coastrider@aol.com*

Classic Riders Association
Wurtsboro, NY
Phone: (914) 888-0286
E-mail: *dtkobo4@citlink.net*

Postal Workers Motorcycle Club
Ronkonkoma, NY
Phone: (631) 737-1361
E-mail: *pwmc6158@aol.com*

North Carolina
Rocky Mountain Motorcycle Club
Tarboro, NC
Phone: (252) 823-3426

Joy Riders
Kinston, NC
Phone: (252) 527-5233

North Carolina Motorcycle Club
Hendersonville, NC
Phone: (828) 696-8248
E-mail: *harleyfan@aol.com*

North Dakota
Rambler's Motorcycle Club
Tioga, ND
Phone: (701) 664-3609
E-mail: *rkenders@nccray.com*

Ohio
Dayton Motorcycle Club
Dayton, OH
Phone: (937) 429-4359
E-mail: *dmc@daytonmc.org*
Web site: *www.daytonmc.org*

Apple City Motorcycle Club
Jackson, OH
Phone: (740) 286-3211
E-mail: *stevei@zoomnet.net*

Treaty City Motorcycle Club
Bradford, OH
Phone: (937) 448-9190
E-mail: *pkneeht@bright.net*

Warren Buckaroos Motorcycle Club
Warren, OH
Phone: (330) 847-9174
E-mail: *fjschaffer@aol.com*

Athens Motorcycle Club
Glouster, OH
Phone: (740) 448-7395
Fax: (740) 592-2777
E-mail: *komen@eurekanet.com*

Pioneer Motorcycle Club
Marietta, OH
Phone: (740) 373-9566
E-mail: *rdhughes@wirefire.com*

Sandusky Valley Riders
Tiffin, OH
Phone: (419) 927-6686
Web site: *http://sanduskyvalleyriders.com*

Canton Motorcycle Club
Canal Fulton, OH
Phone: (330) 854-3597
E-mail: *dweinreb@bright.net*

Western Reserve Motorcycle Club
Salem, OH
Phone: (330) 746-1064
E-mail: *jochenart@aol.com*

Salem Motorcycle Club
Salem, OH
Phone: (330) 533-3341
E-mail: *mi651@raex.com*

Enduro Riders Association
Westerville, OH
Phone: (614) 891-1369
E-mail: *wcumbow@csi.com*
Web site: *www.enduroriders.com*

Glass City Motorcycle Club
Northwood, OH
Phone: (419) 666-8413

Ohio Motorheads
Galena, OH
Phone: (740) 965-9544
E-mail: *wadecon1@msn.com*

Ohio Valley Competition Club
Milford, OH
Phone: (513) 831-6947
E-mail: *pcalsip@aol.com*

Central Ohio Competition
Ashville, OH
Phone: (740) 746-8875

Chillicothe Enduro Riders
Chillicothe, OH
Phone: (740) 775-4694
E-mail: *kevin849@bright.net*

Wheelers Motorcycle Club
Toledo, OH
Phone: (419) 729-3417
E-mail: *hugger736@aol.com*

Zodiac Riders Motorcycle Club
Cortland, OH
Phone: (330) 638-2597
E-mail: *ppeony@aol.com*

Appalachian Dirt Riders
Hamden, OH
Phone: (740) 384-6379
E-mail: *app_dirt@yahoo.com*

Kenworthys Grand Prix Club
Troy, OH
Phone: (937) 335-4763
E-mail: *kenworthymx@worldnet.att.net*

Buckeye Beemers (BMW owners)
Columbus, OH
Phone: (614) 766-2176

Classic British Motorcycle Club
Loveland, OH
Phone: (513) 243-1471
E-mail: *gasmith@goodnews.com*

Michigan Norton Owners Association
Sylvania, OH
Phone: (419) 882-2943
E-mail: *mnosonja@aol.com*

Masonic Motorcycle Club
Painesville, OH
Phone: (440) 354-5599
E-mail: *uncldick@users.oval.net*

V-Twin Cruisers
Painesville, OH
Phone: (440) 357-8256
E-mail: *vtwincruzr@aol.com*

Hard Time Harley Riders
Hillsboro, OH
Phone: (937) 764-1548
E-mail: *ednewk@ameritech.net*

Oklahoma
Outsiders Motorcycle Club
Tulsa, OK
Phone: (918) 488-0929
E-mail: *graybear@outsidersmc.org*
Web site: *www.outsidersmc.org*

Tulsa Ramblers
Tulsa, OK
Phone: (918) 834-1058

Black Diamond Touring Club
Del City, OK
Phone: (405) 670-3911
E-mail: *leroy-r@swbell.net*
Web site: *www.blackdiamondclub.org*

Oregon
Motorcycle Riders Association
Medford, OR
Phone: (541) 779-4267

Rose City Motorcycle Club
Portland, OR
Phone: (503) 532-0886
E-mail: *info@rose-city-mc.org*

Applegate Roughriders Motorcycle Club
Salem, OR
Phone: (503) 585-6359
E-mail: *skturn@aol.com*

Trinity Road Riders
Clackamas, OR
Phone: (503) 774-5149
E-mail: *dale_currier@hotmail.com*

Women's Motorcross League
Bend, OR
Phone: (541) 347-5277
E-mail: *miki@wml-mx.com*
Web site: *www.wml-mx.com*

Emerald Trail Riders Association
Eugene, OR
Phone: (541) 688-5428

Trailsmen Motorcycle Club
Hillsboro, OR
Phone: (503) 628-7332

Pennsylvania
Reading Motorcycle Club
Oley, PA
Phone: (610) 987-6422
Web site: *www.readingmc.com*

York Motorcycle Club
York, PA
Phone: (717) 854-3214

Erie Motorcycle Club
North East, PA
Phone: (814) 725-9447
E-mail: *donald_prindle@lord.com*

Happy Ramblers Motorcycle Club
Carlisle, PA
Phone: (717) 697-1061
E-mail: *info@happyramblers.com*
Web site: *www.happyramblers.com*

Blue Comet Motorcycle Club
Skippack, PA
Phone: (215) 723-8518
Web site: *www.bluecometmc.com*

Bushskill Valley Motorcycle Club
Easton, PA
Phone: (610) 258-3208
Web site: *www.bikehillclimb.com*

Bedford County Motorcycle Club
Sidman, PA
Phone: (814) 487-7580
Web site: *www.digitaliway.com/hillclimb*

Flying Dutchmen Motorcycle Club
Pine Grove, PA
Phone: (570) 345-6340

Phoenix Motorcycle Club
Hummelstown, PA
Phone: (717) 520-9120

Silver Band Motorcycle Club
Lincoln University, PA
Phone: (610) 869-3638
E-mail: *br82454@aol.com*

Back Mountain Enduro Riders
Dallas, PA
Phone: (570) 675-1814
E-mail: *dnoon@epix.net*

Keystone Sportsmen Motorcycle Club
Honesdale, PA
Phone: (570) 253-8192
E-mail: *murman92@socantel.net*

Thunderbird Motorcycle Club
Lancaster, PA
Phone: (717) 898-0871

Cycle Gypsies Motorcycle Club
Bethlehem, PA
Phone: (610) 861-2821

South PA Enduro Riders
Carlisle, PA
Phone: (717) 245-0353
E-mail: *spermc@hotmail.com*
Web site: *http://communities.msn.com/*
southpennenduroriders

Freedom Riders Motorcycle Club
Red Hill, PA
Phone: (215) 679-4766
E-mail: *info@freedomriders.com*
Web site: *www.freedomriders.com*

Three Rivers Competition Riders
Monroeville, PA
Phone: (724) 325-4223
Web site: *www.trcr.org*

High Mountain Dirt Riders
Nesquehoning, PA
Phone: (570) 645-7311

Valley Forge Trail Riders
Oaks, PA
Phone: (610) 873-7010
E-mail: *jamiet@siqinc.com*

East Coast Enduro Association
Jonestown, PA
Phone: (717) 865-0601
Web site: *www.ecea.org*

Susquehanna Off-Road Riders
Lebanon, PA
Phone: (717) 270-9420
E-mail: *mikevan@nbn.net*

Main Line Touring Association
Audubon, PA
Phone: (610) 666-6303
E-mail: *jfbueche@aol.com*
Web site: *www.angelfire.com/pa4/mlta/*

PA Trail Riders
Seven Valleys, PA
Phone: (717) 792-1384
Web site: *www.pamall.net/patra*

Clearfield Cycle Club
Bigler, PA
Phone: (814) 857-7984
E-mail: *djfye@uplink.net*

Black Sheep Motorcycle Club
Sauderton, PA
Phone: (215) 723-2806
E-mail: *inraddad@aol.com*

Motor Sports Riders Club
Mechanicsburg, PA
Phone: (717) 766-2523
E-mail: *chris@hondabmwmoto.com*

Tricky Tryalers Motorcycle Club
New Bloomfield, PA
Phone: (717) 582-8319
E-mail: *partner@mai.igateway.com*

Crawford County Road Riders
Conneaut Lake, PA
Phone: (814) 382-4837
E-mail: *georgecl@alltel.net*

American Gold Wing Association
Mohnton, PA
Phone: (610) 856-7349
Web site: *www.agwa.com*

Benevolent Motorcyclist Association
New Tripoli, PA
Phone: (610) 439-0525

Wyoming Valley Motorcycle Club
Dallas, PA
Phone: (570) 675-6367
E-mail: *dscho18718@aol.com*

Twin Rose Lady Riders
Lancaster, PA
Phone: (717) 291-8999
E-mail: *dmhtrlr@aol.com*

Keystone Off-Road Riders
Cresson, PA
Phone: (814) 886-5464
E-mail: *hmanred@penn.com*
Web site: *www.korr.org*

Arthemis Motorcycle Club
Parker Ford, PA
Phone: (610) 495-2250
E-mail: *arthemismc@aol.com*

Sand and Pit MotoCross Club
Darlington, PA
Phone: (724) 827-8172
E-mail: *nesar@timesnet.net*

Rhode Island
Rhody Rovers Motorcycle Club
Exeter, RI
Phone: (401) 397-3076
E-mail: *billhaas@edgenet.net*

Rhode Island Trails Club
Hope Valley, RI
Phone: (401) 539-0715
E-mail: *scorpa@edgenet.net*

Hoot Owl Scramblers
Chepachet, RI
Phone: (401) 567-0964
E-mail: *info@hootowlmc.com*

Yankee Beemers (BMW) Motorcycle Club
Little Compton, RI
Phone: (401) 682-1102
E-mail: *rcnye@bhcousa.com*

South Carolina
American Gold Wing Association
Ladson, SC
Phone: (843) 875-0526
E-mail: *agwapres@aol.com*
Web site: *www.agwa.com*

South Dakota
Jackpine Gypsies Motorcycle Club
Sturgis, SD
Phone: (605) 347-3418
E-mail: *gypsies@dtgnet.com*

Capital City Cyclists
Pierre, SD
Phone: (605) 224-4296
E-mail: *billysnsd@aol.com*

Tennessee
Memphis Motorcycle Club
Memphis, TN
Phone: (901) 226-5190
E-mail: *bbbukiah@aol.com*
Web site: *www.memphismotorcycleclub.com*

Hillbilly Vincent Owners
Brentwood, TN
Phone: (615) 377-1366
E-mail: *somer@mindspring.com*

Southern Cruisers Riding Club
Christiana, TN
Phone: (615) 804-1050
E-mail: *wgstreb@earthlink.net*
Web site: *www.southerncruisers.net*

Texas
San Jacinto High Rollers
La Porte, TX
Phone: (281) 470-0354
E-mail: *sjhr@biker.net*

Cycle Club of Ft. Worth
Fort Worth, TX
Phone: (817) 926-1346
E-mail: *billcarlton23@yahoo.com*

Montgomery Sport Riders Association
Conroe, TX
Phone: (936) 441-7282
E-mail: *outlawtrax@evi.net*

Magic Dragons
Canadian, TX
Phone: (806) 323-9123
E-mail: *repeka@yft.net*

Track and Trail Sport Riders
Amarillo, TX
Phone: (806) 371-8851
E-mail: *sriffe@aol.com*

Lubbock Trail Riders
Lubbock, TX
Phone: (806) 472-7566
E-mail: *frosty5555@aol.com*

Bent Rims Motorcycle Association
Castroville, TX
Phone: (830) 741-2805
E-mail: *robmoore@flash.net*

Trail Riders of Houston Motorcycle Club
Houston, TX
Phone: (713) 644-8872
E-mail: *chardy@tycoint.com*
Web site: *www.trh-cycle.org*

Austin Moto Sport Association
Austin, TX
Phone: (512) 923-5624
E-mail: *amsa@flash.net*
Web site: *www.texasoffroad.net/amsa/*

North Texas Norton Owners Association
North Richland Hills, TX
Phone: (817) 498-1325
E-mail: *hogleg44@airmail.net*
Web site: *http://pistol1.home.mindspring. com/index.htm*

South East Texas Off Road
Beaumont, TX
Phone: (409) 899-3946
E-mail: *hooper@tex-is.net*

British Motorcycle Owners Association
of Texas
Friendswood, TX
Phone: (281) 482-4769
Fax: (281) 992-2597
E-mail: *kope@flash.net*
Web site: *www.bmoaonline.com*

Mustang Motorcycle Club
North Richland Hills, TX
Phone: (817) 498-1325
E-mail: *pualrr@cyberramp.net*
Web site: *www.mmcoa.org*

Knight Riders Motorcycle Club
San Antonio, TX
Phone: (210) 673-2878
E-mail: *spookytx@earthlink.net*

Central Texas Road Riders Association
Killeen, TX
Phone: (254) 628-2007
E-mail: *cab55@jund.com*

Road Runners Motorcycle Club
Mathis, TX
Phone: (361) 449-1521
E-mail: *scoggins@bcni.net*

Columbus Motorcycle Club
Columbus, TX
Phone: (979) 732-9171
E-mail: *starrfiserman@yahoo.com*

Sidewinders Motorcycle Club
Boerne, TX
Phone: (830) 537-5248
E-mail: *vernonm@gvtc.com*

Red River Dirt Riders
Denton, TX
Phone: (214) 262-5803
E-mail: *pstorrie@esd.dl.nec.com*

Triumph Sport Riders Association
Houston, TX
Phone: (281) 999-4131
E-mail: *tsra@triumphnet.com*

Utah
Sage Riders Motorcycle Club
Springville, UT
Phone: (801) 489-7568
E-mail: *womenoffrd@aol.com*

Park City Motorcycle Club
Park City, UT
Phone: (801) 541-2105
E-mail: *dsanborn@pragdata.com*
Web site: *www.parkcitymotorcycle.org*

Sugarloafers
Delta, UT
Phone: (435) 864-5514

Vermont
Hoosac Valley Motorcycle Club
Stanford, VT
Phone: (802) 694-1233
E-mail: *cc14@nassed.net*

BMW Motorcycle Owners of Vermont
Killington, VT
Phone: (802) 422-3391 Fax: (802) 422-6442
E-mail: *lpdecota@vermontel.net*
Web site: *http://members.tripod.com/ BMWROV*

Virginia
Silverbacks
Newport News, VA
Phone: (757) 595-6236
E-mail: *silverbacks@easyriders.com*
Web site: *silverbacksmc.com*

Northern Virginia Trail Riders
King George, VA
Phone: (540) 653-2959
Web site: *www.nvtr.org*

Virginia Motorcycle Association
Powhatan, VA
Phone: (804) 794-4079
E-mail: *kbrough@vcu.edu*

Potomac Area Road Riders
Mclean, VA
Phone: (301) 443-4500
E-mail: *blackbur@erols.com*

Southern Maryland Dirt Riders
Bealeton, VA
Phone: (301) 782-7633
E-mail: *smdr313@aol.com*

Virginia British Motorcycle Club
Richmond, VA
Phone: (804) 749-3118
E-mail: *centerstand@yahoo.com*

Virginia Touring Society
Norfolk, VA
one: (757) 587-0950
E-mail: *webeeus@aol.com*

James River Vintage Motorcycle Club
Richmond, VA
Phone: (804) 261-6526
E-mail: *wdm20dlbrb@aol.com*

Washington
Tacoma Motorcycle Club
Enumclaw, WA
Phone: (360) 825-5842
E-mail: *tacomaducks@hotmail.com*
Web site: *www.tacoma-mc.org*

Jolly Rogers Motorcycle Club
Tukwila, WA
Phone: (206) 244-4563
E-mail: *greatseymour@juno.com*

Mt. Saint Helens Motorcycle Club
Castle Rock, WA
Phone: (360) 274-9217
Web site: *www.mshmc.org*

Vancouver Black Cats Motorcycle Club
Ridgefield, WA
Phone: (360) 887-8536
E-mail: *everettm@teleport.com*

Bremerton Cruisers Motorcycle Club
Bremerton, WA
Phone: (360) 692-8936
E-mail: *leep@budsters.com*

Rainier Sportsman Club
Rainier, WA
Phone: (360) 446-2949
E-mail: *trophy.1@msn.com*

Puget Sound Enduro Riders
Olympia, WA
Phone: (360) 943-8694
E-mail: *gtoms@home.com*

West Virginia
Appalachian Motorcycle Club
Blount, WV
Phone: (304) 925-6097

Brothers of the Wheel
West Hamlin, WV
Phone: (304) 824-3036
E-mail: *adkin109@hotmail.com*

Moonshine Hill Climbers
Delbarton, WV
Phone: (304) 475-2942

Wisconson
Madison Motorcycle Club
Madison, WI
Phone: (608) 271-0582
E-mail: *jvtroia@hotmail.com*
Web site: *www.madisonmotorcycleclub.org*

Milwaukee Motorcycle Club
Colgate, WI
Phone: (262) 255-5385
E-mail: *sieglegf@aol.com*

Rib Mountain Riders Motorcycle Club
Antigo, WI
Phone: (715) 623-2044

Indianhead Cycle Club
Baldwin, WI
Phone: (715) 684-4821
E-mail: *redktm@aol.com*

Beaver Cycle Club
Beaver Dam, WI
Phone: (920) 887-1469
E-mail: *mx08056@deere.com*
Web site: *www.beavercycleclub.com*

Wisconsin BMW Motorcycle Club
Colgate, WI
Phone: (262) 628-1666

Aztalan Cycle Club
Lake Mills, WI
Phone: (262) 593-5370
Web site: *www.aztalancycle.com*

Wausau Area Enduro Riders Association
Altoona, WI
Phone: (715) 836-7367
E-mail: *momdad9129@aol.com*

Arkansas Creek Cycle Club
Arkansaw, WI
Phone: (715) 285-5679

Index

Everything® **Home-Based Business Book**
  $12.95, 1-58062-364-6

Everything® **Homebuying Book**
  $12.95, 1-58062-074-4

Everything® **Homeselling Book**
  $12.95, 1-58062-304-2

Everything® **Horse Book**
  $12.95, 1-58062-564-9

Everything® **Hot Careers Book**
  $12.95, 1-58062-486-3

Everything® **Internet Book**
  $12.95, 1-58062-073-6

Everything® **Investing Book**
  $12.95, 1-58062-149-X

Everything® **Jewish Wedding Book**
  $12.95, 1-55850-801-5

Everything® **Job Interview Book**
  $12.95, 1-58062-493-6

Everything® **Lawn Care Book**
  $12.95, 1-58062-487-1

Everything® **Leadership Book**
  $12.95, 1-58062-513-4

Everything® **Learning French Book**
  $12.95, 1-58062-649-1

Everything® **Learning Spanish Book**
  $12.95, 1-58062-575-4

Everything® **Low-Fat High-Flavor Cookbook**
  $12.95, 1-55850-802-3

Everything® **Magic Book**
  $12.95, 1-58062-418-9

Everything® **Managing People Book**
  $12.95, 1-58062-577-0

Everything® **Microsoft® Word 2000 Book**
  $12.95, 1-58062-306-9

Everything® **Money Book**
  $12.95, 1-58062-145-7

Everything® **Mother Goose Book**
  $12.95, 1-58062-490-1

Everything® **Motorcycle Book**
  $12.95, 1-58062-554-1

Everything® **Mutual Funds Book**
  $12.95, 1-58062-419-7

Everything® **One-Pot Cookbook**
  $12.95, 1-58062-186-4

Everything® **Online Business Book**
  $12.95, 1-58062-320-4

Everything® **Online Genealogy Book**
  $12.95, 1-58062-402-2

Everything® **Online Investing Book**
  $12.95, 1-58062-338-7

Everything® **Online Job Search Book**
  $12.95, 1-58062-365-4

Everything® **Organize Your Home Book**
  $12.95, 1-58062-617-3

Everything® **Pasta Book**
  $12.95, 1-55850-719-1

Everything® **Philosophy Book**
  $12.95, 1-58062-644-0

Everything® **Playing Piano and Keyboards Book**
  $12.95, 1-58062-651-3

Everything® **Pregnancy Book**
  $12.95, 1-58062-146-5

Everything® **Pregnancy Organizer**
  $15.00, 1-58062-336-0

Everything® **Project Management Book**
  $12.95, 1-58062-583-5

Everything® **Puppy Book**
  $12.95, 1-58062-576-2

Everything® **Quick Meals Cookbook**
  $12.95, 1-58062-488-X

Everything® **Resume Book**
  $12.95, 1-58062-311-5

Everything® **Romance Book**
  $12.95, 1-58062-566-5

Everything® **Running Book**
  $12.95, 1-58062-618-1

Everything® **Sailing Book, 2nd Edition**
  $12.95, 1-58062-671-8

Everything® **Saints Book**
  $12.95, 1-58062-534-7

Everything® **Selling Book**
  $12.95, 1-58062-319-0

Everything® **Shakespeare Book**
  $12.95, 1-58062-591-6

Everything® **Spells and Charms Book**
  $12.95, 1-58062-532-0

Everything® **Start Your Own Business Book**
  $12.95, 1-58062-650-5

Everything® **Stress Management Book**
  $12.95, 1-58062-578-9

Everything® **Study Book**
  $12.95, 1-55850-615-2

Everything® **Tai Chi and QiGong Book**
  $12.95, 1-58062-646-7

Everything® **Tall Tales, Legends, and Outrageous Lies Book**
  $12.95, 1-58062-514-2

Everything® **Tarot Book**
  $12.95, 1-58062-191-0

Everything® **Time Management Book**
  $12.95, 1-58062-492-8

Everything® **Toasts Book**
  $12.95, 1-58062-189-9

Everything® **Toddler Book**
  $12.95, 1-58062-592-4

Everything® **Total Fitness Book**
  $12.95, 1-58062-318-2

Everything® **Trivia Book**
  $12.95, 1-58062-143-0

Everything® **Tropical Fish Book**
  $12.95, 1-58062-343-3

Everything® **Vegetarian Cookbook**
  $12.95, 1-58062-640-8

Everything® **Vitamins, Minerals, and Nutritional Supplements Book**
  $12.95, 1-58062-496-0

Everything® **Wedding Book, 2nd Edition**
  $12.95, 1-58062-190-2

Everything® **Wedding Checklist**
  $7.95, 1-58062-456-1

Everything® **Wedding Etiquette Book**
  $7.95, 1-58062-454-5

Everything® **Wedding Organizer**
  $15.00, 1-55850-828-7

Everything® **Wedding Shower Book**
  $7.95, 1-58062-188-0

Everything® **Wedding Vows Book**
  $7.95, 1-58062-455-3

Everything® **Weight Training Book**
  $12.95, 1-58062-593-2

Everything® **Wine Book**
  $12.95, 1-55850-808-2

Everything® **World War II Book**
  $12.95, 1-58062-572-X

Everything® **World's Religions Book**
  $12.95, 1-58062-648-3

Everything® **Yoga Book**
  $12.95, 1-58062-594-0

Visit us at everything.com

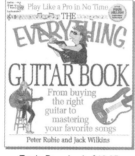

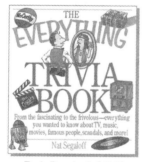